# THE DEEPEST DYE

# The Deepest Dye

## OBEAH, HOSAY, AND RACE
## IN THE ATLANTIC WORLD

### Aisha Khan

**HARVARD UNIVERSITY PRESS**

Cambridge, Massachusetts

London, England

2021

First printing

*Library of Congress Cataloging-in-Publication Data*

Names: Khan, Aisha, 1955– author.
Title: The deepest dye : obeah, Hosay, and race in the Atlantic world / Aisha Khan.
Description: Cambridge, Massachusetts : Harvard University Press, 2021. |
Includes bibliographical references and index.
Identifiers: LCCN 2020047204 | ISBN 9780674987821 (cloth)
Subjects: LCSH: Obeah (Cult) | Tenth of Muharram. | Postcolonialism—West Indies. |
Identification (Religion) | West Indies—Race relations. | West Indies—Civilization—
European influences. | West Indies—Religious life and customs. |
Great Britain—Colonies—America.
Classification: LCC F1628.8 .K46 2021 | DDC 305.8009729—dc23
LC record available at https://lccn.loc.gov/2020047204

# CONTENTS

# NOTES ON TERMINOLOGY AND ORTHOGRAPHY

In *The Deepest Dye*, I use "West Indies" in reference to British colonies in the Caribbean and to contemporary Caribbean countries formerly under British rule. "Caribbean" refers to the region as a whole. I focus on people of African descent and people of Indian descent. Depending on the era and the context, they have been variously called, respectively, "African," "Creole," "Afro-Creole," "Negro," or "Afro-Caribbean; and "Indian," "East Indian," "coolie," "Hindoo," "Mohammedan Hindoo," or "Indo-Caribbean." The term "African" is more recent in present-day West Indian public discourse than is the term "Indian" or "East Indian." I refer to "African" diaspora peoples in the region parallel to my use of "Indian" to refer to the region's diasporas from the Indian subcontinent. Context will make it clear if I am referring to Indians in India or Africans in Africa.

Obeah can be written with a capital *O* or a lowercase *o*. I prefer the lowercase *o* because it underscores that obeah is a "catchall"[*] term with a bricolage tradition.[†] The lowercase *o* conveys obeah's non-doctrinal, heterogeneous constitution, which lacks "the established liturgy and community rituals" that mark organized religions.[‡] By contrast to obeah, Hosay is virtually always written with a capital *H*. This difference between capitalized and lowercase letters reflects the conventional allusion to Hosay's derivation from a canonical religious tradition, Islam.

[*] Jerome Handler and Kenneth Bilby, *Enacting Power: The Criminalization of Obeah in the Anglophone Caribbean, 1760–2011* (Kingston, Jamaica: University of the West Indies Press, 2012), 4.

[†] Diana Paton, "Witchcraft, Poison, Law, and Atlantic Slavery," *William and Mary Quarterly* 69, no. 2 (2012): 235–264.

[‡] Margarite Fernandez Olmos and Lizabeth Paravisini-Gebert, *Creole Religions of the Caribbean: An Introduction from Vodou and Santeria to Obeah and Espiritismo* (New York: New York University Press, 2011), 158.

# THE DEEPEST DYE

# 1

## A PARALLAX VIEW

Emancipation in Britain's West Indian colonies was both an ending and a beginning. In 1834 slavery was officially abolished, and after four years of "apprenticeship" to transition to wage labor, a new era, as conventional wisdom has long had it, was ushered in.[1] And in some important ways, a new era it was. But as I argue, along with a number of other scholars, slavery did not so much end as evolve into other formations of power—restriction, criminalization, and othering. In the West Indies, colonial authorities instituted a replacement scheme that began in 1838 and lasted until 1917—the indenture of immigrant labor on sugar plantations based on the "free will" of work contracts—introducing about 430,000 "bound coolies" from another of Britain's colonies, India.[2] This ending-beginning constituted a moment of overlap rather than one of transition per se: it was a watershed moment in which the older era's ways of knowing and being, although in some important senses over, continued to shape the ways that the new era was imagined, organized, and monitored.

The social and cultural composition of the West Indies and its diasporas today are the historical consequences of the diverse kinds of interrelationships among formerly enslaved Africans and their descendants, and indentured Indians and their descendants. Although indentured Indians entered a society whose power structures and social hierarchies were already in place, they were not simply immigrant add-ons; they were, with their African counterparts, central to the storied histories of development and change in these societies. While European-descended populations remained in West Indian colonies, African-descended and Indian-descended peoples were by this time the demographic majority in all of them. This structure of power relations, set in place by British colonialism and imprinted into the present, define and shape the identities that Africans and Indians and their descendants contend with, as they claim them, reject them, and imagine them in alternative ways.

This book explores the concept of identity in the West Indies—its uses and misuses as a means of instituting, maintaining, and reclaiming the relations of power that structure society. My exploration is concerned with the ways that the interpretive categories of race and religion are animated into identities among people of African and Indian descent that embody them as particular "types" of persons. My central premise is that racial and religious identities necessarily and always work in some kind of conjunction, constituting a nexus where the racialization of religion and the "religionization of race"[3] define, substantiate, and justify identities and the hierarchies that rank them.

In order to peel back and peek behind the identity categories and relations of power that the West Indies have inherited and inhabited, I needed to choose subjects more specific and concrete than "identity categories." I needed to locate where and how identity categories happen, so to speak. In what particular sites of experience and their hierarchical structures do they play a critical role in shaping the conditions and meanings of that experience? What is involved when categories are treated as fixed things but the boundaries that define them are flexible, and how does the meaning of things remain consistent when they are applied to diverse agendas and contexts? How, on one level, are identities mutually defining when, on another, often more overt level, they are viewed as being mutually exclusive? I needed a *thing*, in philosopher Martin Heidegger's sense, on which to focus that has personified "race" and "religion" in the West Indies.[4] At the same time that I was thinking about this, I was working my way through the idea that a comparison of things, and perhaps better yet, ostensibly quite dissimilar things, could be a productive path toward unpacking the historical backstories of racial and religious identities and their shadows today.

My two illustrative cases, the loci where I saw race and religion meeting in ways most suggestive of these issues, are the cultural phenomena known in the West Indies as *obeah* and *Hosay*. Both emerged in the context of British colonialism in the Caribbean, which produced a common indigeneity, or "creole" culture and knowledge system, which obeah and Hosay share. Historically and in the present day, both are complex vehicles of racialized religion and religionized race. Obeah consists of ritual practices and knowledge traditions having to do with healing and divination that involve supernatural powers. Its provenance begins as a broad array of ancient religious traditions that hail from West and Central Africa, which have been fashioned into various and particular customs and practices in the "New World" of the Americas by Euro-colonial as well as African diasporic epistemologies since the sixteenth century, and by South Asian diasporic epistemologies since the nineteenth. Hosay derives from its seventh-century "Old World" origins as Muharram in the Persianate world. It then made its way to India, where multiple religious traditions, including those of Shi'a and Sunni Islam, and Hinduism, among others, were incorporated and brought to the New World by Indians' own diaspora. This book investigates these processes of making obeah, typified as "African," and Hosay, categorized as "Indian," from the nineteenth to the twenty-first centuries.

## Dark Arts and Obeah, Illicit Arts and Hosay

Obeah and Hosay in the West Indies developed within a context of imperialist designs that were based on the extraction of profit on a mass scale for a world market: plantation-based sugar production undertaken by a coerced labor force. From the early seventeenth to the mid-nineteenth centuries, the form of coercion was enslavement of sub-Saharan Africans. These peoples brought with them to the Americas their cosmologies, healing and divination traditions, and existential philosophies, which became congealed as "obeah" under colonial regimes. Following the formal abolition of slavery in Britain's West Indian colonies, the mechanism (although not the motivation) of plantation production and coerced labor shifted. The first shipload of laborers, indentured "coolies" from India, was sent to British Guiana in 1838. What had been unequivocally coerced (enslaved) labor became ambiguously coerced (indentured) labor. The ideological foundation of a European/African, white/black cultural axis that fed the explanation and justification of the production system had to incorporate new others—principally Indians. The mingling of races and religions surrounding the practices of obeah and Hosay also threatened colonial hierarchies, as can be seen, for example, in a late nineteenth-century account of Hosay processions by the Reverend H. V. P. Bronkhurst, author of *The Colony of British Guiana and Its Labouring Populations*. He recounts that "black men hired . . . by the Coolies" were involved in Hosay processions, along with "respectable Creoles and European planters [who] not only countenance these festivals by their presence" but also "encourage them in their wickedness"; Christians "like ourselves" who "attend on such occasions give those who invite them the idea that idolatry is a trifling matter, a harmless amusement, instead of a sin of the deepest dye."[5] This new moment entailed new legal practices and moral imperatives on the part of colonial Britain, and new worldviews and lifeways on the part of the workforce.

The Caribbean region is conventionally characterized as a site of fluid, heterodox religions—combinations of African, Christian, Islamic, and Hindu cosmologies—where creole or syncretic practices, decried or admired, emerge from heterogeneous New World encounters. In some respects, none of this should be remarkable, given conventional characterizations of the Caribbean region. Yet obeah and Hosay typically are studied individually and interpreted, respectively, as "African" and "Indian" traditions, despite the diversity of their heritages and their followers. Because of their shared colonial contexts, when considered together, they represent consummate cases for exploring the construction of interpretive categories, and ways that racial and religious identities are transformed by relations of power and lived experience. This also tells us how scholarship has long understood the Caribbean itself. While many writers acknowledge its mixture and pluralisms in the abstract, their accounts are often stories of separation in the concrete, very much like the popular analytical practices behind race, on which they draw.

Denigrated in Euro-colonial worldviews as a bizarre curiosity and pushed underground by the colonial church and state as being in league with the "dark arts," by the turn of the nineteenth century in the West Indies obeah was practiced largely through secretive rites and masked discourses. Colonial authorities and elites assumed obeah's practitioners to be enslaved (and free) Africans, a supposition that had a good deal of truth to it when one considers the historically important role that obeah could play in organized resistance, from the Haitian Revolution to the continuous rebellions across the Caribbean. What authorities and elites preferred to deny or ignore were their own beliefs about supernatural forces and worlds, which fed their susceptibility to obeah's suggestiveness. Nonetheless, obeah's rites and masked discourses were interpreted by colonial society—and as we will see, still today—as fostering subversion of the social order through the assertion of alternative forms of agency: divination of causality, worship of a pantheon of deities, and invocation of forms of authority at odds with the colonial church. British colonizers, for example, first made obeah illegal in their West Indian colonies in 1760 in response to Tacky's Rebellion, the largest uprising of enslaved people in Jamaica during that century; the rebellion's leaders purportedly had been advised by obeah men. Various ordinances criminalizing obeah have been instituted over the centuries in West Indian

colonies, as we will see in the chapters that follow. Colonial criminalization not only was an attempt to forbid or at least successfully hinder ritual
acts of obeah; it also, ironically, brought "obeah" into being as a particular
kind of *thing*. Obeah has always been elusive, a "catchall term"[6] that was
rendered into "a single unitary phenomenon" largely through "colonial
law-making and law-enforcing"—in other words, its criminalization by
colonial regimes in Britain's West Indian colonies. Elusiveness makes
"obeah" difficult to define with any precision and standardization. It can
be whatever authoritative discourse needs it to be, an elasticity that allows
obeah to signal any number of socially problematic practices and people
as well as socially inspiring acts and agendas. This difficulty in definition
and standardization shows "obeah" to be near ubiquitous and thus not
completely eradicable, yet this same ubiquity makes it easy to find and
therefore to prosecute.

Obeah's bricolage, catch-all quality and its engagement with the supernatural (or, as its decriers charge, the occult) are largely what makes obeah
so hazy and mysterious and so threatening to those who wish to control or
eradicate it. Anthropologist Michel-Rolph Trouillot has suggested that the
"ultimate mark of power may be its invisibility."[7] This certainly includes
obeah's powers, which involve the ambiguity of the unseen, an aspect that,
arguably, contributes to the continuation of obeah's criminalization in
much of the West Indies today. Nonetheless, over the last few decades, a
number of anti-obeah laws have been repealed or greatly revised: obeah
was decriminalized in Anguilla in 1980, in Barbados in 1998, in the Republic of Trinidad and Tobago in 2000, and in St. Lucia in 2004. In Jamaica the last conviction for obeah was in 1964 and the last arrest for obeah
in 1977.[8]

Today obeah retains these complex legacies among cautious devotees,
disapproving skeptics, admiring scholars, and government officials striving
for modernity, in the West Indies and its diasporas. In November 2018, for
example, Jamaica's newspaper *The Star* reported on a "big retirement party"
that was being planned for an "obeah man" who had spent forty of his
eighty years "assisting persons with their careers and other aspects of their
life for years." The "long list of attendees" included entertainers, politicians,
judges, police, and business owners.[9] By June 2019, Jamaica's Minister of
Justice stated that he thought the Obeah Act, the legal prohibition of obeah,
should be repealed.[10] At the time of this writing, it has yet to be done. Despite revisions and repeals, and its eager embrace by some, obeah today

remains not fully accepted throughout the Caribbean; as we will see in subsequent chapters, its stigmatization holds to a certain extent, rejected overtly among its critics and embraced gingerly or ambivalently among many of its devotees. Thus, even in the twenty-first century obeah remains a grey area. It is slowly if reluctantly being recognized shorn of its stigma in the social mainstream of West Indian societies. Yet its insistent set of traditions and the vibrant culture that these traditions generate are kept animated by a historical identity—of individual, of group, of nation—that continues to confer malevolent as well as beneficial qualities that typify self and other. Practitioners and scholars continue to debate the degree to which obeah, past and present, subverts social and moral orders.

Hosay's complex geographical path began as Muharram, the annual mourning ritual commemorating the death of Hussein, grandson of the Prophet Mohammed, at the battle of Kerbala (in present-day Iraq) in 680 CE, and later, in Medina, of his brother Hassan. Centuries of Muharram's observance in India drew in Sunni Muslims and Hindus, among numerous others. Muharram's characteristic heterogeneity in India remained in its incarnation as Hosay ("Hussein") in the West Indies. (As a major aspect of the Indian diaspora in the Caribbean, Hosay also was observed in Suriname, though, as in British Guiana, by the turn of the twentieth century it had faded out of commemoration.) Muslim and Hindu indentured laborers, along with Africans belonging to Christian and Afro-Atlantic religious traditions, avidly participated in Hosay. Its diversity of participants in India and in the West Indies both decentered Muharram's/Hosay's specifically Shi'a significance and emphasized Hosay's signature activity in the West Indies, both historically and today: constructing enormous tadjahs (tazzias), made of wood, paper, bamboo, tinsel, and, later, sequins and Styrofoam, among other materials, which symbolize the tombs of the martyred brothers; organizing Islamic prayers around them, undertaken by religious devotees in the designated spaces in which the tadjahs are built; and publicly marching them, carried by numerous strong men, in procession on the final three days during Ashura, the last ten days of the month of Muharram. Tadjah processions have long involved such accompanying activities as deafeningly loud and rhythmically complex drumming on tassa drums, the martial art of stick fighting, and the singing of marsiyahs, or songs mourning the death of a martyr.

In its incarnation in West Indian colonies, Hosay took on some of obeah's most important connotations as an instance of a disruptive, immoral, and atavistic presence, in a shared context of labor unrest or fears of labor unrest. Trinidad in the 1840s, for example, had become such a violent society that 1844's Ordinance No. 8 was enacted to suppress the widespread carrying and use of lethal weapons such as pistols, swords, and knives,[11] as well as the long sticks that might be used in the stick-fighting martial arts celebrated during Hosay. Discussions about regulating Hosay were being documented and archived as early as the 1850s in the British West Indies. By this time Hosay was organized and visible enough to draw attention from the wider society, and it became the "coolie festival" that received the major (if not all the) attentions of, on the one hand, freedom of religion—as long as it was "genuine" Islam—and, on the other hand, maintaining the social and moral peace—which meant at least basic guidelines about what could be done and where. By the early 1870s pronounced anxieties about Hosay activities in Trinidad were evident because of the "allegedly increasing tendency to riotous behavior."[12] But it was in the 1880s that a prolonged economic crisis due to the fall of the price of sugar exacerbated the unrest of the labor that was directly connected to sugar, specifically, reactions to lengthened task work and reduced wages.[13] Police activity heightened through the 1890s as a result of associations made between the sugar crisis and criminality, notably in the form of plantation labor protests and general unrest.[14] Crime and its punishments were tied to these developments, which drew Hosay—"coolie" laborers' social diversion and political act— under intensifying scrutiny as an expression of this threat. Historian David Trotman notes about Trinidad that the twenty years between 1880 and 1900 "were dotted with battles," numerous protests connected to carnival and to Hosay. This was a time when the British colonial police force was particularly aggressive.[15] My contention is that criminalization was as important to the formation of Hosay as was its comparison to "genuine" Islam by British colonizers.

It is uncertain to what extent indentured Indians on West Indian plantations conducted religious rites during Hosay, or of what these might have consisted; colonial records with these sorts of details are few to none. But there is no reason to assume that indentured laborers did not conduct Hosay-related rites in accompaniment with the annual processions around and off the sugar "estates" (plantations). Balanced between, on the one hand, Victorians' postemancipation position, at least in principle, that religious freedom be fostered in British colonies, and, on the other, the demands of sugar production, Hosay was variously given and denied legal and cultural status as "religion." These attributions involved both nuanced and crude debate about universal rights, "colonized races," and cultural evolution. That said, it was the public face of the processions that were most troubling for West Indian colonial authorities and elites. Hosay was an actual moment when "coolie" laborers from numerous sugar plantations congregated, creating opportunities for work stoppages, consciousness-raising about the injustices that came with the indenture system, and either mock or real physical battles connected to the competitive aspect of each plantation's tadjah procession and accompanying revelries.

Today in Trinidad and Jamaica, plantation-based "coolie" violence has ceased to be Hosay's primary association. Taken up by these countries as emblematic of local culture, Hosay continues to be observed as a variously valued aspect of island history, including the construction and processions of tadjahs carefully attended to by certain Islamic rites, which have been shaped in part by Muharram's long and storied history in India. This history contributes to contemporary debates in the West Indies about Hosay: it is decried by competing schools of Islamic thought that look to canonical rules extrapolated from the Quran and Hadith, and by those who object to what they perceive as the carnival atmosphere of this commemoration. Others celebrate it, either as a deeply gratifying annual personal spiritual journey, or a symbol of resistance to British colonial oppression and its persisting legacies of social inequality such as racial disparities between Indo- and Afro-Caribbeans vis-à-vis Euro-Caribbeans, or, as in nationalist narratives, as a quintessentially multicultural feature of unity that brings together the racial (cautiously termed "ethnic") and religious "rainbow" that is the West Indies.

The religious traditions that served as templates for colonial authority, according to which Hosay and obeah were interpreted and which continue to be so today, were, respectively, Islam and Christianity. Islam is the rubric that has set the terms of the debate of Hosay's demarcation as a problem, historically for colonizers and today for certain Muslim groups. The correct expression of Hosay exemplifies Islam, a religion that had been recognizable to British colonial authorities as they defined it, and a religion that remains recognizable to Muslims today, if debated in terms of Hosay's appropriate fit. Obeah's complex relationship with so-called legitimate religion—either bearing what philosopher Ludwig Wittgenstein called a "family resemblance," or betraying what in Euro-Christianity is divine and holy—also has been the rubric that has set the terms of the debate.[16] Obeah is rarely if ever considered a correct expression of Euro-Christianity, although this valuation may be a celebrative critique rather than a rebuke. As should be clear, Hosay's and obeah's respective histories, social profiles, and cultural multidimensionality make even their seemingly most self-evident differences at times difficult to keep precise. Other factors foreground additional commonalities they share, which I discuss further in later chapters. Among the most important features that it shares with obeah, Hosay was made into a "single unitary phenomenon"—a *thing*—through colonial efforts at its criminalization. Also crucial is that throughout their storied histories in the West Indies, both obeah and Hosay have been sanctioned as valid "religion" as well as tabooed as invalid, "nonreligion." In sum, at work are empirical realities as well as products of the human imagination.

Although there is a growing body of work that explores the imbrication of African and Indian practices in the West Indies, with respect to obeah and Hosay the fundamental constitution of Africanness as black and Indianness as Indian largely remains essentialized—distinct, discernable, coherent, and intact. In problematizing this, however, I am not suggesting that obeah and Hosay have no differences. Contemporary Hosay is decidedly more limited in its recognition than it was historically as a "coolie" observance; "obeah" has been a household word for centuries. Hosay is one aspect of a major "world religion," Islam; obeah's features pervade numerous religious traditions hailing from Africa, Europe, and Asia. One might say that Hosay is a small part of a recognizable, larger whole, and that obeah is the diffuse whole that has virtually always defied precise or uniform definition.

### Racialization of Religion, Religionization of Race

For a half-millennium throughout the Americas, race and religion have been implicated in constructions of "type," embedded in commonsense ways of knowing oneself and others as particular kinds of persons who constitute particular kinds of groups. In Western epistemology everyone is presumed to have a race, whichever way each one may be placed in hierarchies of unequal value. In this logic, "race" in the singular does not come in degrees, despite that "races" in the plural are not equal. Most human groups possessed religion (though not all, even by mid-nineteenth century Euro-colonial thought), yet they did so debatably in terms of proximity to an ideal type. Religion could come in degrees—of approximation to a touchstone, whether of Euro-Christianity or, at times, ideal-type Hinduism and Islam. Both race and religion have, in theory, visible manifestations (phenotype, expressive /bodily behavior, espoused beliefs, enacted traditions), and, given this supposed visibility, everyone allegedly can somehow be traced through them. This traceability became crucial in the power dynamics of the ways that Western countries and colonies saw themselves in terms of their heritages, their progress into modernity, who could legitimately claim and belong to them, and, ultimately, their value and importance on the world stage. Always more than simply a neatly cordoned off, unequivocally "racial" or "religious" question, the flexible and ambiguous identities that resulted from the intersected relationships between categories of race and religion can be manipulated to advantage, depending on a stakeholder's mission.

The principle, as one might call it, of the flexible interconnectedness, or intersectionality, of racial and religious categories of identity is intriguingly evident in an 1898 article from Trinidad's *Mascot* newspaper, a voice of the colonial mainstream. The writer complained that "Coolies [i.e., Indians] will not be persuaded that there is no such thing in existence as *charming powder*," reputed to cause someone, including "an estranged wife," to become "submissive. They fully believe in the "efficacy of the potion."[17] In the *Mascot* story, the sneer at "coolie" resorts to the occult reflects the day's common sense about another kind of naivete, that of the Indian who believes in supernatural powers. This naivete suggests an analogy between Africans and Indians in terms of their comparable lack of enlightened perceptions and lagging development. But the comment also implies that this proclivity among Indians presents an incongruous association with a different racial type, Africans, about whom it would be less worthy of public note, unless scandal or crime were involved, to simply comment on a given: that Africans are devotees of occult practices.[18]

It is probably impossible to know what specifically was in libraries and parlors on any given day that was shaping commonsense understandings of religious and racial identities, their associated practices, and the social hierarchies in which they were structured. We can, however, surmise what people were exposed to in what we can imagine as the everyday life of ideas, imparted in a variety of ways, notably by word of mouth, print media, and the growth of the public sphere.[19] Popularization on this scale had never before taken place, and it spread the boundary-defining, boundary-overlapping stories that people told themselves about each other.

In his account of the "Tazzia" (Hosay) and other "pseudo-religious ceremonies" among "coolies" in British Guiana, Bronkhurst assures readers
that he is objective, making "no comment upon this state of things in the
Colony, but simply mention[ing] the facts, and leav[ing] the reader to form
his own opinion."[20] Nonetheless, his opinions are redolent throughout this
text. He relies significantly on what he knows (or has heard) of Hindu and
Muslim religious festivals in India to explain what he sees in British Guiana,
which, "to be seen in all their glory, must be viewed on the banks of the
sacred Ganges"—the obvious litmus test of authenticity for Bronkhurst. In
the colony, "mobs of Coolies, with their gaudy ('tadjah' or 'tajah' or) 'tazzia,'
flaunting flags, and barbaric music, take possession of the principal streets,
to the unmistakable annoyance, not only of those whom business or pleasure forces to pass in their direction, but equally so of the quiet inhabitants, in front of whose windows the crowd assembles."[21] In his fairly lengthy
description of the procession, Bronkhurst reiterates the conventional rhetorical strategies of his day, emphasizing the element of disruption Hosay
caused and the spectacle it presented: the "shouting out with all their
might" and "dancing before the funeral chapel," the beating of breasts (in
loud lamentation) and tearing of clothes, the male coolies dressed like ti-
gers who "skip about the chapel," the "fencing" (probably stick fighting),
the alleged enmity expressed between Hindus and Muslims when their
respective processions encounter each other on the streets, the "warlike
demonstrations which generally follow the throwing of the tazzias into the
rivers or creeks . . . to show that the followers of the Prophet are ever ready
to fight his enemies, and never will forget the persecutions his grandsons
Hassan and Hosein suffered at the hands of the 'unbelievers'—Kaffirs—until
their deaths have been avenged. It is during these passages of arms that frequently some Muhammedan Coolie works himself up into a perfect state of
frenzy, and attacks any European or Creole who is not a believer. . . ."[22]
Thousands allegedly could bear testimony to this state of things. By the Victorian era, the portrait of the fulminating Oriental was a familiar one, and
formed part of the commonsensical recognition of coolies abroad as well as
their models, "Hindoos" and Muslims at home. But as with obeah, there is
thrill in the danger, the allure of exciting pandemonium—a voyeurism
that reinforces prefigured representations while also conveying an anything-
goes kind of scenario. Coolie tendencies and their behavioral expression
reveal the wildness that lies within; the executors of these (mis)adventures
could be mistaken for their savage brethren in Africa.

The problem of Hosay's (and other "pseudo-religious ceremonies") frenzied Orientals was compounded by the "black native population on the different plantations," who, Bronkhurst describes, "seem to be getting as fond of the annual show as the Coolies themselves are, and they follow the gaudily-dressed temples in thousands with all the appearance of religious fervor that marks the natives of the East." He quotes an 1873 account in the *Royal Gazette* newspaper that a "Creole Tadjah, originated and observed by black natives," was celebrated on the Sparta Plantation in Essequibo, another instance of "the love . . . springing up in the bosom of our native population for the 'Tadjah' . . . ; their passion for it has already broken down the very thin barrier of their Christianity . . ."[23] Bronkhurst concludes that the "heathen Coolies are brought here to till our sugar fields, and it becomes the solemn and responsible duty of the Christian, instead of countenancing or encouraging them in their vile practices or learning their ways, to set before them a holy, pious, and Christian example."[24] Here, Hosay's identification must rely on the very Christians who embrace it (which blurs its definitively "Eastern" borderlines), in order to be presented as not just non-Christian but as fundamentally antithetical to Christianity. Congregants, both black and white (who are, respectively, insufficiently religiously tutored and insufficiently religiously vigilant), are potentially leaking out of the fold, and disorder is fouling proper social harmony.

The assumptions evident in these stories are not unusual in the common sense of colonial West Indian popular discourse. The evocation of race and religion as both conjoined and disjoined "sliding signifiers" piqued my curiosity about how and when sliding signifiers become interpreted as more or less stable *things*.[25] Rather than begin with the "fact" of a particular identity category, however, one might inquire into how it got that way in the first place. The questions become these: How does the idea of something and its conceptual building blocks come into being? Why does it seem to stay that way or to change (whatever "change" may mean)? How, and how much, does it change? And what are the effects of this in everyday life? An interpretive category, an identity, can serve as the entryway to its own construction as well as being taken as final result. We must start with an identity, a focal point, in order to study it. Yet we need not treat it as a constant, but rather as a variable itself, a process or patterned system of identifications.

Today it is in some instances preferable or necessary to understand obeah and Hosay in racial and religious terms—to assert race and religion as being

fundamental and inalienable to them, and hence to their devotees, especially when social justice and civil rights are predicated on certain essential and heritable qualities associated with racial or religious identities. Describing race in Jamaica (and, as I think he would have agreed, in the rest
of the West Indies) as much a "hushed opprobrium" as "full-volume public
commentary," Stuart Hall understood that, there, "the matter of race could
seldom be spoken of for what it was, or barely even acknowledged. It was
all around, in every respect present, but could never quite be located or
articulated."[26] We still need such concepts as race and religion as powerful
means of articulation—daring to speak the name of racism and religious
bigotry in confronting social injustice so long engineered through racial
and religious signifiers yet denied or camouflaged. We speak truth to power
by calling it by its name and then reclaiming that name for other kinds of
projects. What we have in our current moment are identifiers that can be
reworked and redeployed.

At the same time, in order to fully understand the meaning and work of
race as something to be rejected or reclaimed, we must recognize the array
of phenomena that inform race as an interpretive category and that animate it as a mode of identification. Historian Diana Paton rightly points
out that "the prohibition of and hostility to obeah has not just been about
religion."[27] As I approach them, religion is never just about religion, nor
is race ever just about race. Interpretive categories of identity are self-
referential, but only as intersections of other aspects of identity. Many observers would not contest that unequal relations of power give rise to the
social hierarchies of human types according to which identities are structured and made consequential. But my contention is that no interpretive
category or identity is best interrogated as a single analytical object; its gen-
esis and influence happen, to one degree or another, in conjunction with
others. Not foregrounding this can imply that race, or any other identity, is
always and already there; the suggestion of essence is more likely to be kept
intact when we approach something as a touchstone against which all else
is explained. Instead, in any given context, certain aspects of self and other
attain particular importance as organizing principles in common sense, as
I argue race and religion do in the overlap moment of abolition and indenture, which has shaped the way we know obeah and Hosay in the
present. I am not arguing that there is some natural primacy in race and
religion that overshadows other key aspects of identity, such as gender and
class, only that colonial societies emphasized the former as they tried to

make sense of their environments, and that this moment continues to cast its long shadow.

## A Parallax View

As I pondered how to analytically tackle the nexus of race and religion—the racialization of religion and the religionization of race—embodied in traditions that themselves can be surreptitious or ambiguous, I was reminded of something curious that happens when one looks up at a star. Training one's eye slightly to one side gives a clearer image than looking at it head on. I was remembering from childhood practice what astronomers call a "parallax view," which refers to "the effect by which the position of an object seems to change when it is looked at from different positions."[28] A parallax view shifts attention from the objects themselves toward relations among them that entwine them in ways that define, redefine, or reinforce them, in order to attempt different ways of seeing things. This lends to the subjects being compared what may seem anomalous or unusual inferences in order to yield connections or contexts otherwise assumed to be discordant.[29] I look at obeah and Hosay from different points as an exercise in juxtaposition that can open up possibilities of perceiving unexpected formative features or relationships.[30]

Identities are categories that are animated by consciousness of self in relation to other; a parallax view of race and religion focuses on identities as sliding and thus intersectional, where reiterations occur among factors not necessarily similar to each other at the first, head-on glance—"similar" itself being an epistemological question—but which may be responsive to or created by certain shared conditions. As a concept, intersectionality, in legal scholar Kimberlé Crenshaw's theoretical framing, allows critique of the treatment of race and other identities as "mutually exclusive categories of experience and analysis" that understand discrimination as occurring "along a single categorical axis." Instead, multiple and interlinked forms of discrimination are at work in any given moment; no single aspect of identity, or discrete subset, overshadows, and thus marginalizes or erases, another.[31] Building on Crenshaw, I argue that the nexus of race and religion is a key expression of intersectionality, where what are conventionally conceived as mutually exclusive categories of experience are, when not viewed telescopically, drawn together into intersections in which aspects of identity may retain the appearance (and strategic utility) of being distinct but that, always in mutual reference, generate and give meaning to the ranked human "types" that both substantiate and justify them.

Intersectionality, and its categorical typologies, is part of how personhood is structured and made meaningful in Western societies, including those of the Americas. It relies on inherited Victorian race classifications that construct quintessential human types of person, meaning that we are today, to borrow from writer and social justice activist Audre Lorde, still working with the master's tools. The fundamental problem of the concept of intersectionality, as critics such as political scientist Adolph Reed argue, is the categorical typologies on which it is premised: they are ontological and idealist, presuming that "ideas are real things and have a real force and can do things in the world," and that "they have essences, ultimately, and the essence can be realized in the world." The concept of intersectionality, the critique goes, ultimately reiterates these typological distinctions: "instead of resolving the problem of essentialism by dissolving the essentialized categories," intersectionality increases them; "it's like fission," producing more discrete and sharply defined categories, which, in the process, are reified.[32] Yet in striving to contest essentialism, I argue, we must also scrutinize how the identity categories which ratify that essentialism serve and challenge structures of power. Analysts still engage these race science–derived identity categories precisely because this is how personhood is structured and made meaningful, in Western societies, at least, including those of the Americas. But analysts can do this while at the same time scrutinizing the truth-value of the identity categories according to which we live. Intersectionality is a conceptual tool, a way to capture how these reified typologies are presented as intersected or as discrete, according to the agendas of power, and a way to understand our *selves* while emphasizing the ways that they work in reference to each other.

Taking a parallax view helps to avoid the "race reductionism" that Reed, among others, warns is arguably a danger in working with reified typologies,[33] and it does so without eliding the concept of race and thereby denying the rac*ism* that variously and undeniably fuels much of how societies, including those of the Americas for the last 500 years, have been structured and operative. The challenge of a parallax view is to keep the objects of study themselves in proximate focus without reifying them, reserving ultimate focus on the relationships among these objects, which generate new or enhanced ways of understanding them. This goal requires a balancing act that necessarily has to shift analytical registers as objects and relationships are traced. Through a parallax view of obeah and Hosay, these registers are seen in concrete terms: as repeated themes that arose in various ways yet contain recurrent messages. Thinking about them in relation to each other invites a parallax view that emphasizes networks of analogies that can reveal the bigger picture of ideas about identity and identity's relations of power, which open up when obeah and Hosay are treated, so to speak, as larger than themselves. Robert Borofsky and his coauthors have lamented that "anthropological comparison in the traditional sense—as involving two or more social units—seems to have gone out of fashion."[34] The value of a parallax view is to advance comparative analysis by rethinking the boundedness and stability that "two or more social units" can imply, and to seek out the themes that, together, turn processes into "social units," or *things.*

In my exploration of obeah and Hosay through a parallax view, key themes emerged from the larger story that contextualize obeah and Hosay and that make them meaningful as racialized-religious identities. These themes—heritability, the rogue individual, and what I call an Atlantic common sense—collate ideas that emerged within climates of crisis. I argue that racial-religious anxieties were particularly salient under British colonial rule, providing an anxious context for both obeah and Hosay, and whose ways of knowing the (putative) identity of the other produced the racialization of religion and religionization of race, which remain in today's West Indies and its North American and North Atlantic diasporas.

### Heritability

The "president's problem is that he was born a Muslim, his father was a Muslim. The seed of Islam is passed through the father like the seed of Judaism is passed through the mother. He was born a Muslim, his father gave him an Islamic name," the Reverend Franklin Graham, son of the late Reverend Billy Graham, said in a CNN interview in August 2010, discussing a Pew Research Center survey taken that same year indicating that nearly one out of five Americans believed that the U.S. president, Barack Obama, was Muslim. Graham went on to say that he could only take President Obama's claim to Christianity on faith, so to speak, because Obama still carries the "seed" of religion, recessed in his genes, inherited from his progenitor father. Islam (and Judaism), it seems, is an unavoidable trait, much in the way that the president's race, "black," or, depending upon context, perhaps "black" and "white," is inherited. The metaphor of the seed lends both religion and race substance; through their common means of conduction, race (blackness) and religion (Islam) reinforce each other. Invisible ontologies thus can be traced through their visible expression as identity.

Graham's conviction that in certain cases religious identity is a dubiously escapable genealogical inheritance carried by seed arguably expresses his own parallax view. He reimagines a still tenacious truism of Western epistemology, which literary scholar Ania Loomba explains as the understanding of religious difference that is "rooted in culture, affiliated to discourses of faith and belief rather than those of the body, and therefore, at least theoretically, less rigid. But the history of racial formations testifies not to a neat separation between these categories but to their deep interconnection."[36] It is within the nexus of race and religion, in which the racialization of religion and the religionization of race takes place, that racial and religious identities are reinforced—naturalized as mutual expressions of each other even as they are treated as separate phenomena.

These processes of "naturalization" occur throughout the Atlantic world through what I argue is a notion of *heritability*: the quality through which religion becomes materialized and race becomes an intangible property, and by which both are substantiated by the persons who typify particular racialized-religionized identities through their practices—for example, those associated with obeah and Hosay. My approach to heritability as the conduit through which race is religionized and religion is racialized is in terms of the particular qualities that are thought to be transmitted through heritability, rather than substances and qualities that are in fact inherited. As historian Rebecca Goetz writes, the idea that religion might be hereditary has "long roots"—for example, the Spanish Inquisition's notion of blood purity (*limpieza de sangre*)—but it "found its full expression in the Americas."[37] In developing my ideas about the meaning and significance of heritability, I have drawn from anthropologist Diane Austin-Broos's work on contemporary Jamaicans' ideas about race and class as heritable identities, "constituted and reproduced through the sustaining of distinct environments," and Goetz's work on seventeenth-century colonial American ideas about religion as an inborn determinant of identity, which she terms "hereditary heathenism."[38] I am also mindful that there is a fine line between the Western notion of "heredity," based since the start of the twentieth century on the concept of genes, and the Western concept of "herita-bility," based on the premise of inherent and unchangeable human devel-opmental features transmitted genealogically through racialized-religionized groups. I therefore treat heritability as an "epistemic space" akin to Staffan Müller-Wille's and Hans-Jörg Rheinberger's approach to heredity, which they view as an epistemic space where "various historical and cultural realms," and the "knowledge regimes" these constitute, contribute to the formation of a given concept or idea.[39] Although, says Ian Hacking, "so-cial change creates new categories of people" and "people spontaneously come to fit their categories," new categories are actually variations on abiding themes.[40] Even social constructionist approaches to identity do not entirely escape this, albeit complex, notion of inherited identity. It rests on an implicit essentialism that persists—even despite objectives to the contrary—as the cornerstone of the concept of identity itself. These inherent qualities are the "natural" inheritances that constitute religion's essential core, an intangible "spirit," and race's essential core, a palpable embodiment. With Stuart Hall, we can think of discourses as cumulative archives that go on "unfolding, changing shape, as they make sense of new circumstances," but which also "carry many of the same unconscious premises and unexamined assumptions in their blood-stream."[41] As I noted above, however, race and religion each takes on the essential quality of the other as race is religionized and religion is racialized. In this sense, what is in the "blood-stream" can be both evanescent and inherent at the same time.

## The Rogue Individual

Vital to debates over proper social behavior in the colonial and postinde-pendence West Indies is an improper, disruptive social figure—what I call the *rogue individual*. He or she is a dangerous foil to propriety and confor-mity, a crucible of cultural values and attitudes about unacceptability and who not to be.[42] Rogue individuals are social figures who crystallize the changing dynamics of given archetypes in different circumstances.[43] My notion of the rogue individual in the West Indies is an archetypal deviant who contravenes the model of the proper subject who, directly or ultimately, reinforces the social and moral order. The Enlightenment's and post-Enlightenment's figure of the individual possesses free will and rational thought that is in the Cartesian sense separate from the body. Freedom is an interior state of mind that determines capacity and potential; it is an exterior condition realized through the practices of the civilized. More-over, by the turn of the eighteenth century, individual identity was under-stood in terms of a morality about right and wrong, an intuitive feeling that contrasted with an immoral approach to right and wrong through the cal-culation of consequences.[44] "Calculation" can easily slip into "crafty" and "duplicitous." The rogue individual carries this legacy, exercising the wrong kind of individuality and the wrong kind of agency, which are expressed through the body rather than the mind. Colonial experts debated these endowments of individuals, located along a developmental continuum: the capability to experience and handle freedom, to be rational persons and thus able to control one's passions and adjure one's sensibilities.[45] All of these capacities represented responsible members of society capable of advance-ment, just as incapacities represented those who were not.

My choice of the term "rogue" to describe individuals so problematic to British colonial authority rather than more general terms like "subaltern" or "marginalized" is meant to signal a tension in Western epistemology. This tension involves, on the one hand, the romanticization of insubordi-nate agency within normative ideals about the individual, such as, for ex-ample, the individual's ability to express contrarian "free will," but which ultimately upholds a society's moral imperatives about conformity (think of Robin Hood, an "outlaw" who performs Christianity-compatible social justice work—robs the rich, gives to the poor). On the other hand, there is the anxiety about an individual's insubordinate agency that perverts nor-mative ideals of individualism by challenging society's moral imperatives. In the West Indies, as we saw in the examples above and will see in subse-quent chapters, the figure of the rogue individual could titillate or amuse (and thus perhaps be associated with the "literary exoticism" of Britain's Romantic Period),[46] but this expression of individualism did not enjoy moral redemption. Being branded a "rogue" was not a trivial charge—whether implied in British colonial references to intractability and misconduct (no-tably in the context of labor) or, as in one document I read, explicitly la-beled as such.[47] This figure finds particular gravity at the intersection of race and religion in the nineteenth- and twentieth-century West Indies, and was salient as a way that obeah and Hosay could be identified. The rogue individual is one angle in a parallax view meant to capture the com-plex of ideas that worked to imagine, embody, and recognize both obeah and Hosay as encapsulating the troubling and at times terrifying tenor of daily life in these colonies, undermining the common sense that comprises their norms and values and yet whose threatening power also made them larger than life.

The figure of the rogue can be evoked in diverse sorts of imagery, suggesting different degrees of impropriety and nonconformity. Bronkhurst's description that "Coolies" participating in Hosay work themselves up "into a perfect state of frenzy," attacking "any European or Creole who is not a believer," is one extreme. Perhaps not as fearsome but certainly problematic is another rogue individual figure, described in a story told by British colonial administrator Hesketh Bell, who spent twenty-four years (1882–1906) in the West Indies and the Gold Coast. Bell recounts in his obeah memoir, *Obeah: Witchcraft in the West Indies*, an experience imparted to him, he says, by a West Indies "planter friend." The planter advises Bell that "as you are fresh from England and consequently know but little of the character of the negro, you can hardly realize the depth and extent of their superstition, or their unreasoning belief and dread of anything coming under the head of what they call 'Obeah.'"[48] Nonetheless, precisely identifying an obeah practitioner was a challenge, particularly "in these days" of the late nineteenth century, when an obeah man "would be hard to distinguish from other blacks." He "might only be known by wearing his hair long, or some other peculiarity, or else by possessing a good substantial house, built out of the money obtained from his credulous countrymen, in exchange for rubbishing simples or worthless love-spells." In earlier times, obeah men "were usually the oldest and most crafty of the blacks, those whose hoary heads and somewhat harsh and forbidding aspect, together with some skill in plants of the medicinal and poisonous species, qualified them for successful imposition on the weak and credulous. . . . A veil of mystery is cast over their incantations, which generally take place at the midnight hour, and every precaution is taken to conceal these ceremonies from the knowledge of the whites."[49] A decade earlier the Reverend Bronkhurst assured his readers that the "Obeahman, generally speaking, is deformed, ugly, with a lot of wrinkles on his face, and altogether a frightful object."[50] By the time Bell was writing *Obeah*, these were stock images of obeah practitioners and their doings, which had long circulated throughout Europe and its Caribbean colonies. Nonetheless, there also remained an uneasy opacity about this figure, difficult to make out, secretive, and potentially harmful, yet potentially also all the more entertaining for it.

The rogue individual emerged as a key figure from the labor coercion and criminalization that are the cornerstones of West Indian colonialism.

In presenting illegitimate versions of Enlightenment and post-Enlightenment notions of the ideal individual, which were based on particular conceptualizations of free will, autonomy, and self-realization, this figure symbolizes the "savage" and the "coolie" in ways that draw racialized-religionized identities together by analogy. The colonizer's rogue individual—the obeah practitioner and the Hosay enthusiast—represents a more encompassing yet nonetheless objectionable kind of blackness, which garbles the typological line between "African" and "Indian" yet does not erase it. In other words, the proper kind of individual manifests the correct kind of religion. Given the West's evolutionary hierarchy that defines "legitimate" religions and ranks them accordingly, the individual implicitly is European-white and the rogue individual implicitly is nonwhite. In the mid-twentieth century, on the eve of and after West Indian colonies' independence from Britain, governance transferred from British authorities to a new administrative elite comprised largely of black and brown leadership. Although always an important factor, class stratification became reinforced in the process, as an index of the rogue individual that emphasized intragroup—racial, religious, and so forth—differences between the socially proper and the socially rogue. The importance of class stratification to the identification of rogue individuals remains the case today. But like every facet of identity, class always works intersectionally with race; each mutually reinforces individual types and the groups they comprise rather than negating one category or the other.

One could say that British colonizers thought there was not enough that was communal in obeah, and that there was too much that was communal in Hosay. In both scenarios, however, the rogue individual perverts Enlightenment and post-Enlightenment ideals. The noncompliance of the rogue individual among subordinated populations—from alleged occult traffic with the devil, to the supposed wild abandon of festivals, to the clear and present danger of workers' rage—was explained by British colonial authority not in terms of structural inequality and gross injustice but in terms of the racial and religious identities of subordinated peoples, identities drawn from categorical types that dictated, and predicted, behavior, values, and aspirations. These identities were at times understood as separate, existing independently of each other; at other times they were treated as mutually constitutive. Either way, they were the primary focus of colonial anxiety, so apparent in the records that colonizers left. Both positions formed part of the common sense of West Indian societies so committed to the moral justification and practical maintenance of the sugar industry on which they were dependent and, postindenture, committed to the explanation of what appeared to be unequal development, stalled progress, and worrisomely incomplete modernity. In what one might call an Atlantic common sense, the figure of the rogue individual is both a character and a characteristic of the region.

## Atlantic Common Sense and Climates of Crisis

Assumptions about African and Indian identities and the work of "types" that characterize and explain West Indian peoples and societies in the past and in the present are undergirded by a tenacious system of logic that establishes the order of things, as Foucault termed it: what is given in things as their inner law, the hidden network of analogies that determines how they confront one another but that does not exist except in the grid of identities, similitudes, and analogies, the coherence according to which similar and different things are categorized.[51] This system of logic is produced within the race-religion nexus and kept alive as common sense.

As I employ it in this book, common sense is not a generic, positive term for received wisdom; rather, it is a depiction of the multitude of disparate, and sometimes contradictory, certainties that constitute the matrix within which "epistemic habits" are "easy to think"[52] or are, by association, "unthinkable."[53] I treat common sense as what Antonio Gramsci terms a "collective noun," a "relatively rigid phase of popular knowledge at a given time and place" which persists as the "folklore of the future."[54] Common sense organizes the basic landscape in which individuals are socialized to interact with each other and chart their life courses.[55] Common sense, the persistence of presumptions, is an optic through which to detect the historically contingent certainties and uncertainties of a particular moment, which produce particular climates of thought and feeling—"climates of crisis," as I call them.

The Caribbean's historical record, the official documents of colonial authorities and popular media typically produced by local elites, reveals a "prototype of the colonial mind and the fears that animated it.[56] British colonial authorities tried to manage the tension between, on the one hand, observing indentured laborers' rights as (putative) voluntary agents of their own free will who were aware, to one degree or another, of these rights while, on the other hand, profiting from their exploitation. In the colonial and postindependence West Indies, subordinates orchestrated threatening events such as rebellions, strikes, and more ambiguous presentations of noncompliance exemplified by alleged sociocultural developmental lag. These events had a cumulative effect: they produced an imaginary bloated with supposed and anticipated anxieties based on what might happen. The letters colonials wrote to each other, the ordinances they decreed, and the punishments they debated throw into relief the unnerving, ad hoc realities of a system that was presumably a streamlined machine of capitalism and civilization based on coerced labor. The perpetual state of uncertainty about this balancing act contributed to the climate of crisis that characterizes this era.

In the interest of social and moral order, West Indian authorities and elites needed to draw homologies among ostensibly unlike things, raising family resemblances when necessary, and to draw distinctions among ostensibly like things, negating family resemblances in the process. Categorical typologies of "African" and "Indian," their members' allegedly inherent inimical feelings about each other, and their inferiority to Euro-Christians were the epistemological foundation of colonial authorities' and other elites' reasoning about the climates of crisis in which they lived. These climates of crisis were exacerbated by the contrary possibility that through their shared primitivism (sometimes "savagery") Africans and Indians might be drawn toward each other rather than away, thus becoming collaborators against the colonizer. Official and popular media were preoccupied with the racially-religiously defined types so present and so threatening.

Well into the mid-twentieth century, British accounts continued to shape and reflect local ideas about African and Indian identity through their religious traditions. In his self-published study of obeah in Guyana, John Campbell wrote that it is believed that Indo-Guyanese "were attracted to the field of obeahism for its lucrative commercial value."[57] This presumption "could be traced back to the early twentieth century when Buckridee, an East Indian obeahman was convicted with others for the murder of Molly Schultz, the two year plus daughter of a white coffee planter on the West bank of the Demerara."[58] This assertion implies that although obeah itself may not be a natural proclivity among "East Indians," the stereotype of their predictable (natural) cupidity meshes well with this lucrative (and evil) "field" of the occult. The story continues that Buckridee allegedly told his clients to procure the eyes of a "buckra" ("white") "picnee" (child) in their request for his help to get them a promotion on the sugar plantation. Buckridee's defense was that in his language, "buckra" means "goat," and that goats were commonly sacrificed at the religious ritual known as "Kali Mai Puja."[59] Nevertheless, the jury sentenced him to hang.[60] Campbell added that during "the same period there were several reports of children being sacrificed in India in what was described as ritual murders."[61] Whether elaborating on the context of this murder case or suggesting the obeah man's culpability, Campbell implies that India is the logical link between dark rituals, the deeds of sociopathic behavior, and the guileful attempts at self-exoneration.

Campbell portrays Indians and India as sharing with Africans and Africa both malevolence and cunning—in the form of obeah. Coolie obeah men might also have been regarded as evoking an esoteric engagement with the universe's mysteries, including such "oriental" talents as telepathy and mind reading, popularized by late nineteenth- and early twentieth-century mystic philosophers like Madame Blavatsky and publisher Lauron William de Laurence.[62] Yet the special talents of coolies *as* coolies may be employed toward obeah's end goals, but they are still primarily identified as "coolies," the racializing term for indentured laborers. In other words, as long as they are "coolies," they do not own the obeah of an Afro-demographically dominant (and historically older) population; their essential spiritual qualities simply make them good at it.

As this illustration suggests, the crisscrossing movements among presumably stable categories allow access to customs and traditions of other types. But it is a postancestral borrowing, which is not the same as ownership. The types themselves are fluid and stable at the same time, not one or the other. In a paradoxical sense, movement reinforces stability in terms of the way that the events and people are represented in popular discourse. There is an implicit distinction between *individuals'* practice of something and the ways those practices create family resemblances, and the categorical *thing* itself. Indians keep their ostensibly inherent spiritual qualities, which are "oriental," not black or African. Obeah implicitly remains exclusively black or African. Yet both easily can be made analogous: an uncivilized human evolutionary stage. This backward, inferior condition became frightfully ignited in the form of obeah and Hosay, in their association with labor and social order in the sugar plantation–engraved societies of this region.

In these representations, race and religion variously intersect, and directly or by implication circulated throughout the West Indies, and the greater Atlantic world, as its common sense. In their intersections, race and reli-

gion are compressed into different kinds of things which share family resemblances that, perhaps counterintuitively, reinforce their familiarity and
thus their truth. Obeah and Hosay are such things—vehicles of race and
religion attainting particular meanings that indicate certain human types.
In the postemancipation period obeah became even more problematic for
the social and moral order.[63] In the colonial optic, obeah and Hosay were
never entirely separated from their ancestral origins, but their shared forms
of racialization and religionization made former slave and coolie—laborers,
not proprietors; heathens, not Christians; vestigial "savages," not civilized—
often more analogous than not.

Making sense of the meaning of relationships among subordinated populations in the West Indies—characterized as constitutionally either antithetical or interconnected—and determining their significance for interpreting social and cultural reproduction under unequal relations of power
(that is to say, "creolization") remains in the West Indies today among the
more insistent preoccupations among scholars, policy makers, activists, and
ordinary people. No longer are models of unequally ranked stages of human
development and accomplishments central to scholarly thinking, although
in commonsense wisdom these ideas are far from entirely disappearing.
Moreover, still shadowing common sense about social interaction and cultural reproduction is the premise that identities are heritable, and that
their fundamental differences are the root of mutual hostilities which must
be managed, either through top-down (colonial) governance or through
rhetorical (national) strategies about sameness.

## Rethinking Boundedness

As a student of mine once summed up evocatively, "History has a lot of
secrets."[64] I think of history's secrets as a kind of historical and sociological
reality, empirically observed and verified, and imagined into palpability
when they are not. The paradox of secrets, as philosopher Georg Simmel
understood, is that something can only be a secret if it can be revealed;
secrets are seductive precisely because they are always subject to revelation.
For Simmel, secrecy is a universal sociological form.[65] My attraction to secrets is more particular: they are what is unsaid but present, or misspoken
but axiomatic, and, living between the lines of history, they constitute evidence that is always more than what it seems and that can be excavated by
reading between those lines. These "mute meanings," as anthropologists
John and Jean Comaroff call them, are "transacted through goods and

practices, through icons and images dispersed in the landscape of the everyday."[66] The question is the excavation: guided by what methods and theoretical goals? Reading between the lines of evidence for mute meanings is an anthropologist's stock in trade, one of the techniques of the ethnographic method. The diverse kinds of texts that anthropologists interpret—"books, bodies, buildings"—are "scattered shards from which we presume worlds."[67] Anthropology gives me permission to extrapolate, helping me to imagine documented pasts as interlocutors' stories; even the most stilted of formal documents contains an ethnographic footprint—lived experience that is no less lively than it is assumed to be in such seemingly spontaneous or unself-conscious expression as "novels, songs, or children's games."[68] I treat documentary materials as if they were dialogues and conversations freighted with obvious, subtle, and oblique messages that can be decoded with sufficient knowledge of, and educated speculation about, the cultural and historical contexts in which these dialogues and conversations take place. Often these stories purport to prove a single truth, especially when they are generated by governing authorities and their representatives. What a parallax view can do is refract that "truth" into its numerous and unevenly empowered constituent parts that represent different stakes and vested interests. In this way a parallax view can forge new units of analysis that produce storied histories of the local.

Given my starting point of the mid-nineteenth century in the colonial world, all of my subjects are people *with* history, whose lives were indelibly shaped by the historical forces with which they contended. I mined the texts of history that are housed in archives for as much as I could glean of the perspectives of those subjected to documentation—the unequally valued "people without history"[69]—as I could glean from the perspectives of those doing the documenting (and the subjugating). To both I applied an anthropologist's interest in meaning and interpretation, and an ethnographer's practice of scrutinizing quotidian experience, treating, as much as possible, the long gone as I treat the alive and well. I did not problematize disciplines and their boundaries; I moved across them in what I would like to think is in the spirit of a comment John Comaroff made forty years ago, that "there ought to be no 'relationship' between history and anthropology, since there should be no division to begin with."[70] I have consulted colonial documents housed in the National Archives and British Library in England, and in the National Archives and main library of the University of the West Indies, in Trinidad, and gathered ethnographic data in Trinidad and Guyana. My research mission in the archives was to capture "mute meanings" as well as to glean key patterns, assumptions, and reiterations from official correspondence, reports, and popular media such as newspapers and memoirs that constituted the common sense of the day about regimes of truth and of rule during the era when Britain replaced enslavement with indenture in its West Indian colonies and Indians joined Africans in the landscape of production—in the process associating both as antithetical or as analogous.[71] If pressed, I would say that this book is largely a work of historical anthropology, based on extensive archival work, which then pivots to the current day in its later chapters.

I am indebted to earlier and current scholarship on Hosay and obeah and have drawn from the literature on both, as well as from my own three decades of ethnographic and archival research. Hosay enjoys a good foundation of historical and anthropological work, although this body of literature is far smaller than is obeah's.[72] Obeah has a longer history in the West Indies; it is a catchall term that is applied to a multitude of phenomena;[73] there is a great deal of contemporary scholarship on obeah; obeah remains pervasive in popular culture, often signifying "voodoo," magic, or generic African folk traditions. Obeah also has been viewed by numerous scholars as an entry point into broader issues of domination and resistance.[74]

My analysis began with this chapter, which introduces these two racialized-religionized traditions living in the space of overlap between the end of slavery and the beginning of indenture in the West Indies. Chapters 2 and 3 focus on the nineteenth- and early twentieth-century West Indian colonial plantation, looking in particular, respectively, at Hosay's and then at obeah's relationship to the key anxieties about racial and religious others that were central aspects of colonial lifeworlds, and the ways that this relationship molded Hosay and obeah into cultural traditions as well as sets of practices. I follow this period through the end of the British colonial indenture system in 1917 and the decades of its aftermath. Chapter 4 takes up obeah in the contemporary moment, approaching it as a constituent of racialized-religionized diasporic identities brought by and developed among the "Windrush Generation" of postwar-era West Indian immigrants to Great Britain and by present-day immigrant communities in North America. I highlight the imagery of obeah in two of its major social presences—creative arts and legal systems—different social fields that are nonetheless interlocutors in the ways that obeah lives on today. Next, in Chapter 5, I explore Hosay in present-day Trinidad in terms of its diverse and multilayered meanings among devotees as they craft for themselves personal and public statements about religious (or spiritual) devotion, racial and other diversity, and the genealogies of heritage. I conclude, in Chapter 6, with an exploratory critique of the concept of identity, as it informs and animates the forms of agency and personhood that race and religion, obeah and Hosay embody and express.

*The Deepest Dye* is not about obeah and Hosay per se, individuated and adjacent, compared as clearly boundaried social units. But neither are obeah and Hosay essentially the same processes with different manifest ideological content. Thinking about them through a parallax view can reveal the bigger picture of ideas about identity and identity's relations of power, which open up when obeah and Hosay are treated, so to speak, as larger than themselves. The value of a parallax view is to advance comparative analysis by rethinking the boundedness and stability that "anthropological comparison in the traditional sense" of "two or more social units" can imply,[75] and to seek out the themes that, together, turn processes into social units, or *things*.

Race and religion, and any other identities, are not inevitable conditions of being in the world that simply require fine-tuning to be in service of justice and equality—however those may be defined. This book represents my own efforts to understand race and religion as always multivariate, necessarily intersected by certain other social-structural factors that, in a given moment and context, lend race and religion their substance, their meaning, and their effects. How do we understand and value the racialized and religionized selves we have inherited? How might we attempt to challenge those constructions when the fundamentals of that heritage still remain? A book that begins with the West Indian plantation and colonial authority and ends with West Indian popular culture and religious practice today will, I hope, challenge readers' understandings of obeah and Hosay, and expand our interpretations of what they can tell us about the ways we know our racialized-religionized selves and others.

# 2

## PLANTATIONS AND CLIMATES OF CRISIS

In this chapter I look at what I call climates of crisis that colonialism's long shadow cast in the West Indies, and the influence of crisis in shaping understandings of obeah and Hosay.[1] Their reification into dangerous *things* emanated from that costly, precarious, and vulnerable Euro-colonial capitalist venture, the sugar plantation. It was a risky business to establish settlements and colonies far from the metropole that relied on a monocrop (sugar) economy based on coerced and often insufficient labor. That risks were taken, and some great fortunes made, did not do much to dull the apprehensions which saturated the societies that formed around the plantations. Nothing in that life was reliable, not the least being the organization and control of labor, whether enslaved or indentured: always simmering to a boil, ready to erupt—which it did. For much of obeah's and Hosay's history in the region they have been represented by governing authorities and privileged citizenry as an ever-present danger to the racial and religious social order that structured and justified colonial society. The unease and sometimes alarm with which they were associated was fueled significantly by currents of social unrest, particularly labor unrest, partially explained by Euro-colonial models—Enlightenment and post-Enlightenment derived—of the uneven evolutionary progress of different human types, from "savage" to "civilized." The threat posed by obeah and Hosay was policed through the criticism, criminalization, and persecution of beliefs that purportedly encouraged social disobedience in espousing alternative worldviews; policing was also enacted through criticism, criminalization, and persecution of the human types who embodied these beliefs and carried them out.

Obeah takes center stage in the next chapter; here the main focus is on Hosay, which comes into popular awareness, and concern, in conjunction with postemancipation, plantation-bound indentured Indian immigrant labor. Rather than organize my discussion as a chronology of events, I wish to capture a mood—of uncertainty, of anxiety—and key circumstances that contributed to it. In this spirit I offer illustrative material from a number of decades between 1838 and the turn of the twentieth century—the heyday of postemancipation plantation life and labor. Two broad periods characterize the plantation context. One begins at the end of the 1830s, when slavery was working its way toward abolition, and continues through the 1870s. This is a time when the "experiment" of indenture was attempting to find its footing through control of process and people. The second period is roughly from the 1880s to the early 1900s, a time of escalating labor unrest, sugar market uncertainty, and vilification of Hosay as cause and consequence of the "coolie problem." Subsections highlight different aspects of crisis that together constituted a climate in which indenture had to be justified and promoted, labor had to be secured and controlled, plantation production had to conform to the demands of a global market, and the racialization of Indian "coolies" and their traditions, like Hosay, was construed in the pall of a labor regime now renounced but whose racialization of Afro-Caribbean former slaves remained a vibrant touchstone.

### Colonialism's Long Shadow: The Twilight Zone of Existence

Climates of crisis is a trope of West Indian plantation society and, more generally, throughout the Atlantic world. These climates emerged at the inception of Euro-colonial capitalism's accidental entry into the region in 1492 and lasted well into the postindependence era (at which time other, newer yet related crises would come to characterize the region, which I consider in later chapters). My focus in this chapter is on West Indian societies at the end of slavery and the commencement of indenture, both marked by the year 1838. Although the indenture system was officially ceased in 1917, I end this chapter around the turn of the twentieth century. History's endings and beginnings are rarely if ever abrupt; changes unfold in overlapping transitions rather than as neat cleavages. I treat this period in two ways: as a historical moment in which slavery's end and indenture's beginning are conjoined, and also as a site of production that was subject to the vicissitudes of nature uncontrollable and human folly in the form of profound mass oppression. Various crises charged this atmosphere. The frequency, intensity, and widespread dispersal of hurricanes kept colonists in a worried state about their economic and social futures throughout a region Matthew Mulcahy calls the "British Greater Caribbean," conveying the great range and shared impact of these devastating natural disasters.[2]

Near-constant subaltern rebellions, most notably those among enslaved Africans, reverberated throughout the region, one that Vincent Brown characterizes as "an archipelago of insurrection" throughout the North Atlantic Americas, where war in the form of slave revolts was a way of life, leaving colonies like Jamaica in a state of perennial anxiety.[3] By the time the era of Indian immigrant indentured labor was in full swing, Gaiutra Bahadur tells us, "Everywhere in the sugar colonies, the suicide rate outstripped that in India."[4] Whether from natural calamities like wild weather or man-made disasters like slavery and indenture, the unpredictability that was always a predictable aspect of life in West Indian plantation societies generated a steady climate of crisis, which obeah and Hosay were viewed as both fueling and exemplifying.

This climate necessarily, then, consisted of the commonsense knowledge, largely involving feared calamities, through which people—the empowered and the vulnerable—understood their societies and the lives that they lived in them. The coolie laborer and the indenture plantation emerged on the heels of emancipation. There were important differences in these two systems of exploitation, notably the ideal of universal individual liberty that characterized postemancipation society. But this signal change was less a clean transition from one system to the other than a space of overlap between them. Madhavi Kale rightly describes this overlap as an ambiguous space between slavery and freedom that derived from indenture representing both "investment opportunities" and an "instrument for civilization."[5] My interest is in this ambiguous space's fostering of commonsense assumptions about obeah and Hosay, which cast labor into ranked and intersected racial and religious types of people and interpreted the cultural practices that identified them. These ways of knowing were based simultaneously on inference and empirical observation, blurring the lines dividing such ostensibly stable binaries as African/Indian and civilized/savage that ordered plantation life.

Crises of various kinds, real and imagined, texture the social and cultural contexts in which obeah and Hosay came to be known as particular kinds of *things*: worrisome to some, welcomed by others, but always bellwethers of colonialism's crises. For many decades scholars have made abundantly clear that colonial Caribbean societies were almost always on the edge—cauldrons of fear, force, and tense braveries. My aim is to highlight key arenas of indenture plantation life on the edge, the locus of tensions that contributed to the making of societies experienced as socially unstable, in need of careful monitoring and precise "understandings" of the identities of laborers on which these societies were aversely dependent.

Indenture plantation society had the same "recurring dynamic" of disruption as did slave plantation society: insubordination, uprisings, and flight.[6] This continuing dynamic perpetuated a crisis climate in the postemancipation era that maintained slavery's principle means of social control: the criminalization of noncompliance. Retaining its emphasis on labor and violence, criminalization was at the center of indenture plantation life both as practical strategies of discipline and insistently lingering epistemic habit. The indenture era also marked the projection of Britain's self-image as enlightened global leader in terms of its credibility and claims to moral superiority in an antislavery, postemancipation new, and not so new, world order. This perceived responsibility complicated criminalization's implementation, making the lines between free and unfree, legitimate and illegitimate more equivocal. The uncertainties of indenture plantation societies were aggravated, moreover, by a major contradiction: civil matters like workers' obligations and rights stipulated by contract were treated as criminal issues; simply withholding labor was punishable according to criminal law.[7] David Trotman aptly calls this "half-free nature of indentureship" the "twilight zone of existence."[8] It is in this anxious atmosphere of attempts to interpret events and situations and to justify their control that race and religion, as properties that define human beings, are treated as both analogous and unrelated, and, either way, as heritable properties. This context is also a formative moment in the ways that obeah and Hosay define types of person. Whether mentioned by name or not, they remain intersected, implicit interlocutors and reference points. The plantation was both symbolic site of "coolie" identity and material factor in their (working) class location; as such, it evoked coolie savagery and backwardness, a racialized resemblance to African laborers.

Despite indenture contracts that stipulated the obligations and rights of planters and the indentured, measures were often draconian in practice. This reflected some ad hoc elasticity in the formalized agreement, which arguably mirrored conditions under slavery. Britain first forayed into its indenture scheme, known as the Gladstone Experiment, in 1838 in British Guiana. A driver on Gladstone's plantation, Vreed-en-Hoop, was reported to have "freely used the cat-o'-nine-tails on the backs of coolies and had then cleansed the wounds with salt water."[9] These kinds of atrocities went on routinely when indenture was the business of private companies, as in

Cuba.[10] In 1839, 53 out of 405 indentured laborers died; five years later, in 1844, almost 25 percent of British Guiana's indentured labor population—98 persons out of 405—had died.[11] Despite its stated principles, British government-sponsored indenture never entirely made the separation from slavery in real terms. Eight decades after indenture ended, the noted Jamaican scholar, activist, and artist Rex Nettleford wrote that in contemporary Jamaican society, "rich East Indians" are not "negrified' as their racial counterparts on the estates [plantations]," "negrified," he explains, being "a special feature of the Euro-African complex" that "implies a metropolitan European perspective of the African essence in the New World and more generally of the creole culture."[12] The former slave and the coolie share a blackness through their "negrification" in connection with the plantation; views of colonized labor overlapped, linking one system of exploitation to another.

The ideals of individual liberty promulgated in postemancipation society were susceptible to the pressures of production and profit. Starting in the 1850s the British government began to reduce certain rights associated with free persons, including indentured laborers. These changed priorities, wrote Edgar Erickson, "can be attributed to the decrease in the influence of the humanitarian interests on the colonial office and the recognition of the natural improvidence of the Indian immigrants."[13] Indians were a type that was by nature lacking in foresight and the ability to plan for the future. True to form, Trinidad's Governor Harris (1846–1854), for example, characterized "coolies" as "naturally dissolute and depraved," yet likened them to "wayward children."[14] This representation of the childlike colonized (which was never fully abandoned, even well into the twentieth century)[15] confirmed an Enlightenment-based cultural evolutionary model that now needed to be "enlightened" (magnanimous, paternalistic). The experimental frontier of indenture fluctuated between fixed certainties and fragile hypotheses. More pronounced than under the earlier system of slavery, these fluctuations arguably made indenture an equally, or even more precarious bet.

Fluctuations between certainty and hypothesis also disrupted the "racializing surveillance" that the requirements of the indenture contract amounted to. As Simone Browne defines it, racializing surveillance is a method of social control where surveillance practices produce norms relating to race, thereby determining what is in its proper place and what is out of place. These processes "reify boundaries, borders, and bodies along racial lines" that result in discriminatory treatment of those who are "negatively racial-ized by such surveillance." Browne sees these strategies of domination as connected to Euro-colonial expansion and transatlantic slavery, and con-siders a range of cases of the reification of blackness through racial surveil-lance of African American and Afro-Atlantic diaspora peoples.[16] But pre-cisely because racial surveillance is temporally and spatially contingent, and is therefore dynamic rather than static,[17] transatlantic indenture and its plantation societies also were laboratories, if more experimental than intended, of what amounts to racial surveillance. Whether the race of "coolies" seemed more "African" than "Indian" or it emphasized their In-dian/Eastern/Oriental qualities, the plantation watch was potent both symbolically and literally. Mobility and compliance were guarded—if clearly often unsuccessfully—through targeting, and conflating, "coolie" cultural and genetic heritage (themselves similarly heritable), phenotype, behavior, and customary traditions. Surveillance techniques symbolized particular races in a tautology of behavior-proves-race/race-predicts-behavior, and affected coolies in literal terms—for example, by close tracking of their daily work tasks and requiring by law that they secure of-ficial permission (and paperwork) to leave the plantation. These strategies reified the racial "coolie" as they had reified the racial "slave."

Despite its reliance on unmechanized human labor, the plantation pro-duction on which indenture societies depended aspired to be a well-oiled machine. But it is more accurate to think of the rationalized management of their operation as a wish list, an aspiration energetically striven for, but also the seedbed of grey areas incompletely or contradictorily enforced. Co-lonial authorities spent a good deal of the indenture period they helped create trying to assess general conditions and to anticipate and manage in-dividual situations and events. Regimentation was unpredictable and con-flictual, with ongoing attempts on the part of those in power to suppress conflict and unpredictability, at times seemingly figuring it out ad hoc as they went. Indenture's regimentation was often uncertain, confusing, wor-risome, and thus always in need of flexible oversight. Under slavery the exploitation and caprice of the plantocracy had few institutionalized forms of monitoring. Indenture's plantocracy were "employers" rather than "mas-ters" who underwent more scrutiny. Indenture was de jure a system of ex-ploitation more in line with the insistence central to capitalist rationale: that workers enter freely into contractual agreements to sell their labor power rather than laboring by means of force. Contracts represented this "freedom," but workers represented a different type of human being than Europeans: they were suited to a certain kind of labor, and life, according to race—a character comprised of physical, mental, and emotional essences. This distinction between a racialized coolie and political-economic theory's generic proletarian was another of indenture's major contradictions.[18]

Thus indenture was de facto more complicated than simply the "free will" arrangement that helped to morally condemn and correct the evils of enslavement. This system, required to be watching itself as much as it had to watch its others, was all the more inexact and worrisome for this balancing act of gentility with extraction by any means necessary that would not get caught. The familiar scholarly debate between indenture being "a new system of slavery"[19] or "a form of slavery by another name"[20] versus being a different arrangement whose regulation indicates an improved existence for its "bound coolies" continues to dominate the discussion.[21] Oversimplified, it fosters misguided comparison between the supposed liberties of indentured life, particularly in the domains of cultural expression like religion (notably Hosay) and the exigencies of enslaved life, with slavery's attempts to repress cultural expression like religion (notably obeah). The enslaved made their own religious worlds, and indentured laborers struggled against the restrictions placed on theirs.

Correspondence between British Guiana governor Sir John Scott and Earl Granville, the colonial secretary, about Ordinance No. 16 of 1869, captures the tensions between liberty and restriction. Ordinance No. 16 provided for "the due regulation of the Festivals and Processions of East Indian Immigrants in this Colony." The reason for the ordinance was "to prevent as far as possible the sometimes violent proceedings of these immigrants, often leading to breaches of the peace amongst themselves." The religious festivals of the indentured laborers were clearly threatening in terms of the violence that instigated the disruption of "due order." Although the letter stated plainly that it "is not intended to prohibit any of these religious festivals, or in any way interfere with them," the Ordinance stipulated that "any contravention" of its regulations, which were empowered by the governor, were "penal." Yet "after full consideration," it was deemed that "the best plan would be to authorize the Governor from time to time to issue regulations by Proclamation which could be varied to suit different localities and to be amended or altered as circumstances and experience might render expedient." The letter adds, almost as a reassuring afterthought, that the religious festivals "only take place once a year."[22] There is, on the one hand, the problem of not betraying the postemancipation commitment to freedom and free will (essentially the white man's burden), while, on the other hand, keeping labor on site and tractable. The pull between a noninterference directive, a fear of violent chaos and possible social upheaval, the need to keep costs low and profits high, and an ultimate decision to play things by ear suggest the uncertain, work-in-progress character of the indenture system. In 1906, just eleven years before the indenture system ended, the Colonial Office's *Memorandum on East Indian Immigration to the West Indies* noted that in "British Guiana alone no less than 98 Ordinances have been passed for the regulation of immigration since the system began, the main Ordinance (25 of 1891) containing no less than 240 clauses."[23] Arguably, indenture never entirely ceased its experimental character, as the various parties involved sought to standardize as they could, justify as they felt was warranted and according to the tenor of the times, and maximize or at least maintain profit as much as possible. The *Report of the Committee on Emigration from India to the Crown Colonies and Protectorates*, published in 1910, summed up both indenture's vexing contradiction and its dependence on factors that were unpredictable. The committee wrote, "There is much to be said in disfavour of imprisonment for breach of a civil contract, but the proposed remedy—getting judgement in court for damages—is worse than the disease; it would be impoverishing the man; and, as to branding him as a 'rogue' and repatriating him, let the knowledge of this once get abroad and immigrant ships would become tourist steamers for as many as cared to try it on."[24] As this comment makes clear, stakes and uncertainties were high.

At times the charge of wage-depression through the importation of scab labor was the critique, and this was voiced throughout indenture's duration. Other of indenture's opponents recognized the need for steady agricultural labor but drew a distinction between local, "immigrant," and "indentured." For example, in 1903, British Guiana's *Daily Chronicle* newspaper printed an editorial arguing that "there is today a superabundance of coolie labor"; that "although the sugar planter . . . asserts that . . . coolie immigration is necessitated by the natural laziness of the negro and his unreliability for steady and continuous toil," the only "true" reason, according to this writer, is "the planter's desire and determination to obtain cheap labour, which is secured, partly at the cost of the general tax payer, by means of the indentured coolie, since the black or native is unwilling, from his more civilized habits and greater needs, to work for less than a fair living wage."[25] Here, the "black or native," by now suitably "Western," is more civilized, indicating the virtues of asserting one's sovereignty and individuals' rights and appreciation of fair play. But also evident are strains resulting from the pressure of cost: Who financially underwrites the system, and who profits from it? It involves some powerful if convoluted logic about race and its hierarchies, and their association with unrest and disorder.

The *Memorandum* of 1906, however, reflects greater ambivalence about the capacity of its subjects, an ambivalence between praise and disdain. It asserts that "the coolies are infinitely better off in the West Indies than in India." Coolie children born in the colonies "revert to a higher type of civilization. The daughters of men who do not require them to work, they lead a happy life, free from the care and toil which aged their mothers before they had reached their prime. . . . The immigration system of this Colony (British Guiana) stands as an example to all the world of British fairness, honesty, and organisation in the beneficial control of a humble and dependent race."[26] The self-congratulatory tone of paternalism is plain, but it was always in conversation with another sort of white man's burden: ungrateful and dangerous beneficiaries.

Other forms of (mis)recognition reinforced racial and cultural hierarchies. In a letter sent almost six decades earlier, in 1849, to circuit stipendiary magistrate W. B. Wolseley from C. A. Goodman, acting stipendiary magistrate in British Guiana, Goodman enters what was already an animated discussion about the relative value of immigrant labor versus indentured labor. He was "strongly of opinion that a system of Indenture is absolutely necessary for the class of Immigrants imported to this Country, there can be no question as to the utility of the contract in producing steady and certain Labor on an Estate, the habits of the Immigrants both from India and Africa are decidedly migratory," thus they must be "placed under some kind of restraint on their arrival to gradually impress on their minds the necessity of sober and steady labour."[27] It is a win-win situation, Goodman argues, where planters get a continuous, ostensibly guaranteed labor force, and among indentured immigrants "a vast good accrues"; for "besides learning industrious and steady habits," it is a "humane measure to Indenture for a limited time the barbarous African or demoralized and Ignorant Coolie."[28] The critical, underlying consideration in these discussions was that of race: How to permit, and by implication valorize (or not), the natures of racially inferior peoples?

Another example of the vestigial forms of racial thinking even among those in whom one might not expect to find it is the Canadian journalist and lawyer William Grant Sewell. In 1861 he published *The Ordeal of Free Labor in the British West Indies* in which he assured readers that he was presenting "information" based on his "actual observations." As much as the colonies profited from indenture, it was "scarcely equal to the blessing that this immigration scheme has conferred upon the coolie himself. . . . A poor pagan, he is brought in contact with civilization, and soon forgets and abandons the gross superstitions in which he was wont to put his faith. . . . The coolies who go back after an industrial residence [i.e., indenture], go back to spread abroad the seeds of civilization and Christianity."[29] As "perfectly free men and women," and, importantly, by their own free will–driven choice, coolies "leave the squalid filth and misery in which they have been accustomed to live . . ." When they begin their indenture they are "a set of naked, half-starved, gibbering savages, ready to eat any dead, putrid animal, fish, flesh, or fowl that lay in their path." But those who return to India "are clothed, sleek, and well-fed, strong and able-bodied, speaking English with tolerable accuracy and looking the intelligent people that they really are. I have seen them arrive and I have seen them depart and speak from actual observation," Sewell testified.[30] Thus the true nature of coolies' potential is released with the civilizing forces of indenture. "It seems to have been decreed in the providence of God," Sewell opined, "that these fair and fertile islands should ultimately become an asylum for millions of wanderers from heathenesse [*sic*]"; indenture, then, should not be condemned but rather "upheld, defended, and perfected . . . as a plan most happily devised for the elevation of a degraded people and for the restoration to prosperity of a splendid inheritance."[31] Another win-win scenario.

By this logic, shared among a number of commentators of the day, as emancipation uplifted former slaves, so did indenture among coolies. "Freedom" is what both ostensibly shared. Defending the rights of coolies as, for example, the Protector of Immigrants in each West Indian colony was charged to do, served the purpose of not only supporting antislavery efforts but also of emphasizing freedom as a condition, the measure of man rather than the more delimited principle of a labor scheme. Nothing short of evolutionary progress was at stake for both ex-slave and coolie, but for the former it meant the achievement of freedom by *not* being bound; for the "bound coolie," freedom was achieved *with* such binding—labor's legal contract. When coolies "rioted," for example (went on strike), more was at stake than just plantation production. Such acts chipped away at, or contradicted, the rationale of freedom embedded in the notion of voluntary labor, a notion that under slavery was held in esteem only for the already and necessarily free.

### Between Departure and Arrival

Plantation labor in the West Indies initially included a range of immigrant labor—Africans, Madeirans, and Chinese, as well as Indians. Indians soon became the majority population on plantations. In 1851, for example, they were 16 percent of British Guiana's plantation labor force; by 1891 they were 80 percent.[32] In 1872 Indians in Trinidad were about 75 percent of plantation labor; by 1889 they were about 81 percent. Even by the mid-1870s in Trinidad and British Guiana, "sugar worker" and "Indian worker" were equivalent.[33] Yet this predominance of coolie labor belies the challenges faced in their procurement and thus underestimates the climate of crisis in which indenture functioned. Tensions arose, and never entirely subsided, around the need for labor and methods for labor's recruitment. It is difficult to control the message (rules and expectations of indenture) when the messenger (agents and recruiters) and the recruited (potential "coolies") are not within firm grasp and have their own agendas.

Recruiters sought above all else to deliver bodies to the depots. But departures were not certain. Indenture had only nine years of life left in 1908, yet A. Marsden, government emigration agent for Trinidad, Jamaica, Fiji, and Mauritius, wrote to London's under-secretary of state for the colonies about the emigration depot on the Hooghly River and the need to find a new site for it because British colonial "tenure of this Depot" was ending. There were important factors to consider as decisions were made about the establishment of depots, not the least being that in this case, and assuredly others, emigration depots were not permanent sites. "There will have been no less than 4 changes in the Emigration Depots here in 15 years," Marsden reported, "owning to the growth of Calcutta and expansion of trade and also to the fact that the Colonies have been tenants and not landlords."[34] Added to the inexorable changes over which the British had no control yet which dictated to an extent the kind of presence they could exercise in India was the problem that an "indentured Emigrant," Marsden advised, "is not like a prisoner to whom force can be applied, or a pilgrim inspired with religious enthusiasm about to visit a shrine, and it is therefore essential that the Depot should be in close proximity to the river side or a dock, so that embarkation may take place smoothly as possible and without wayside temptations to desert. . . . Were the depot some distance from the steamer, many emigrants would avail themselves during periods of famine of the entertainment afforded by the Depot during the days of collection and preparation for shipment, only to disappear in transit when the day for embarkation arrived, and although such conduct is actionable, experience has shown that it is not worth while prosecuting except in exceptional or aggravated cases, and then the delinquent has to be caught first."[35] Here is a use of emigration depots neither intended nor anticipated by the indenture system. The "entertainment" during famine periods clearly refers to access to food, and the resolve of locals not to starve.

Nonetheless, as much as the exercise of agency among the subjugated reveals hegemony's gaps and crevices, it does not suggest a balance of power. Depots were warehouses of both human capital and capital in other material forms, notably what was required to maintain plantation-bound coolies in minimum fitness for the voyage across and for work on arrival. This maintenance was meant for coolies-to-be, not for sojourning locals. But prosecution, as Marsden notes, was a complicated matter. Besides having to apprehend the "delinquent," which was apparently often a hit-and-miss effort, punishment was inadvisable because it would not be good for business if indenture became associated with draconian treatment on the departure side. Much of the historical record and contemporary discussion of indenture on the arrival side in the colonies—including virtually all of the literature on Hosay—deals with labor's penalties and punishments. But the coolies were not being courted by then. They were already there.

Hurdles did not disappear once the ships were at sea. Competition for coolies occurred at all levels. In a testy letter in 1908 to the crown agents for the colonies in London, Marsden requested "that when future arrangements for the shipment of Emigrants to Trinidad by the steamers of Messrs James Nourse Ld's line are made the steamers may not convey Emigrants for Dutch Guiana as well as Trinidad." The steamer S. S. Ganges was chartered for Trinidad, carried 191 laborers to Dutch Guiana, 100 of whom already "had previously been passed by our Medical Inspector and registered for Trinidad by one of our contractors in the United Provinces." The immigrants were transferred to Surinam because Surinam's Dutch agent tempted Britain's subagent with 50 percent more in recruiters' fees than British authorities had been paying. "A transaction of this kind," reminded

Marsden, "is an offense under the Emigration Act and it is probable that we will suffer through losing our largest contractor owing to his irregularity in yielding to the temptation," and "conduct such as that now complained of is to say the least reprehensible. . . . Experience has shown that the organization of British Emigration is only used as a handle by foreign Agencies who are lacking in organization of their own and whose general arrangements are of a very primitive description." Marsden ended that it behooved the British-conducted emigration system not to give the Indian Government the impression that they were working with "outside Emigration Agencies."[36] At this late date in the indenture scheme, there were still potentially very costly risks.

Other costly risks plagued indenture. One situation "of such Paramount importance to our West India Colonies" was relayed by Henry Barkly, governor of British Guiana, to Earl Grey in 1849 as part of the ongoing discussion among planters, officials, and the Colonial Office about how to regulate and discipline the labor of immigrants—"liberated Africans" as well as Indians. The threat was the "struggle in which they [the colonies] are now engaged with countries where Sugar is produced by Slave-Labour. . . . The disadvantages over which most of the British Colonies labour in this Competition, do not arise, I firmly believe, from the Dearness of Free Labour, as compared with Slave Labour—they are attributable almost entirely to the great difficulty of commanding continuous labour." Daniel Hart echoed this persisting concern, writing in 1866 that the "existence of the Sugar Planters of the Island [Trinidad] depends on the power within themselves" because "the increase of Sugar Cultivation in Cuba, Porto Rico, &c., must supplant the British grower in the British market." Hart decried that "planters here must suit their expenses to those of the adverse and competing party which threatens to overwhelm them."[37] Postemancipation planters could not be certain how long slavery would remain costly competition.

Governor Barkly continued his case for indenture by contract because, he wrote, planters cannot force free labor to work, which jeopardizes the planter's "capital of so many thousand pounds invested in his estate." If "half the labourers choose to go fishing," or if "they are taking advantage of the weather to plant their own yams," the cane crop is at severe risk, which is compounded by the possibility of being "ruined by the competition of his slaveholding rival, who suffers none of these inconveniences." Consequently, immigration, although "the readiest palliative for this evil," is not worth much without contracts; moreover, the introduction of "a multitude of African Savages subject to no restraint and exempt from all Supervision" was inadvisable, to say the least. The solution was contractual arrangements, which "must of necessity form part of any sound plan of African Immigration." The only "problem" left to be solved is how long the contract should be—which evidently was not really much of a problem, since Barkly finishes his thought by reiterating the need to make sure that the period of indentured time gives "the Immigrants that external civilization which will render them useful members of society."[38] In December of that year a letter was sent in response, signed by "C.," emphasizing the necessity of making immigrant laborers, "these rude and ignorant people," into "useful labourers by [submitting?] them to work control as is necessary for their own good & by placing them in circumstances in which while they would find it necessary to labour they would at the same time be stimulated to industry by finding that they reaped the natural reward of their [exertions?]."[39] A work ethic whose conceptualization drew from Euro-Protestant Enlightenment values was applicable to all indentured laborers, who, in the sense of their uncivilized bloodlines, backward ways, and fitness for manual (rather than mental) work, could be thought of only as "coolies."

At seemingly every step of the way, securing labor was a process plagued by chance and contingency and certainly by potentially great risk. Recruitment entailed paying careful lip service to the imperial self-image by asserting time and again the moral safeguards of procurement while in practice striving to corral, confine, and successfully ship out sufficient numbers of coolies. Local recruiters needed to meet stipulated standards of "fitness," which included colonial safeguarding against forced emigration, but everyone, recruiters and colonizers alike, also had per capita motivations to produce bodies. At every turn, indenture faced a sense of urgency—about cost, about risk, about morality, about profit—that constituted a slow burn climate of crisis. In 1896, for example, the West India Royal Commission was appointed to "enquire into the depressed condition of the Sugar-producing Colonies of the West Indies."[40] Among their conclusions were that the "sugar industry in the West Indies is in danger of great reduction, which in some colonies may be equivalent or almost equivalent to extinction." Some years earlier, in September 1884, Trinidad's *Port of Spain Gazette* newspaper warned its readers not to forget that "these Asiatics now form one third of our population, and that, fanatics of an effete superstition and a most corrupt form of ethics, they must, as a matter of self-preservation, be kept in subjection to our laws under pain of the most disastrous results."[41] Reminiscent of colonizer attitudes toward enslaved Africans, the very people depended upon to sustain the industry were mistrusted and feared.

## Shocks and Aftershocks

In many colonial societies in the Americas there were tensions between the home government and local administrations—colonial governors, stipendiary magistrates, town mayors, local police, and, in the case of indenture, the Protector of Immigrants and Agent General of Immigration. Add to this each society's plantocracy and its vested interests, newspaper owners and editors, and the general population, all of whom divided according to their various locations in the social hierarchy. Although responsibility for governing and keeping order in the West Indies was ultimately the charge of the British government and the UK Parliament, the day-to-day running of the colonies was under the aegis of colonial governors and governments. London at times made demands on colonial authorities, and they in turn conceded or repelled these demands. By and large, however, Britain's colonies were governed domestically rather than from the imperial center.[42] During the indenture period, the debates that ensued between imperial center and colony and among variously grouped local interests included concerns about the vicissitudes of the sugar economy and its depressed market throughout the 1880s, a flashpoint for labor unrest on and off the plantations (exacerbated by lengthened task work and reduced wages).[43] Debates also concerned the defense or critique of the indenture system and whom it benefitted or burdened, in terms of establishing the norms of civil society on the plantation, where civil contracts were policed by criminal law. All of this was happening in an atmosphere of fear and doubt derived from anxiety mixed with dreaded anticipation, as memories remained acute about previous slave rebellions, such as Jamaica's Tacky's Rebellion in 1760 (in whose aftershock Jamaica's assembly enacted a law to penalize and defeat obeah),[44] Jamaica's Great Maroon War (1795–1796), Nat Turner's slave rebellion in the United States (1831), the Muslim slave uprising in Bahia, Brazil (1835), and most disturbing of all, the Haitian Revolution of 1804. The aura of obeah not only hung on but became stronger after emancipation, intensified by the new forms of agency among its now free supposed practitioners.

Multiple reverberations of this kind also shaped the management of and attitude toward indentured laborers, who contributed to the aftershock with their own acts of resistance. The 1880s were particularly marked by labor and other forms of unrest, partly due to the depression of the sugar economy in the 1880s and 1890s, which was largely the result of competition from beet sugar grown in Europe and, to a lesser extent, in North America. The Colonial Office publication *Notes on West Indian Riots 1881–1903*, for example, was prepared "in view of the impending removal of white troops from the West Indies."[45] It is a list of brief summaries, or "notes," of ten "riots" occurring over the course of twenty-two years, almost annually. Listed in chronological order by colony, these eruptions were critical enough to be covered in a document that explained itself as providing the "causes and results of the principal disturbances which have taken place in West Indian Colonies in recent years, and especially the extent to which the assistance of His Majesty's forces, naval and military, has been necessary for the preservation of the peace."[46] Trinidad's "'Camboulay' [Canboulay] Riot" in 1881 was included, which was Trinidad's harvest celebration and featured parading with torches, music, dancing, the martial art of stick fighting, and drumming. After emancipation, Canboulay transformed into the Carnival familiar today. Trinidad's major "Coolie Riot" in 1884 was also included; also called a "Riot" were unrests in Dominica (1893), St. Kitts (1896), British Guiana (1896), Montserrat (1898), and Jamaica (1902), among others. In Trinidad alone, the years 1849, 1859, 1860, 1865, 1872, 1881, 1882, 1883, and 1884 saw major "riots," and again in 1891 and 1903.[47]

Years before the sugar depression, however, the institutions of indenture plantation law and order were kept busy. In 1872, for example, an incident major enough to garner extensive official documentation occurred in British Guiana. The "coolies" of Devonshire Castle plantation had walked off the plantation on September 27 "armed with hackia sticks" in protest of the treatment of one of their fellows. Three days later, "coolies" from Anna Regina plantation surrounded the home of one Sergeant Loughran armed with cutlasses, shovels, and stones.[48] Using interpreters, depositions were taken from parties involved, revealing the cause of the protest. Peraag, an indentured laborer from Devonshire Castle plantation, stated that he had been in the boiling house simply eating his breakfast when the Buildings Overseer "caught me by the back of the neck, and gave me two blows with his fist." Then the plantation manager, Peter Abel, ordering Peraag to leave the boiling house, struck him twice on the chest with his fist. Peraag fell to the floor; the manager then told a rural constable (Mr. Reid) to take Peraag into custody. "The Coolies interfered," saying that if Peraag had to go to the "Lock-up," then the overseer, manager, and head boiler, who also reportedly had pushed and beaten Peraag, should also have to go. The laborers said that they wanted to go back to work, but the manager sent for more police. The laborers prevented Peraag from being taken into custody. Peraag testified that he "and the other Coolies then proposed to resume work. The Manager would not allow us to do so," and sent for five policemen. Peraag signed his name with an "X." According to another indentured deposant, Pertaub, "all the Coolies" said that they would all go to the Lock-up in Georgetown, and would "complain to the person who brought us to this Colony that the Manager would not give us work to do nor pay us wages." Pertaub continued that they "had to work from 3 o'clock in the morning until 11 o'clock at night. We had to eat our food in the Buildings. We were only paid two shillings for all this work." Pertaub signed with an "X."

For his part, Mr. Abel swore that he never "used violence" against any of the plantation laborers. He deposed that he "found a coolie named Periag [Peraag] making a great disturbance" in the buildings. "He was cursing and stamping. He shouted out in his own language that he would cut the head of any one who would come near him. I told Periag not to make a noise and to leave the Buildings. He refused to go. He told me that if I put my hand on him he would cut off my head. He then dashed the ladles about the copper-wall. He stated that if a Constable were sent to arrest him, he (Periag) would kill him." Peraag agreed to accompany the rural constable, Pompey Reid, who was there to arrest him for "violent and disorderly conduct," and to remove him from the building as his "prisoner." While leaving the buildings Peraag threatened Abel and an overseer, James Robertson, "with death if he (Peraag) was taken to the Police Station." About forty yards away, he called out to his fellows to "rescue" him, and, Abel states, "about thirty Coolies did come." Peraag tried to strike the constable with a pole, and then hit him with his fist. Two more overseers showed up. Abel says that when he "saw the other Immigrants closing around the Constable I ordered him to let the prisoner go." The "prisoner" and his supporters "shook their fists" in Abel's face and threatened him and an overseer. Later that day more laborers, the shovel gang and the buildings hands, left the plantation "in a body."[49]

One can envision the mayhem of this incident; events such as this were not uncommon on West Indian indenture plantations. It is likely that the violence toward the laborers on the part of plantation staff is accurate reportage. But we do not really know how Peraag was behaving or, at that moment, why—apart from the deposition about rage over the ongoing, general problem of work conditions and assignments, wage compensation, and subjection to abuse. How did Abel know what Peraag was allegedly saying about cutting his head if Peraag was speaking in his own language? Peraag seems to have been having a tirade about something in particular, and it was met with a physical response. His fellow laborers banded together and supported him, brandishing the weapons at their disposal—the cutlasses and shovels of their occupation, and stones from the ground. This is a story of diffuse violence: that of words, that of bodies, that of community disruption, that of terror imagined. These forms of violence got minimally, reductively reported, and maximally, fulsomely repeated, throughout the different sectors of indenture society, each with its own slant and rationale. But the overarching theme was the common sense of the day: the embedded image of the wild coolie and the precarious plantation.

Historian Bridget Brereton remarks that soon after their arrival in Trinidad, Indians "acquired a reputation for violence" and that a fundamental element of Trinidadian reaction to them was fear: "fear of their potential for violence and rebellion."[50] This reputation was not confined to Trinidad. Most if not all of this "rioting" was related to worker unrest and to the demand to occupy public space. But in colonial documents "rioting" was rarely connected to injustices of the indenture system; rather, it was an expression of nature, an inner character embodied by enslaved and indentured persons that made its way across the Atlantic. An important example is India's 1857 Sepoy Mutiny, or 1857 Rebellion, which reverberated across continents and loomed large in indenture plantation society. A newspaper editor in Trinidad wrote in 1870 that the Sepoy Mutiny's "horrors" were "fresh in the recollections of Englishmen . . . , and we do not need to be reminded that the race to which our immigrants belong is easily roused."[51] Britain's move away from such an ignoble enterprise as slavery required that it exercise care in maintaining the appearance of indenture as something not only different but reputable. This pressure was compounded by the Indian government's concern about the treatment of its labor diasporas. The Sepoy Mutiny was an additional factor that tempered Britain's stated policies toward the colonized—in the West Indies, notably indentured labor.

Until 1857 the British East India Company ruled India on behalf of the British crown. That year *sipahis*, or sepoys, the company's "native" soldiers in its army, engaged in a major uprising that spread throughout the subcontinent. The rebellion was suppressed by the British in 1858, but the company's rule in India ended, replaced by the British Raj. The force and consequences of the rebellion caused great alarm throughout the colonized world, in the way that major uprisings and revolutions were reminders to those in command that power is brittle and temporary. The Sepoy Mutiny resulted in an official "Proclamation, by the Queen in Council, to the Princes, Chiefs, and People of India," which was "presented to both Houses of Parliament by Command of Her Majesty."[52]

The proclamation promises to "respect the Rights, Dignity, and Honour" of native princes and subjects, which will lead to enjoyment of "that Prosperity and that social Advancement which can only be secured by internal Peace and good Government." Two full paragraphs deal with the relationship between religious freedom and colonial rule. "Firmly relying Ourselves on the Truth of Christianity," it stated, "and acknowledging with gratitude the solace of Religion, We disclaim alike the Right and the Desire to impose our Convictions on any of Our Subjects. We declare it to be Our Royal Will and Pleasure that none be in any wise favored, none molested or disquieted by reason of their Religious Faith or Observances; but that all shall alike enjoy the equal and impartial protection of the Law: and We do strictly charge and enjoin all those who may be in authority under Us, that they abstain from all interference with the Religious Belief or Worship of any of Our Subjects, on pain of Our highest Displeasure. And it is Our further Will that, so far as may be, Our Subjects, of whatever Race or Creed, be freely and impartially admitted to Offices in Our Service, the Duties of which they may be qualified, by their education, ability, and integrity, duly to discharge."[53] The proclamation ends with the reiteration that "internal Tranquility" will be restored, and the "peaceful Industry of India" stimulated, promoting "Works of Public Utility and Improvement." Prosperity is strength, contentment is security, and the gratitude of one's subjects the "best Reward."[54]

The uprising was a "major push factor" in the emigration of Indians.[55] The *Port of Spain Gazette* reported in May 1865 that the Trinidad Immigration Report for 1865 mentioned "a retired Mohommedan soldier or sepoy" who was not suitable for agricultural work and possessed an "unChristian" attitude, but "the number of sepoys is unfortunately too scanty to admit proof of the latter."[56] Still, official reports from the West Indian colonies expressed concerned conjecture about sepoys' experienced marksmanship and soldiering being part of the plantation coolie labor protests—for example, in *The Coolie Riots in Essequebo [British Guiana]: A Report, 1872.*[57] Other speculations were as anxious. In his memoir, *My Missionary Memories,* about being a Canadian Presbyterian missionary in Trinidad early in the twentieth century, the Reverend Kenneth Grant mentioned that in a sermon he had recently given, he included remarks about a "riot" that had "occurred on a sugar estate [plantation] within our sphere of influence." It "was of a very serious character," he continued, "the local constabulary were unable to cope with it, and a strong force was called from the capital." Implicitly linking plantation labor uprisings to Indians' violence in general, he voiced concern that "we should be exposed to the tragedies of 1857 in India."[58] Part of the "legacy of the Mutiny was a fear that the Indians could no longer be trusted"; a "Frankenstein monster in the colony" might one day "get out of control."[59] Nonetheless, Victoria's proclamation provided a language for the policing of laborers' activities that suggested, instead, an innocence that derived from respect for personal liberty and cultural tradition. Religious protections would preserve colonial hegemony.

Massive social unrest and its potential multiplier effects hinder profit, the main reason to establish a colony in the first place. But occasionally concessions and compromises must be made, at least on paper, in an attempt to contain the challenges of rage and refusal. British colonizers, who labeled the rebellion a "mutiny," interpreted it as the reaction of disgruntled sepoys against the introduction, in 1857, of a new firearm, whose bullets had to be bitten by the soldier before loading. There were rumors that the grease used on the bullets was from cows and pigs. Hindus consider cattle sacred and Muslims revile pork; sepoys refused to use the bullets, interpreting them as an attack on Hinduism and Islam, a defiling of caste and religion, and as a plot on the part of their "Christian masters" to coerce them into conversion.[60] Many British officials claimed that the cause of the rebellion lay in the "cartridge affair and nothing else"; . . . that the revolt was consequently nothing more than an irrational panic on the subject of caste among credulous and superstitious sepoys."[61] This mid-nineteenth-century period in India was one in which various kinds of liberal reforms were attempted on the part of British colonial authority. The precept of religious tolerance derives from Enlightenment liberal ideals:

freedom from religious persecution, civil equality irrespective of religious affiliation, and freedom to practice one's religion.[62] Far less lofty was the characterization of this situation as religious canons devolving into irrational superstitions: basically, fear of fat.

Reducing resistance to religious taboos (which fall short of "reason" on the Enlightenment's developmental scale) yet appearing to honor them at the same time may have the unintended consequence of appearing to contemporary scholars as favoring Indians over Africans on West Indian plantations. But considering the rebellion/mutiny narratives, it seems more likely that in the proclamation, respecting religious rights was an effective but not power-jeopardizing recourse. Religion became a red herring, but in its "proper" form it also stigmatized those allegedly without it, or with a perverse version of it—that is, "coolies."

The proclamation's primary concern was to maintain a smooth-running, profit-making operation in the aftermath of the rebellion. Toward that goal, race and religion were conceptually disentangled: race could be (needed to be) eschewed, while religion was one very useful means of fostering the ideal of human rights. The aim was to reassure British colonial subjects that whatever their race, they would not encounter hiring bias in the colonial service but would be held only to the standards of educational competence, ability, and integrity. This is a clear allusion to racial bigotry, which would not be tolerated. The proclamation pairs creed (religion) with race, seemingly, from the language of the document, the two equally notable variables in the identification of subjects who require promises of respect and protection. As important is the assertion of the document's "truth," that of the superiority of Christianity, at the same time that it acknowledges "the solace of Religion" in general. This inalienable right to spiritual comfort and salvation holds the moral high ground of implied equivalence between colonizer and colonized, a presumptive unity through shared observance of, and obeisance to a higher authority who ultimately subscribes to the same values and moral imperatives. The very idea of "religion" is useful sacred ground; it connotes the higher qualities of humankind that, if shared, means a common equality (in some fashion). Religion is a domain of experience that is safe to honor as long as its categorical definitions and their substance can be stipulated and enforced by those who have an interest in doing so. This is a kind of monitoring of the discourse of common sense that can discourage problematic outliers with the soft power of suggestion: propriety, legitimacy, and permissibility allegedly are based on intrinsic, timeless values, not socially engineered, situational decisions. But the latter is exactly what the proclamation tendered. In application, however, race and religion work conjointly in the creation of human types. This makes their protection by decreed rights a force that reifies and reiterates who they always and already are.

The indenture system depended on numerous arrangements and protocols it could not entirely control. Access to sufficient labor and at least superficially appropriate recruitment of that labor remained a challenge. Retaining potential indentured immigrants in India's depots long enough to ship them out was a delicate matter. Filling the chartered ships was not a sure bet. The poaching of labor both en route to the Caribbean and among plantations in one colony presented serious competition and potential loss through deficient delivery of working bodies, and it was evidently difficult to prosecute although it was illegal. There was even "wastage" with which to contend, "caused by term-expired immigrants emigrating to other colonies."[63] Another sort of competition, this from slave plantation societies, was a more troublesome threat. Ensuring labor compliance once on the plantations was both fragile and potentially dangerous. The twenty-year depression in the world sugar market during the third quarter of the nineteenth century did not help. Quixotic efforts led to the pyrrhic victories of subjugating labor and producing sugar. There were many edges to be on the edge of in indenture plantation societies.

## Maintaining Plantation Peace

Historical accounts from eighteenth-century Danish Virgin Islands reveal that on occasion planters would join their slaves in revels, which included alcohol, drumming, fireworks, gunfire, and trooping from one plantation to another, enveloping town and country in mobile carousing.[64] In the nineteenth century, during the West Indies' Christmas season, enslaved and masters together engaged in the "tumult of lively celebration and gala ceremony."[65] This pattern of plantation hopping was already an aspect of expressive culture in the Caribbean when Indian indentured laborers arrived there. They were familiar with mobile processions in home villages and towns; Hosay's source, Muharram, was a variegated spectacle before it ever left India. In November 1884 the *Times of India* noted that Bombay's Muharram was "a carnival . . . the like of which for extent and eccentricity, is to be found in few other cities of the world."[66] Thus, important cultural and social precursors contributed to what would become the metonym of the "coolie problem," Hosay, which entered into an entrenched pattern of public culture—the social commemoration associated with festivity and relaxed or inverted rules of structural inequality, such as hierarchies of race and class—carrying its own "eccentricities." For centuries plantation groups moved from site to site, encountered other plantation groups, and picked up people along the way. This customary tradition of celebration through raucous mobility, even if only annually and brief, was familiar to people living in these societies. But the assembly of throngs in public space always presents ruling authorities with a challenge to social control—of behavior in the moment, and of thought (consciousness) after the moment, when energies are still fermenting. Public merriment often has an implicit air of incipient bedlam. At their most peaceful, popular celebrations were a cultural tradition that produced their own sense of social vertigo throughout colonial society. At their least peaceful, they could look a lot like rehearsals for uprising. By the 1840s, Trinidad, for example, had become such a violent society that Ordinance No. 8 of 1844 was enacted to suppress the widespread carrying and use of lethal weapons such as pistols, swords, and knives, as well as the long sticks that might be used in the stick-fighting martial arts of Hosay.[67]

The Guianese newspaper *The Creole* reported in 1867 on the "Tadja festival of the Coolies," which had brought together six plantation communities in a "fatal affray" in which two "combatants" were mortally wounded and several others "dangerously wounded."[68] Interestingly, the manager of one of the plantations, "Peter's Hall," was charged for his part in the incident, along with two of the "combatants." Some of the men had "loaded guns and other deadly weapons," but it is not clear that everyone involved was either a "coolie" or a laborer. Nonetheless, the newspaper reported that "these coolie orgies have long been complained of as dangerous nuisances . . . requiring an exertion of the strong arm of the law to put them down." Besides the "hazardous" obstruction of the highways, of which the laborers at times take possession (hindering travelers), the gangs commit "frightful excesses" "under the maddening influence of their heathenish rites." More outbreaks are occurring, fretted the article, "produced by the same cause, pagan fanaticism." The situation must be brought under control because the "lives and limbs of even Coolie laborers are valuable—at least to the planters. . . . But it is not only the lives and limbs of the reckless Coolies, drunk with rum and religion, that are to be regarded." The "jealous fervour of their superstition," the article explains, is what induces the participants to place themselves above the law and prevent travelers from passing their "idol." But some "gentlemen" do not wish "to stand on the Queen's highway, sweltering under the sun, until it pleases a parcel of howling pagans to let them pass. And in the struggle between British liberty and heathen aggression, valuable life—more valuable than that of the sturdiest Coolie that ever wielded shovel or bill—may be sacrificed. It behoves [sic] the Government, therefore, to take some measures whereby the planters may be compelled to compel their labourers to confine their pagan orgies to the particular plantations on which they are located." *The Creole* was not known for its open-minded point of view, and violence involving several plantations is a matter of concern for anyone potentially subject to it. Moreover, in British Guiana's 1869 Ordinance about "the due regulation of the festivals and processions of East Indian immigrants in this colony," obstruction of the public highway is mentioned in the first paragraph's lead sentence.[69]

The issue of "disorder" and its public demonstration was still being pointed to more than four decades later. The 1910 report by an official committee looking at Indian emigration to the crown colonies and protectorates observed that "Indian festivals were . . . regulated by law in 1882, before which time there had been much disorder and obstruction of the public highways in certain districts."[70] But this reportage also encapsulates much of the manufactured fear of foreign enemies that permeated indenture plantation society. Clearly what is being described is a struggle over public space, the right to visibility and presence, exercise of mobility, tensions between the local plantocracy and the imperial metropole, and control of the liberties invented by the Enlightenment and idealized by a role model empire but problematically applied across the board.

Just as Hosay's processions would become the linchpin of its disruptive visibility, so were the earlier Canboulay and Carnival festivities. Trinidad's prohibition of torches for the Canboulay of 1881 catalyzed the "Canboulay Riot," which some scholars deem "the most serious confrontation in the history of Trinidad Carnival."[71] Trinidad's Governor Freeling wrote to the Earl of Derby on March 8, 1884, reminding him about what had happened three years earlier during Carnival: "It will be remembered that disturbances were occasioned in Port-of-Spain during the Carnival of 1881 by the Police attempting to extinguish the torches used in these processions without giving timely notice that they intended to do so, and that although in 1882 the Carnival passed off quietly, the experience of the disorder which prevailed at the Carnival of 1883 induced me" to quell "any disorder in future." Surmising that over the next few years such measures would "lead to increased respect for the Government," Freeling noted that "Coolies" were a large percentage of the population in the district in which the "disturbances" took place, that they had been duly warned, and that those who had suffered were reaping the consequences of their "own folly."[72]

Freeling anticipated the eventual demise of Carnival once it would be shorn of what the "lower orders" found attractive about it.[73] The eventual dying out of undesirable practices and traditions, notably including obeah, is a common refrain in colonial West Indian discourse. It followed, implicitly, a racial and cultural evolutionary developmental model that was a legacy of Enlightenment thinking. Considering all that was henceforth not to be allowed, one wonders what kind of festivities any enthusiast would have been able to envision that could both conform to these restrictions and yet express the exuberance of the season. But this was not merely a simple choice to make between being restrained and obedient or not. In the Euro-colonial imagination, drawing from Enlightenment/Protestant epistemology, expressiveness itself was a measured manifestation; too much of it—passion, bodily responses, audibility—were the racialized exaggerations of the savage or near savage.

Canboulay, Carnival, and Hosay all emphasized mobile gatherings of laboring peoples across public space. As Nicholas Dirks observes about nineteenth-century British India and religious rituals, "Colonial concern was immensely heightened when an event was by some definition public, and so religious functions that took place outside of the provenance of the temple or home became objects of regulation."[74] This concern was about potential social disorder as well as the implied governmental sanction conveyed by allowing visibility in public space. In Britain's West Indian colonies the plantation took the place of the "inside" that was represented by temple and home; it was an enclosure demarcated from public space by virtue of being both workspace and home space at the same time (conflating public and private spheres), and in which mobility was, at least in legal principle, monitored by pass laws or curtailed altogether. Trespass into the public roads and highways had to be protected, as colonial authority saw it, not only from violence and conflict but also from implications that the ruling regime approved of this kind of occupation of public space. Public space is social space, but "social" as defined by certain understood mores, rules, and expectations. Here again is the issue of how "social" a ritual can be before it is ceded from "religion" and bequeathed to "popular culture." Hosay was the wrong kind of "social" because its presence troubled public space and because, in so doing, it troubled religion and unleashed race.

Discussions about regulating Hosay were being documented and archived as early as the 1850s in Trinidad and British Guiana; anxieties about Hosay in Trinidad were especially pronounced in the 1870s and 1880s due to the "allegedly increasing tendency to riotous behavior."[75] The unrest of the 1880s was followed up with heightened police activity through the 1890s, a result of associations made between the sugar crisis and criminality.[76] Crime and its punishments were tied to these developments. David Trotman describes how the twenty years between 1880 and 1900 in Trinidad were "dotted with battles," numerous protests connected to Carnival and to Hosay; this was a time when the British colonial police force was particularly aggressive.[77] Where "obeah" was identified, it was always to some degree associated with its genealogy of rebellious and savage Africans. Where "Hosay" was identified, it took on some of obeah's most important connotations as an instance of a disruptive, immoral, and atavistic presence, in a shared context of labor unrest, or fears of labor unrest. In his report of April 15, 1885, Trinidad's inspector of prisons, Lionel M. Fraser, included a list of "Contraventions as Distinguished from More Serious Offences." Included are such breaches as "Driving Cart Quicker than a Walk," "Non-Maintenance of Wife," "Disturbing Divine Worship," "Trespass," "Gathering Alms," "Practising Obeah," and "Dancing to Drums."[78] What is striking is the respective numbers of people charged with practicing obeah and dancing to drums over the course of a five-year period. In 1880, 869 persons were charged with practicing obeah; in 1881 it was 799; in 1882 it was two; in 1883 it was one, and in 1884 it was four. The number of people charged with dancing to drums in 1880 was fourteen; one in 1881; twelve in 1882; eleven in 1883; and eighty-one in 1884. The drop in charged obeah practitioners and the increase in persons charged with dancing to drums may be a reflection of the kinds of attention being paid to certain socially disruptive activities in this period of "coolie" discontent, particularly its apex in 1884, when charges of dancing to drums increased almost sixfold from 1880 and the watershed "Hosay Riot" occurred. Drumming was at best an objectionable, and at worst an unlawful, feature of "disorderly assemblies in Houses and Yards," as Fraser's report noted. But drumming is also key to Hosay and its assemblies, and thus Hosay almost certainly was included under drumming's violations, as well.[79]

Trinidad's so-called Hosay Riot made 1884 a banner year for associating the crisis of social, particularly labor, unrest with "coolie festivities." "Coolie disturbances" of all sorts at times overlapped with the Hosay commemoration and thus were encompassed by the symbolism of Hosay as trouble. Kelvin Singh's discussion of the Hosay Riot, or, better put in his terms, "massacre," made an early case for looking at 1884's Hosay observance in terms of the pressures of production and discrimination that eventuated in what was widely referred to at the time in catastrophic terms.[80] Catastrophe it was, from any point of view. On October 30 a confrontation took place in Trinidad's second-largest town, San Fernando, between collected bands of Hosay commemorators, primarily indentured laborers from surrounding plantations, and local police. This was a period already punctuated with confrontations—"riots"—on the part of "coolies." The issue on October 30 was the curtailment, decreed by previous ordinance, of the mobility of these bands (ideally keeping them within the bounds of their respective plantations) by preventing them from processing along the public roads and going through San Fernando toward the sea, where the tadjahs would be cast off at the end of the commemoration. With umbrage, and defying the regulations, the bands continued to advance. The police took aim and fired into the crowd. In the *Port of Spain Gazette*'s reportage on "the Hosein Calamity," "sixteen coolies" were shot to death, "three or four of the coolies [were] still in the hospital, whose wounds are fatal," "four of the coolies are crippled for life, and . . . in addition to the ninety-four admissions to hospital, there are fully thirty-six wounded who have been received in estate's [plantation] hospitals." The official inquiry into the circumstances of the "calamity" concluded with the coroner's opinion that the police were "acting under the orders of the magistrate, . . . that the magistrate was fully justified in giving such orders, and that he (the Coroner) is of the opinion that no person was guilty of felony."[81]

This comforting verdict may have reflected in part the ongoing efforts of colonial authority to figure out the delicate balance between the rights and regulation of rites. Trinidad's Executive Council had met three months earlier, on July 10, and had discussed a letter sent from the Protector of Immigrants on June 24, "together with all the previous correspondence on the subject." The letter reported "the results of the enquiries made by his

Department from the principal Mahomedans throughout the island as to what was considered necessary for the performance of the religious portion of the festival." The plan was to make the "Indian population" aware "as soon as possible of the restrictions which it was proposed to impose on the conduct of the Festival."[82] It is not recorded here what the "principal Mahomedans" advised about the "religious" content of Hosay, or what, if any, of their input was taken into consideration. But simply having it on record that local religious leaders were consulted was likely useful. Perhaps reinforcing this tactic was the charging of plantation laborer headmen with redirecting Hosay away from what was "strictly necessary for the celebration of the religious rites of the Hindoos" because of their "pecuniary interest in the gorgeous display of castles and pagodas which is yearly acquiring greater and greater proportions"—an interest allegedly demonstrated by the headmen who collect "large sums of money . . . for the purpose." If the "parading" of the tadjahs were prohibited and only the strictly necessary religious aspects were allowed, then the laborers, who feared their "priests" too much to complain openly, would privately "rejoice that the blackmail annually levied on them will no longer have its *raison d'etre*."[83]

Also likely useful in its symbolic value was the internal dissention that could arise among Muslims about the practice of Hosay. A few years earlier, about 1881, a group of Muslims submitted "a petition to the Government not long ago protesting against the procession of Tazias as a vain and useless ceremony and an insult to their religion." The petition was signed by "respectable Mussulmen in San Fernando."[84] This *Port of Spain Gazette* article on "coolie insubordination" was published a week after the Hosay massacre, and it aimed in part to "assist those who are unread in oriental literature to explain that the celebration of the Moharran [*sic*] . . . is held in great respect by the Shiah [*sic*] sect Mussulmen especially in commemoration of the death of Hosein the son of Fatima and grandson of the prophet who was killed at the Kerbala A.D. 680. . . . Mussulmen in India are divided into two distinct sects; the Shiahs just mentioned who reject the oral traditions of Mohammet, the authority of the four Imaams [*sic*] and the martyrdom of Ali Hassan and Hosein and the Sunnis who may be considered orthodox and differ with the Shiaha [*sic*] on these points." Following this peculiar religious edification, the newspaper opined that "the Moharran" should be restricted to "Mohammedans" and that, in any case, its significance was limited to just a "small portion only of the faithful";

Hindus participate in it simply "from habit," following "Musselmen," who were their "former masters in India." Along with the "creole" (Afro-Caribbean) population, Hindus' motivation was not from "any religious or superstitious ground, but was dictated by a pure spirit of opposition to authority."[85]

As the West Indian sugar industry limped along, and as the temperature of its workforce ran high, the local populations were at the ready, primed for violence and to be violent in return. Two months after the Hosay massacre, on December 17, 1884, the mayor of San Fernando, Robert Guppy, wrote a letter to His Excellency John Scott Bushe, Administrator of the Government of the Island of Trinidad, about a public meeting that had been held on November 15, two weeks after the massacre, at which ninety-one of the town's (male) residents offered "their services to the Government as members of a Volunteer Rifle Corps." San Fernando had had a volunteer rifle corps previously, but it failed in part due to lack of government support. The "circumstances of the times," however, had "greatly changed since the former corps came to a premature end." Trinidad had become overrun by "a vagrant and lawless element quitting the neighboring islands and working a precarious existence here, and which is always ready to join in popular disturbances, with also an unruly and mutinous spirit has been developed [*sic*] among that class of our people who until recently were noted for quiet and orderly submission to authority. And this lawless spirit seems likely to increase rather than diminish."[86] While it is not clear exactly who Mayor Guppy thinks were formerly quiet and submissive, it does seem clear that the good citizens of San Fernando thought the time had come for "those amongst them who are of suitable age and ability to form a body which may be useful as auxiliaries in the event of troubles occurring for which it would be a fatal mistake to be unprepared." Bushe wrote to London in support of the idea, and asked for the necessary funds.[87] Three months hence, on March 25, 1884, an official report on the proper use of firearms stated that the police needed to be "instructed sufficiently" in order to "enable them to act together," in the use of the rifle and the bayonet "without danger to themselves and with effect against others." An enclosure (No. 2) notes that "before the end of June," that is, in three months' time, "there will be no less than 38 Police Stations throughout the Colony, not counting Head Quarters and San Fernando."[88] This state of presumptive readiness reflected a population whose various sectors felt, in their own way, under threat.

The language remained overblown and self-contradictory in this 1884 Hosay moment. In March 1884 the *Port of Spain Gazette* wrote that in its connection with the "abominations of the Carnival," the "Coolie Hosein" was taking on "abuses" that had "crept into what was, formerly, a simple religious rite"; where the "purely religious rite" ended and the abuses began required ascertaining.[89] The *Gazette* wrote two weeks after the "Hosein Calamity," as it called the event, that "we believe that in every well regulated community, but especially in countries possessing an ignorant and semi-savage, and therefore excitable and easily misled peasantry, the supremacy of the law should be upheld at all times, and regardless of consequences." The "peasantry" referred to Afro-Trinidadians. Underlying the contemptuous racism toward the "peasantry" and the "coolies" both, real fear is evident, indicated by the call for control irrespective of its consequences. In the effort to further stigmatize the "coolie" by representing this human type as a threat to vulnerable, culturally underdeveloped Afro-Caribbean peoples (despite the depredations of their own, abominable Carnival), the most effective imagery from which to draw was, ironically, Euro-colonialism's racist ways of "knowing" the African. Even by contrast, analogies were drawn.

Early the following year, in February 1885, British Guiana's newspaper, *The Argosy*, wrote about the "Tadjah riot" in Trinidad that "this festival has gradually degenerated into a Saturnalia in which Hindus, Mohamedans, and Negroes mingle promiscuously, and rum and ganja add to the religious fervour of the processionists. A free fight is the usual termination where rival factions meet, and as lethal weapons are not wanting in the crowd, many are wounded and some are occasionally killed. . . . They are not only highly objectionable, but fraught with danger to the more law-abiding of the community." The "festival" has "gradually assumed the proportions of a riot rather than a religious gathering. . . . About eight thousand men took part in this [Hosay] riot. . . . The Tadjah in Trinidad has long lost all pretensions to a religious festival."[90] These few examples illustrate a wordplay of propaganda that obfuscates what actually might have happened that day—for example, different numbers are given for the Hosay "rioters," none of which are reliably corroborated. It also reinforces the epistemic habits of racial thinking that were conjoined with religious traditions. Although sometimes contradictory, commonsense understandings of the persistence of heritable traits typed all Indian immigrants, indentured or free, as "coolies," as, for example, Sir H. W. Norman noted in his *Report on the Coolie*

*Disturbances in Trinidad.*[91] Moreover, often against intention, this common sense drew Indian and African together under a shared religio-racial rubric of inferiority and threat.

The prevailing religious and racial thinking of this era—the epistemic habits that colored the "overlap" society that was the indenture plantation—did not allow either a fuller grasp of what Hosay was (its substance, its meaning) or who its proponents and participants were. The tension between making good on moral imperatives, with whatever motivation, and believing that this was not a futile—and endangering—exercise was palpable, always in the air. By 1915, just two years before indenture's end, there was still discussion about the punishment of those who harbored plantation deserters. Punishment "should be substantial," James McNeill and Chimman Lal advised in their report on behalf of the government of India about Indian immigration in the West Indian colonies. Although evidence sufficient to convict them was hard to acquire, people who harbored plantation deserters "sometimes instigate credulous immigrants to desert, and exploit them subsequently."[92] The supposed (or invented) credulity of coolies was an important identity feature of which colonial authorities had long taken advantage. The childlike developmental stage of this less-advanced people needed paternalist protection from unscrupulous parties and also explained the wayward behavior that called for this paternalism. As these official investigators explain, "Immigrants are as a class credulous and excitable but are neither habitually unreasonable nor opposed to the just and firm exercise of lawful authority."[93] This kind of rhetorical tightrope, balancing between acknowledging the manifestation of innate qualities and the need for evenhanded but unflinching control of those qualities, blurred the boundaries dividing hierarchical racial formations, sliding closely to a heritable quality of "blackness" that was not necessarily specific, or unique, to Afro-Caribbean laboring people.

At this tail-end moment of the indenture scheme, McNeill and Lal could write in their report on Indian indenture in Trinidad that their "personal experience did not suggest that immigrants were too timid to say what might displease their employers. They are by no means in a state of terrified subjection."[94] This was a double-edged sword for colonial authority: freedom to speak one's mind and act according to one's conscience was a valuable Enlightenment affirmation; freedom to speak one's mind and act according to one's conscience was also a worrisome Pandora's box. As simultaneous narratives, protecting naivete, on the one hand, and conceding economic pressure, on the other, are mutually buttressing representations of what were the dilemmas of discipline. This theme of rhetorically miti-gated criminalization had been part of colonial discourse about indenture for a long time.

Indenture was an insecure system, contending with contingencies not within its control despite ongoing attempts to do so. In addition to the promise of criminalization and colonizer violence directed toward offenders of the plantation peace, compromises were attempts to keep things running smoothly. Guianese planters, for example, attempted to offset disgruntle-ment among plantation workers by resorting to what Basdeo Mangru calls the "safety valve of the indenture system, the immigrants' rituals."[95] Surely prompted by Queen Victoria's proclamation, if not also perhaps encour-aged by Britain's earlier, postemancipation sense of itself as a model of moral virtue that would awe and inspire the world, plantation owners resorted to that sacred-secular public sphere of (selected) rituals and festivals. Even pass laws and other forms of mitigating marronage off the plantations, or, as in Trinidad, for example, the offer of Crown lands in lieu of return passage at a contract's end, could not guarantee that laborers would stay put. Planters hoped they could "create an atmosphere of contentment" through festival freedom that would "induce laborers to prolong their industrial residence"; festivals would also "provide an opportunity for physical relaxation from the rigours of the plantation system and help to foster a sense of belonging."[96] We do not know by a complete count to which "rituals" and "festivals" the plantocracy was referring. By the 1850s, when Hosay was organized and vis-ible enough to draw attention from the wider society, it would have been the "coolie festival" that received the major (if not all the) attentions of, on the one hand, freedom of religion—as long as it was "genuine" Islam—and, on the other hand, maintaining the social and moral peace, which meant at least basic guidelines about what could and could not be done, and where. The production-driven need for law and order often took local pre-cedence over metropolitan reformist agendas. Therefore, although "reli-gion" was the great conundrum for British colonial authority, it was a means to an end, not an end in itself. That end was status quo order and increased profit. In other words, because of prevailing common sense about religion and cultural evolution, even the more or less venerable religions of Hinduism and Islam were not of real interest, except perhaps to a handful of European scholars. Notwithstanding that British colonial authorities were very clear about what they thought "religion" and "religions" to be, real interest lay in public peace and sugar's dividends. The two narratives, social and moral order and religious liberty, were never very far apart.

Hosay's context of labor unrest reinforced the suggestion of "religion" bursting out of its structure by simultaneously drawing upon Islamic canonical religious themes while evincing unrestrained, profane liveliness, literal and figurative intoxication, and a protean responsiveness to local environment that defied the fixed replication of doctrine—if Muharram in India and Hosay in Trinidad ever really had one. Hosay's heterogeneity confounded its "religious" legitimacy; in order to contain the out-of-bounds danger of Hosay's collective action, it had to be reinforced as "racial"—an *Indian* thing. Stipulating Islamic criteria also racially reinforced its "Indian" qualities, especially given the relative paucity of Caribbean Muslims who were not Indian. This policing of Hosay through this kind of racial thinking differed from but worked in tandem with an earlier mode of racialization through overtly expressed bias and bigotry. At the same time, Islam deracinated African Muslims from the Euro-colonial concept of blackness—not completely, of course, but enough to distinguish them, in the gaze of slavers and other colonizers, as being "a little more enlightened" than those "weak and credulous" "savage brethren" with whom they shared the continent.[97] Although the "menace" of Islam was that "it challenged Catholicism [and Christianity more generally] on its own terms, with a universal monotheism and belief in a mysterious, unseeable, and eternal god,"[98] these shared terms also allowed a different kind of racialization among even those Muslims who were "black" and "African." The combination of the "exalted rank"[99] they purportedly held in the stratified societies of their lands of origin, literacy, knowledge of Arabic, and presumed developmental distance from African animists made African Muslims, if not undeserving of New World bondage, then at least more recognizable in terms of progress along the cultural evolution models of Euro-Christian colonialism.[100]

The alarmist imagery of coolies, rogue individuals en masse, evoked the coolie as a type of being—a testosterone-laden horde brandishing weapons of vast destruction. The disordering and martial dimensions of Hosay were essentialized in the terms of coolie heritability: the genealogical inheritance of a racial type defined in part by overt, uncontrolled passions that infected religious heritage through its racial packaging—that is, through the biologically reproduced conduit of the coolie body. British colonial epistemology contained fear-fueled critiques of "superstition," the wrong expressions of "passion," and secrecy, blurry boundaries that dubiously distinguished among religious traditions—all religious reference points that were signal in defining the race of Hosay's "coolie" participants. In a model of tautology rather than trajectory, these supposedly areligious (or antireligious) qualities helped define and transmit the "race" of coolie labor, and, in turn, their racial identification predicted how far coolies slid from possessing legitimate religion and, therefore in part, legitimate humanity.

Taking a parallax view, we can see that Hosay and obeah were proximate targets; the ultimate target was social peace, defined in certain terms. The worker status and labor conditions of coolies were in a mutually defining dialogue with race and religion; all four—workers' status, labor conditions, race, and religion—were coextensive factors in shaping the rights that defined Hosay. We do not know now and probably cannot ever know precisely what indentured laborers and other Indians, or anyone else who did not write it down, thought about Hosay—religion, resistance, recreation, or something else—especially given that in the recorded, archived media (newspapers, reports, letters) it is couched in terms of two sides of one coin: plantation labor unrest and primal essence. What we can surmise is that Hosay lent itself to public collective action; in fact, its performative aspect depended on public visibility, mobility, audibility, and reenacted (and at times real) confrontation. The British colonial optic read Hosay primarily through emotion and its bodily expression, through atavistic characteristics, and through excess, largely identified as bodily manifestation and sensation. One way to "explain" coolies' behavior away from the harshness and injustice of plantation life was to redirect it to their intemperate character, a heritable genealogy of savagery visible through the phenotype of race and the excesses of fanaticism. Expressed through the body, religion is in the blood: religion is heritable, either as genuine touchstone or as warped departure; it comes out in race, and, in turn, race materializes religion. Religion and race are thus passed along through the routes, and roots, of heritability, ever channeled in Hosay.

# 3

## THE PERFORMANCE OF SHADOWS

In his discussion of racial and color hierarchies in British colonial discourse, Stuart Hall comments that visibility—of skin color, for example—is race's "greatest discursive value" and "facilitates instant recognition" of that which the naked eye cannot otherwise see. As such, visibility "becomes the synonym for truth."[1] Hall would have agreed that color is not the only indicator of the "truth" of race; the relationship between what is empirical (visibility) and truth is complex. Various phenomena are substantiated by evidence drawn from a society's storehouse of common sense that does similar ideological work. "Seeing is believing," but such persuasions can either support social inequality or call it into question.

### The Magic of Evidence

Among the most illustrative examples of the relationship between race, religion, visibility, and evidence connected to early West Indian indenture plantations is what was known as the "hookswinging festival." I frame this chapter with a discussion of hookswinging before I turn to obeah and Hosay, focusing in particular on obeah, because hookswinging illustrates so well the ambience of fear, disbelief, perplexity, and bravado that permeates colonial discourse about obeah and Hosay, both of which shared within the colonial gaze—each in its own way—the unwelcome specter of the unseen through its material as well as conceptual tool kit. Seeing may be believing, but often it is predicated on a presupposition or suggestion of what ought to be there. Despite hookswinging's limited and short-lived existence, it is precisely its elusiveness and the consternation it generated on the part of colonial authorities that invites a closer look at the way it, like obeah and Hosay, reinforced how the unseen and the supposed were made visible material realities, provable by evidence and traceable along the channels of religio-racial heritability that demarcate human types.

Hookswinging was a ritual associated with Hinduism in India that involved physical duress as a demonstration of devotion—notably, swinging of the body suspended by hooks inserted into flesh. This ritual was brought to British Guiana with the first indentured Indian laborers in 1838. It was practiced there from at least 1848, and was outlawed in 1853. (It apparently was not practiced in Trinidad.)[2] The criminalization of hookswinging coincided with the renewed postemancipation efforts at the criminalization of obeah—for example, Jamaica's first stand-alone anti-obeah act in 1854. In the 1850s the British government also increased its efforts to diminish the rights of indentured laborers, along with other free persons in its West Indian colonies (as discussed in the previous chapter). Forty-four years after Jamaica's Obeah Act of 1854 was passed, the Obeah Act of 1898 doubled down on attempting to ensure that obeah remained a crime by making criminal convictions easier to attain.[3] To this end the legal category "instrument of Obeah" was created, whose deliberately capacious definition covered "any thing [*sic*] used, or intended to be used by a person, and pretended by such person to be possessed of any occult or supernatural power." This rubric included any suspect material object, loosely defined, whose owners were expected to prove were not instruments of obeah.[4]

In the Reverend H. V. P. Bronkhurst's *The Colony of British Guiana and Its Labouring Population*, he included a description of hookswinging. His detail was impressive. He wrote, for example, that the "Sheddal" (apparatus)

> is a beam about forty or fifty feet in height, across the top of which is placed a transverse pole of smaller size, to each end of which is tied a rope, one end of which trails upon the ground, while to the shorter end are attached two iron hooks, strong, pounded smooth, and sharp pointed. The devotees are retained in an adjoining place or temple (as I may call it) until the fitting time arrives, when one of them is led out, preceded by pujaries or priests, musicians, drummers, and male and female relatives, and other friends. The devotee approaches the upright pole and lies upon his face while the hooks are thrust under the flesh on either side of the vertebrae below the shoulder blade, and is then hoisted up in mid air [*sic*], where he swings round and round from ten to thirty times, according as strength allows, or vow makes necessary. Twenty or thirty may sometimes go through this ceremony

in succession, manifesting total indifference to pain. They do this to obtain *Sivalogum* (or heaven of Sita). After the devotees undergo this painful and torturing ceremony, they retire and keep at home for some days—their co-religionists say, to propitiate the favour of the gods—and many valuable presents are given them by their friends.[5]

Bronkhurst wrote this thirty years after the ritual, or "ceremony," or "festival" as it was sometimes called, had been banned—by British colonial authorities and at least one outraged Wesleyan reverend.[6]

It is a truism of plantation societies that labor, bound by chain or by contract, had to be monitored and controlled. Discipline, in its numerous forms, was a central preoccupation and challenge for colonial authorities. Methods to coerce work from physical bodies were geared toward the production process, but to preserve the social and moral order other practices also had to be policed. What colonial authorities could see, they could try to contain: absenteeism, shirking, mass gatherings, open conflict. However, it is what they could *not* see but "knew" was there that arguably equally troubled them. Perhaps foremost in this state of epistemic haze were subordinates' rituals involving the supernatural and the ineffable. Colonial authorities typically attempted to suppress these practices, and yet knew they never really could, because so much of the rituals' power lay in the unseen—the elusive and fantasized practices that stoked colonial fears and titillated colonial sensibilities. Ambiguous or even absent visual and aural cues were difficult to deny because unseen does not mean nonexistent. A kind of magical thinking—a combination of empiricism and supposition—pervaded these societies, which provided comparable "truths" that upheld the logic of domination.

Policing rituals necessarily relied on what I think of as the performance of shadows. By this I mean the retrospective inferences about a ritual, its choreography, performers, and supposed significance that observers made when that ritual practice was not seen in action. They based their retrospective inferences on material evidence: the objects that allegedly indicated the occurrence of a ritual practice. Colonizers engaged in a kind of forensic, anxious investigation of the ephemeral traces of these ritual practices through inference: they reconstructed (materialized) the illicit or problematic ritual from its traces—the stories that a ritual's objects allegedly left behind. The traces that the objects suggested then could provide evidence used to police what were criminalized practices. We can say that the objects and the messages they supposedly conveyed are what cast the shadow—the hint, the suggestion, the implied act and its intentions—of certain actions that are unseen but still ephemeral traces, sources of power that must be contained or eradicated.

In his discussion of ephemerality, performance studies scholar José Muñoz argues that ephemera comprise "a kind of evidence of what has transpired but certainly not the thing itself"; rather, it is the traces of lived experience and its performances. Such ephemera as "traces, glimmers, residues, and specks of things" must be recognized as a "mode of proofing."[7] Whereas Muñoz associates this "proofing" with subordinated groups, my focus here is the perspective of the dominating group, the colonizer. This is perhaps not surprising given that the nineteenth-century Caribbean's historical record on the points of view of the colonized is slim. That notwithstanding, the supposed practitioners of rituals—through their persons, their acts, and the identities that these persons and acts substantiate—also cast a shadow of sorts in that their actions could only be suspected, guessed at by colonial authorities and other observers who were not privy to empirical observation but were nonetheless heady with fantasies that filled in, or underscored, what could not otherwise be known.

The empirical evidence authorities had were the material objects associated with a particular ritual. Those objects indicated at best a performance of shadows—suppositions about the unseen that confirmed and predicted the performance of racial type, and the racial terror that type could provoke. This kind of post facto investigation of "shadows," the performances that cast them, and the imaginaries that interpreted them had implications for the racialization of colonized subjects. Racial categories based on Enlightenment- and post-Enlightenment-based models of human evolution served as an interpretive grid in West Indian colonies, but these categories had to be flexible when clear-cut divisions among types of people—according to Euro-colonial epistemology—were blurred by seemingly comparable or overlapping practices or beliefs. The retrospective inferences that colonial authorities and other observers drew from material evidence (ritual objects), which indicated a ritual practice when that practice was not seen in action, turned what was *not* visible (it was either otherworldly, or it was hidden, or both) into what *was* visible. Visibility was never a complete explanation of these elusive forms of power, which could spite mortal efforts at domination as well as harness immortal capabilities.

Still, visibility possessed significant truth-value for colonizers: it concretized, or reified, subordinated peoples' forms of power to dissent by inventing crime, illegal offenses that could be more easily (and justifiably) policed than ephemera that left only suggestive traces or no trace at all. The unseen, therefore, is treated like material evidence through the objects that represent it, allowing certain conclusions, racial and otherwise, to be drawn about the presumed users of those objects. For colonizers, one or two remnants of the hookswinging ritual established not only its existence among plantation coolies but an entire epistemological vision of racial and religious identity.

The ritual objects of nineteenth-century non-Christian West Indian Africans and Indians were neither well known nor well understood by colonial society, and they were often random in their discovery by colonial authorities despite the efforts to rout out the criminalized activities associated with them. Partly as a result of the desire to fill in these gaps, the shadow stories that the objects were thought to relay were much more encompassing, not limited to ascertaining the nature of the ritual itself. They told tales not only of ritual practices but of racial traits. As Nicholas Dirks observes about nineteenth-century India, from the perspective of colonial officials and Christian missionaries, "the fact that hookswinging appealed to the baser passions of the lower groups in society . . . seemed every bit as troubling as the barbarism of the rite itself. Indeed, civilization itself, in every possible sense, seemed up for grabs."[8] Once again, tradition and type (of person) were not really separable. In the West Indies, Indians' religio-racial identity always has been relative to "African"/"black" and "European"/ "white" referents. Such "primitive," atavistic traditions as hookswinging and firewalking defined indentured Indians *as* "Indians" of the lowest castes, of the so-called hill tribes, and of "coolie" plantation labor—all of which were their own racialized categories that were arguably closer to "Africans" than to the proper, recognizable "Hindoos" and "Mohammedans" within the colonial gaze. In other words, "African" was always "black," but "black" need not always be "African."

In 1853, the same year that British Guiana outlawed hookswinging, E. J. Williams of Georgetown, British Guiana, sent a handwritten letter dated March 1 to Governor Barkly reporting on his inspection of the Melville sugar plantation "for the purpose of inducing the Coolies . . . to abandon their intention of celebrating the Swinging festival," which had been planned for the coming Saturday. Williams followed procedure, presenting to the plantation owner, Mr. Smith, the communication of the Government Secretary to the Inspector General confirming Governor Barkly's "commands" about preventing the "festival." Smith "collected the Coolies who were at home," about twenty-five, "all from Calcutta," Williams added parenthetically. He "explained in as mild a way as [he] was able all the points of the case, giving them to understand that no interference would be exercised in regard to any part of their observances" except for hook-swinging, which "from its barbarous character and demoralizing tendency could not be permitted."[9] The mildness with which Williams says he conveyed his directive and the clarification about not interfering with other of the coolies' "observances" was a reassurance among officials about their following British colonial mandates about respecting the religious traditions of the colonized. This had been spurred in part by the need to distinguish coolie from slave and indenture from slavery, one stepping on the heels of the other.

Williams and the inspector who accompanied him on this investigatory mission went to the indentured laborers' barracks (Williams called them "cottages") to look for clues to the imminent swinging. They saw the center pole lying on the ground not yet erected, and the "crosspole," from which the hook, and thus the person, was to be suspended. They noted the length and circumference of the poles and, significantly, that the center pole "had only a day or two before been brought from the bush"—that is, the Amazon rainforest. The "bush" loomed large both materially and symbolically: it had resources like wood and, sometimes, small game animals, and was a nearby space of wildness and other sorts of freedoms, a connotation it also had in slave plantation society. Williams admitted that they were not able to ascertain with any certainty the number of those intending to be swung, but he guessed about twelve. He did include that the back of one of the Melville Plantation men was "still swollen at the part where the hooks had passed." The planter, Smith, assured them that he could tell from the coolies' "manner and [his] knowledge of them" that they were now dissuaded from "their design."

The policing team then advanced to another plantation, "Supply," to report to the plantation manager that they had heard rumors that these coolies, too, were planning a swinging ritual. The manager was away; they convened the coolies anyway and questioned them. "To our astonishment," Williams reported, they learned that in the previous month eleven coolies had swung, their names provided by the laborers themselves. Another devotee, thirteen or fourteen years old, showed them his back, "on which," Williams recorded, "were 20 distinct scars, he having already swung no fewer than five times, in five successive years, and all in this Colony." This time they spied the center pole, still upright, "standing within sight of the manager's house. . . . Neither police nor, it would appear, the inhabitants of [this area] generally, were aware of any such thing having occurred." Disappointed, the team never found the hooks that would have been prepared for the ritual; Williams speculated that "they may have been concealed from us, or the party with whom they were deposited may have been absent. I am inclined to think the latter." In other words, defiant secrecy was not involved, only missing testimony.

Perhaps Williams wanted to convey the suggestion of coolie innocence because it implied their satisfaction with being indentured. Relatedly, perhaps his intention was to contradict for the record the simmering dissent that colonial officials knew full well was an aspect of indenture. In any case, concealment was an issue, something Williams felt required explanation. He prudently ended his letter with a suggestion to the governor that throughout the coming week all the plantations be visited by the police sergeant of the area and that "the police be directed to exercise a diligent surveillance" over the plantations and so that the plantation attorneys or other management could be notified of the (would-be) goings-on—"in order to prevent its repetition in future."[10] Three weeks later a government notice, written in Tamil for the "Madras Coolies" as well as in English, was posted by S. Gardiner Austin, the Immigration Agent General. It was a reminder that hookswinging was prohibited, that prohibitions had often been issued previously "upon its frequent celebration," and that it would "hereafter be strictly enforced by the police" in all districts of the colony. They were certain that it was occurring but this seemed based on innuendo rather than on having been able thus far to catch this elusive practice in the act (archived documentation of which I have not found). An explanation was given for the strictness of enforcement: "The reason of this prohibition is not that His Excellency [the governor] would prevent those who have come here to labor [*sic*] from observing the rites of the religion they profess, while those observances are not calculated greatly to demoralize the uneducated black population . . ."; but the hookswinging "being considered calculated greatly to blunt [devotees'] feelings and strengthen them in vice, His Excellency is pleased to issue this prohibition, as in the British dominions the Honourable East India Company have forbidden the drowning and burning of widows with their deceased husbands, and the casting of themselves beneath the wheel of the idol car, and the destruction of infants."[11]

This notice was a handy reminder to "coolies" and everyone else about the general category of unsavory, uncivilized traditions of coolie culture (note, not "Indian" culture, which would have suggested "legitimate" Hinduism and Islam). The notice also holds other messages, other shadows of the performances that colonial authorities surmised must have taken place. These inferences were based on the statements of devotees, whether voluntary or in some way coerced—statements seemingly corroborated by such embodied messages as scarred backs. Inferences were also based on the most minimal of material objects—wooden poles and metal hooks, the latter presupposed rather than viewed in their implementation. These inferences were also based on the symbolic significance held by those objects. They were procured from the "bush," a space of unruliness, of underdevelopment. These objects represented coolies' indulging in pain and "torture," and yet these inferences also represented coolies' insensibility to pain—the kind of contradiction that racial thinking has always contained. Connected to these symbolizations that nested between the lines of the government notice was an Enlightenment-resonant focus on body rather than on mind. This emphasis relegated these particular human types closer to animal levels on the evolutionary scale than to more developmentally successful human types—who had long lost, or who had never had such "barbarous" traditions—thereby confirming the category of person within which these devotees fit.

These inferences are shadows whose performance registers a certain definitiveness—all that is air congeals into solids, to reverse Karl Marx's famous phrase. Each perceived indication of ritual performance—the deployment of objects, the choreography of bodies, and the expression of type—are pieces of evidence, material or otherwise, that constitute ephemeral traces that are at the same time both flexible and resolute. As Western psychoanalysis has long held, fantasy needs at a minimum a certain external object or stimulus in order to project its own, in this case colonial, imaginary. The traces, no matter how minimal, reify a colonial worldview and with it racial types.

On April 14, 1853, six weeks after Williams wrote to Governor Barkly, Barkly sent a letter to the Duke of Newcastle about his efforts to "stamp out the hook swinging festival" in British Guiana. "I have endeavored as far as possible, with the valuable aid of the Revd [Reverend] Mr. Williams the Wesleyan Missionary to the Coolies, to explain the grounds on which I have thought it necessary to interfere." The "public exhibition" of the swinging, which "from its novel and exciting nature seldom failed to attract large crowds of the Negro Youth," was "accompanied almost invariably with intemperance and immorality." Barkly did not state outright that he had been an eyewitness to hookswinging, only that he had "interdicted" it a number of times—yet based on precisely what we cannot be sure.[12]

Despite that "it may be easily imagined" that these exertions to prohibit hookswinging had "not yet produced much visible effect," the chance for their success was better on West Indian plantations "than amid the associations, and influences of Heathenism."[13] One might infer that this "Heathenism," so prevalent and so concentrated, was a synonym for India. For many Euro-colonizers (and perhaps some Indians as well), lower caste Hindus were barely Hindus, and their near brethren, Indian hill tribe peoples, even less so. The rubric of an overdetermined "primitive," with the imagined ritual of either embodied ecstasy or sensorial imperviousness (a kind of polarized, no-win option), framed the practice as superstition rather than faith, a defiance of authority that condenses "African" and "Indian" into the generic figure of the "savage," antisocial rogue. This performance of shadows reified not only Christian superiority but also racial hierarchy, identifying Indians as primitive and disturbing, tantamount to Africans.

### Other Suspect Evidence

The "farrago of materials" that comprised the tool kits of obeah were both the stock-in-trade of obeah practitioners and the criminalized objects of colonial domination. They were "enumerated," for example, "in the Jamaica [*sic*] law, viz. 'Blood, feathers, parrots' beaks, dogs' teeth, alligators' teeth, broken bottles, grave-dirt, rum, and egg-shells,'"[14] and were itemized decades earlier in Jamaica's 1761 anti-obeah law.[15] Obeah's assortment of perplexingly mundane or unappealing objects[16] was far from the votive offerings of Euro-colonialism's so-called legitimate religions—notably Christianity. Votive offerings are "agents of faith" offered to a saint or deity to make a pledge or fulfill a vow.[17] Obeah's objects historically have been represented as functioning outside of the moral good, as magic. In this perspective, obeah's objects are not "votive," and obeah's acts cannot be acts of faith; they are tainted, allegedly committed to the dark arts of superstition and malevolence. This kind of visibility also indexed racial traits and the racial hierarchies that these traits substantiated. What was not seen was present in the form of the shadows (the hints, inferences, extrapolations) created by ritual objects and their presumably intended uses. These shadows confirmed the fact of a ritual act and also the racial types who perpetrated it. But just as speculation can be uncertain and unclear, Euro-colonial racial typologies did not necessarily remain as distinct as the classificatory grid defined them.

In his history of the West Indies, merchant, politician, and slave trade supporter Bryan Edwards footnoted a common definition of the *"Obi"* ("obeah") of enslaved Africans: "a species of pretended magic."[18] This definition of obeah, common in its day and long after, had abiding consequences in British colonial imaginaries, notably obeah's associations with magic, fraud, and their rogue perpetrators.[19] This definition suggests, on the one hand, that obeah was epistemologically counterfeit, a pretense to relations with supernatural power because it was, or was tantamount to, "magic." On the other hand, it was only bogus magic, which reaffirmed an implication that there was "real" magic—always a contentious possibility in Euro-Christian worldviews. "Pretending" to possess supernatural and occult power can mean that those powers do not exist (as in some canonical forms of Christianity), or it means that occult power does exist but only illegitimately, through the Devil, for example. Both magic and its swindle, fraud, are kinds of deception; deception is the illusion, and elusion, of evidence.

That said, for colonial chroniclers much of the unseen was interpreted as "real." This is clearly indicated, for example, by planters' fear, or at least wariness, of the obeah purportedly worked by slaves and former slaves. In his *History*, Edwards included a story about "Obeah practice." It was ostensibly from "a planter in Jamaica, a gentleman of the strictest veracity, . . . ready to attest the truth." As the story goes, it was 1775 and this planter had returned to Jamaica after being away for a time. He discovered that "a great many of his Negroes had died during his absence" and at least half the ones still alive "were debilitated, bloated, and in a very deplorable condition." The deaths continued, two or three each day; "others were taken ill and began to decline under the same symptoms." This went on for a year, and the planter and "the doctor and other white persons upon the plantation" "strongly suspected" "the *Obeah practice*," which was known to be common in that part of Jamaica. But suspicions could not unequivocally be verified because "the patients constantly denied their having any thing [*sic*] to do with persons of that order [obeah practitioners], or any knowledge of them." Eventually, one of the afflicted, a "Negress," saw it as her dying duty to "impart a very great secret" in order to stop the "mischief." She identified her octogenarian stepmother to be a longtime obeah woman, who "put *Obi upon her*" and others who had recently died. The other "Negroes" on this plantation "confirmed the truth of it," saying that ever since she had arrived from Africa she had been the "terror of the whole neighborhood." The planter took "six White servants" with him to the "old woman's" house, forced open the door, and took visual inventory of "the implements of her trade," which were under the whole of the roof and stuck in "every crevice of the walls." These implements included "rags, feathers, bones of cats, and a thousand other articles," such as a large earthen jar hidden under her bed filled with various size balls of clay mixed with hair, rags, or feathers and bound with twine, human teeth, colored glass beads, eggshells filled with a "gummy substance," and small bags of various items. The house was razed to the ground and burned. Magnanimously not wanting her to be legally charged and thus punished with death, "from a principle of humanity," the planter "delivered her into the hands of a party of Spaniards, who . . . were very glad to accept and carry her with them to Cuba." As soon as she was gone, the "malady" ceased to spread, but over the fifteen years preceding this discovery the planter's losses totaled at least one hundred deceased persons.[20]

Exile off-island was among the legal punishments for obeah in the eighteenth- and early nineteenth-century West Indies. This handing her off to some Spaniards, however, may have been a gray area in the legal transactions involving human property. It is interesting that Edwards implies it is a kind of gifting rather than a sale of human chattel. We can be fairly sure that the octogenarian alleged culprit would have fared pretty horribly as this group's property, on their way to a place foreign to her. The kind of informing the planter reported the stepdaughter doing may have happened during slavery, and it did happen in the courtroom among postemancipation litigants.[21] But we can never know whether the enslaved Africans on that plantation were genuinely happy that their fellow sufferer turned in her stepmother so that the obeah would stop. We also cannot know for certain what was killing them. In fact, we do not know which, if any, part of this story happened at all. As is the case so much of the time, we have only the word of Euro-colonial observers towing their agendas. But at the time, the veracity of this narrative was not of paramount importance. Obeah's entertainment value overlapped with its truth-value, the two together constituting its discursive value.[22] The firsthand attestations of the truth by gentlemen of "the strictest veracity" reinforced through storytelling the meaning and importance of visibility as the synonym for truth. The climax of the story does not involve the unseen malevolent forces unleashed by the old obeah woman; rather, it is the immolation of the itemized objects of obeah and the house in which they were stored. Eyewitness testimonies lend empirical credibility, identifying and reifying the unseen through its manifestation in the quotidian material culture of subordinated peoples.[23]

In an 1868 ordinance dealing with "rendering certain Offenses punishable on Summary Conviction," decreed by Arthur Gordon, governor of Trinidad (1866–1870) and his Legislative Council, there is a section devoted to "Superstitious Devices." Item XXXI of this section stipulates that "if it shall be shewn, upon the Oath of a credible Witness, that there is reasonable Cause to suspect that any Person is in Possession of any Article or Thing used by him in the Practice of Obeah or Witchcraft, it shall be lawful for any Justice of the Peace, by Warrant under his Hand, to cause any Place whatsoever belonging to or under the Control of such Person to be searched either in the Day or in the Night, and if any such Article shall be found in any Place so searched to cause the same to be seized and brought before him or some other Justice of the Peace, who shall cause the same to be secured for the Purpose of being produced in Evidence in any Case in which it may be required."[24] Whether operational through the mysteries of witchcraft or the pragmatism of deception ("fraud"), obeah's objects are key. Literary scholars Kelly Wisecup and Toni Wall Jaudon note that obeah's "classic representation" is "obeah-as-assemblage."[25] They rightly contend that the colonial interest in obeah objects was part of a larger project to transform obeah, in part through its objects, "into a set of knowable practices."[26] The objects serve as conduits of revelation; they are the empirical evidence that concretizes the unknown and the unseeable. Hence, the power of suggestion and deduction from the performance of shadows are important qualities of obeah. The slipperiness of obeah, like trying to catch smoke, suggests that it is inherently duplicitous—as opposed, for example, to hard-and-fast dogma, seemingly easy to apprehend, seemingly stable in meaning and injunction. Because of these very qualities, obeah's formation is based as much on what is said about it as what is actually done; the spoken or written word is another stand-in for the unknown and the unseeable, a kind of empiricism in the form of reportage that could help reify it for purposes of its criminalization, the named objects that identified its existence and its user(s), endlessly repeated.

An additional motivation to establish empirical indicators of obeah in order to stifle it may have been to offset the Victorian era's expanding science-based epistemology, which emphasized the observable and the measurable world. For example, the traveler-physician R. R. Madden published his classic memoir *A Twelve Month's Residence in the West Indies* in 1835, on the cusp of the Victorian era, one year into apprenticeship. Writing about obeah, Madden asserted that it is "evident to any medical man who reads these [obeah] trials, that, in the great majority of cases, the trumpery ingredients used in the practice of obeah were incapable of producing mischief, except on the imagination of the person intended to be obeahed."[27] Madden's notion of empiricism falsifies the reality of obeah (its palpable consequences) on the basis of "trumpery ingredients"—worthless or useless articles without power or agency. Africans, "weak in intellect," brought their superstitions to the colonies.[28] Madden adds that "ignorance was essential to slavery; and no pains were spared . . . to keep the negro from enlightenment, which is the door to liberty."[29] By contrast to Madden's commitment to empirical verification that trivializes obeah's objects, colonial authority's valuation of these very objects was the empirical evidence colonial authority needed, the materialization of the shadows professed but not visible in obeah acts. Visibility was "truth" for both, but visibility was defined in terms of different ideas about what needed to be seen. Yet both Madden's Victorian science-based truth and British colonial law-based truth were informed by racial thinking that led back to the savage—in obeah's case, specifically African. This label was not always synonymous with the more encompassing savage quality of blackness to which the "coolie" could also be subject. But both reinforced obeah's supposed provenance and its degraded (both sullied and stigmatized) race-based essence.

Some anti-obeah laws in the West Indies referred to "instruments of obeah" but did not specify what they were, or did so vaguely and, occasionally, tautologically. In 1898, Jamaica's Obeah Act stated that an "'Instrument of Obeah' means any thing used, or intended to be used by a person, and pretended by such person to be possessed of any occult or supernatural power."[30] "It was not always easy," David Trotman observes, "to distinguish fact from fiction in obeah cases." Trotman cites the case of a man arrested for practicing obeah in Trinidad in 1871. The man was found to be in possession of objects considered to be obeah paraphernalia: "two bottles (one of rum and one of sweet oil), two fowls (one dead and one alive), a piece of bone, some powder, and some shells."[31] Such a collection may well have been intended for some kind of occult mission, but how to be certain? Possession is telltale of behavior only if stipulated by legal or other social means (such as moral dictates)—that is, there is no intrinsic essence that is a necessary or automatic catalyst. Trotman is right that the "fact" of having an assortment of (disparate) objects does not confirm or deny their use, which makes usage a "fiction" until shown to be otherwise. But it was proof enough in 1871's Trinidad. At the same time, the ambiguity created by fact versus fiction is exactly how mysterious things work. Being unsure of the meaning of an experience is the source of mystery's power.[32] In other words, obeah's power significantly rests in its abstruseness, and this same quality facilitates obeah's criminalization and persecution through vague or blanket definition of its tool kit.

The challenge for colonial authority thus came in the plural: obeah's objects must visibly represent the unseen; obeah's practitioners must be identified broadly but according to some kind of rationale (largely through possession of objects); obeah's charges that detected practitioners must (in theory) be substantiated with appropriate proof, not promiscuously; obeah itself, and its effectiveness (the results of its powers), must be denied even as they are confirmed by the very policing that seeks to accomplish this. This twisted reasoning, contradictions that operated simultaneously in common sense, likely lent a surreal quality to the pursuit of law, order, and conformity. The intent was to maintain categorical distinctions between what could be thought of as credible evidence and what could be thought of as incredible invocation. The "magic" of evidence, its capacity for persuasion, could not be magical; in theory, at least, it had to be scientific. But "science," a label more flexible than strict nineteenth- and early twentieth-century empiricism generally allowed, also came in occult, invisible forms; and tangible, visible forms could take on a number of associations and meanings that transcended the bounds of the empirically observable. This labyrinth of logic ultimately led to the rogue individual. Criminalization materializes the unseen; we "see" things by inference rather than empirical observation. The juxtaposition of objects into collections of things reinforced their identification as insidious tools of mischief; a single object may have been suggestive, but an aggregate was proof. Identifying and policing obeah objects thus rendered criminalization of the objects' owners easier: the occult *things* in a person's possession were obvious (seen by the naked eye), and they were encompassing (a broad assortment of everyday items). Still, the objects' power lay not so much in being individual instruments as it did in their gestalt—the whole that is greater than the sum of its parts. In conjunction with each other, this power-gestalt required manipulation by certain specialist individuals.

Whether or not nineteenth-century colonizers were convinced that there was a clear divide between animate and inanimate things, all things still had roles and purposes that should remain intact. In 1854, for example, the Lieutenant Governor of St. Vincent, Windward Islands, Richard Donnell, sent a letter to one Colonel Colbrooke in Barbados in reply to a letter Colbrooke had sent him concerning the punishment of obeah and "other occult sciences." Donnell assured Colbrooke that legal prohibitions would be "directed only against an improper use of those 'occult sciences.'" He made his position clear by means of an analogy: "The use of the Bible is similarly not forbidden by English law in our churches or for purposes of Family Worship, but the use of the Bible as a means along with a key of discovering stolen property and thereby obtaining money from simple people would consign the party so using it in England to the Treadmill."[33]

The appropriate usage of discrete religious things was important in order to keep the sacred properly defined and separated from the profane, the immoral, and the occult. But a collection of incongruous things also can generate a kind of power, possibly but not necessarily produced by each item alone. Odd groupings produce a kind of perverse power, the power associated with "dark arts." Each of the diverse objects recorded by contemporary observers—grave dirt, nails, hair, bones, insects, animal parts—likely brought a certain meaning with it. I have not seen colonial documents that contain analyses of the meaning or symbolism of alleged obeah objects except in sweeping statements about their nefarious capabilities. But the lists exemplified often have many of the same or very similar items, which suggest that obeah's incongruent assemblages are not random; there is significance to their groupings. Although the particular meanings of both single objects and collections of objects are elusive (unrecorded, ambiguous, mysterious), the boundaries that conventionally differentiate obeah objects are drawn together in what Wittgenstein called a "family resemblance"[34] that creates the power of the whole (the gestalt), a resemblance that also can become evidence—of practices that are otherwise either unseen or uncertainly understood by devotees as well as by observers.

The power of the whole, obeah-as-assemblage, derives from the fact that family resemblance does not negate the "abomination" of "hybrids and other confusions."[35] As Mary Douglas argued, "Holiness requires that different classes of things shall not be confused." Obeah's objects are used for purposes not in their presumed nature—that is, their categorically appropriate function or use. Their family resemblance lies in the suggestion of disorder that is produced by things together out of place; the contradiction between "what seems and what is" is a kind of "dissembling"[36] that helps to confer on obeah's objects its disturbing implications about agents that carry out immoral intentions. Ridiculous, frightening, and alluring to colonial authority, and alluring and frightening to the colonized, obeah's shadowed performances called for materialization, most readily of the tools of its trade and the rogues who manipulated them. Criminalizing objects and individuals created evidence that made policing appear less arbitrary and therefore moral and just.

The alleged propensity for superstition and belief in magic was shared among African and Indian subjects. Given their savage natures and simple minds, Africans (metonymized as the slave) were invested in obeah and its objects. Given their savage natures and simple minds, Indians (metonymized as the coolie) were also invested in ritual objects, whether poles and hooks or the tadjahs that were characterized by some Euro-Christian observers as "idols." Both types also shared a propensity for irrational and uncontained expression of "passions." They were evincing ritual excess, acutely different from exercising religious freedom.[37] This included slaves' resistance to their enslavement (uprisings, marronage) and socially unnerving merrymaking (Canboulay, Carnival), and indentured laborers' proclivity for uncontrolled violence, fanaticism, excitability, and, at times, being "perfectly mad" in their "coolie orgies" called Hosay. Not only did these charges reiterate the inherent inferiority of these colonized peoples, but they reinforced the truth of the differences that separated them from their local Euro-colonial superiors.

A significant factor in this difference was condition of mind, measured significantly by a peoples' understanding of the cosmos and extranatural phenomena—that is, "religious" orientation enabled by "racial" type. Magic and magical thinking characterized the unenlightened, non-Euro-Christian other. However, magic and magical thinking had never left Euro-Christians' lifeworlds. A salient dimension of magic in its quintessential form is that it is ritual action that has intrinsic and automatic effectiveness, engaging forces and objects independent of deities, a notion that goes back to the early Judeo-Christian legacy in Western thought.[38] The ideas that magic is automatically effective and that its forces lie outside the scope of divine (sacred) entities are connected to other ideas about magic: it is self-serving and strategic, particularly applied to worldly interests rather than generically focused; its results are rapid and its methods mysterious. These aspects require management by a specialist, one who is expert in summoning, manipulating, and controlling dark forces whose energies, when unleashed, are very dangerous. This human middleman, a leader in mischief, has had for millennia various personifications.

In the colonial West Indies this person was the obeah worker, an individual who by virtue of their craft was antithetical to proper social formations. This was the individual so vaunted in Enlightenment thought, but one gone bad. There were two kinds of inadequacy to this spoiled (and spoiler) figure. On the one hand, this person was an insufficient individual, exemplified in the idea that enslaved Africans represented an "absence of sovereign will" and were in thrall to "other, unseen forces, [who] were their masters."[39] On the other hand, and equally (if not more) threatening to established order, this kind of individual exercised a perverse agency, a duplicitous leadership in malevolent forces. The rogue individual is not limited to the obeah worker, nor is it exclusive to one racial type. The figure of the rogue individual fed British colonial imaginaries about moral communities, functional societies, and modern futures. Fraud involves intentional deception—false claims and empty promises. This hidden contradiction of truth, in the form of fraud, was an important dimension of colonial criticism of traditions and practices that were feared to dishonor its moral imperatives or threaten its rule. Colonizers policed the fraudulence exercised upon one subordinate by another, but they did not really care about the harm done to the colonized themselves, which most of the time was not life-threatening in any case. The concept of fraud in law discounts the truth factor of the fraudulent acts (and thus discounts the legitimacy and merit of those committing the fraud) but still keeps fraudulent acts a punishable violation. Belief is denigrated while punishing the act, which is legally interpreted as extortion of some kind—for example, the obeah practitioner is allegedly extorting something from the client dupe. Fraud embodied in the individual is an attempt to prosecute something within the law without conceding belief in it.

Obeah and Hosay presented different, equally prosecutable forms of fraud. The "fraudulence" of Hosay was not an intentional deception but rather its motley crew of heterogeneous participant-observers: Hosay's fluid combination of religious traditions and the "barbaric" customs of noncanonical religions both Indian and African, its exuberant expressiveness, and its primacy in the context of secular protests led by a congeries of individuals gone rogue (notably, labor unrest). But the detection of fraud was focused primarily on theoretical concerns about meaning—on the one hand, Hosay's relationship to "religion" (Islam, Muharram), and thus how to manage it between philosophical commitments to freedom and individual agency; on the other, the demands of economic production and moral responsibility. Obeah's fraud lay in its allegedly deliberate deceptions, its performance of shadows through which its objects made visible its pretense and misdirection.

In his 1854 letter to Colonel Colbrooke about the practice of obeah in Saint Vincent, Lieutenant Governor Donnell lamented that "obeah practices are very general, I regret to say, in this Island. They are practised by a few Charlatans, who here as in England impose on the credulity of the Vulgar by pretending to discourse[?] stolen goods and to administer for all sorts of diseases, specifics [sic], and charms, which they sell at an exorbitant rate. As I believe that in one form or another similar modes of cheating are practised all over the world whether selling winds in Lapland or scraps of the Koran in Africa. I consider Barbados especially fortunate in not being infested by such imposters. At the same time as pretended witchcraft, fortune telling, astrology and similar impositions [?] are punishable in England and they who pretend to practice them can be sent as vagabonds to the treadmill. I cannot imagine why the same protection by law should not be extended here to the ignorant and credulous 'till more enlightened views and a wider system of education shall enable us to dispense with legal enactments on the subject."[40] It is not clear why Donnell thought Barbados was imposter-free, but whether referred to as an extant problem or a nonexistent one, fraud, imposters, and credulity loom large in discussions about objections to obeah.

The reification of credulity as a thing to monitor and ostensibly to guard against was also useful to other policing endeavors of colonial authority besides the criminalization of obeah and its practitioners. For example, in their report on Indian indenture in West Indian colonies, James McNeill and Chimman Lal advised that newcomer coolie laborers should not be punished "for being a fool and being easily duped," as they were vulnerable to being cheated, for example, by "the sale or barter of rations."[41] These efforts—protecting the vulnerable from the dangerous chicanery of obeah and the lure of distracting tangible temptations—were meant to keep plantation peace (avoid conflicts over deception) and fasten labor to production (punish the enablers). Ultimately, the priority was labor control and the extraction of profits from production while maintaining a global profile of model morality. As McNeill and Lal advised, "it is very desirable" that the coolie "should be broken into harness gently."[42] Obeah was decidedly subversive, and its practice exemplified in the colonies the African atavism of blackness. But obeah never has been exclusive to Afro-Caribbeans except in Euro-colonial racial thinking, being shared in one form or another by the cultures of all peoples in the region. In the context of plantation society, neither has "black" been solely an association with African peoples. Credulity among West Indian Africans and Indians is an aspect of what makes race and religion heritable identities; credulity might be stimulated by unfamiliar circumstances (like plantation indenture), but it also is a primary mark of superstition, the legacy of ancestry, and stage of mind.

Credulity, then, is also the target of the rogue individual. As so many colonial ordinances, amendments, and other documents indicate, obeah's dupes must be protected from their own childlike, savage mentality. In the context of obeah, credulity is associated with belief in supernatural instrumentality—magic—the pursuit of immediate objectives and instant gratification by means of an individual expert's interventions. Under the guise of protecting the mentally inferior credulous from themselves (not incidentally reinforcing the racial thinking of the era), credulity served as a kind of evidence. As part of an inferior belief system, credulity was the flipside of pretense. Credulity is materialized into evidence as a manifestation of the power of the unseen to influence people's behaviors—for example, the obeah acts sought, feared, and denied.

## Communities, Individuals, and Belonging

Those who put fraud into specific action are pretenders; pretending designates that one is aware of being fraudulent, that one is cheating people deliberately. To pretend is to fake something in order to delude others; to claim something might be self-delusion (the claimant may truly believe in her or his claims). Claiming and pretending, then, are different; pretending involves consciousness of word and deed. Intention, motivation, and self-consciousness are at issue. Criminalized as fraud, to pretend is one dimension of the larger bad bargain called obeah. It represents a perverse (wrong) kind of *self*-awareness; in other words, pretense is self-awareness of one's antisocial behavior and character. (In Euro-colonial thought, behavior expresses character, and character authenticates type.) The pretender engaged with antisocial activity is a "rogue individual," someone who allegedly does not contribute to the formation and continuity of community and thus threatens it. A rogue individual is the person not committed to freedom and self-realization in pursuit of a moral good, bound by a social contract. It is the person whose individual will is solely self-fulfilling, going against the grain of enlightened agency and, instead, being in concert with nefarious means to accomplish one's own, or others' self-centered, destruction-oblivious, immediate desires. Another way of thinking about what constitutes a rogue individual is that he or she is someone who is not "public" in the sense of being socially visible but instead remains "private," not customarily meant to be widely viewed or known. Being seen and recognized (visible) is a kind of conformity to the social body. Conformity in this sense does not necessarily mean acceptance; visibility may be an act of resistance to certain aspects of that social body. But it is predicated on the demand for belonging. Following the logic of the West's Durkheimian legacy, visibility is community.

The concept of "the individual" that infused the West Indies is an aspiration of Enlightenment and post-Enlightenment thought—that is, the ideal of (hu)man's capacity for self-realization, the exercise of free will that enables rational decisions, the capacity to determine one's own destiny. This Western existential model of the individual (presented as a universal model) is understood in relation to the concept of "community" or "society." Individuals either work with or against communities; either way, they are viewed in relation to one another. One of the ways that scholars have tried to understand West Indian religious traditions is to distinguish between those that are highly structured and based on canon, and those that are not. Scholars have defined the latter as lacking the "established liturgy and community rituals" that are the mark of organized religions.[43] Obeah and Hosay certainly fit among those so categorized when charged with having no formally institutionalized roles or orthodox liturgy. Being an obeah man or woman takes relevant knowledge and skill, but in theory anyone may exhibit these.

The eighteenth-century interest in the nature of society and social institutions was continued throughout the nineteenth and early twentieth centuries, largely in terms of questions about the impact of modernity on traditional societies and how the latter developed new institutions, remained cohesive, and exemplified developmental progress (or did not) according to still-vibrant evolutionary models that had arisen almost two centuries earlier. A number of social theorists came to prominence in this period; some left an indelible mark that continues to shape Western ways of knowing human society, social institutions and organization, and relations of power. Particularly relevant for my purposes are Emile Durkheim's ideas about religion, the individual, and community—a legacy still authorizing commonsense assumptions about what constitutes religion and what forces produce it.

Religion is the cornerstone of Durkheim's attempts to understand modern society as a whole, not as simply "disparate individuals pursuing private projects" but rather as "'a moral being' that transcends its members even as it resides within them and fashions them."[44] Durkheim was developing his ideas at a time when liberal humanism emphasized the individual, an entity that was greatly invested with free will.[45] Enthusiastic about the idea of free will, Durkheim understood the meaningful functions of religion in terms of a social good. He held that "all the most characteristic manifestations of collective life"—"religious beliefs and practices, the rules of morality and the innumerable precepts of law"—are "ways of acting and thinking [that] are not the work of the individual but come from a moral power above him, that which the mystic calls God or which can be more scientifically conceived."[46] The idea of a moral community is central to Durkheim's definition of religion; the "moral community" and the "Church" were interchangeable in his writing.[47] "Religion" consists of beliefs and practices that build a moral community; they are synonymous, and one cannot exist without the other. This shared morality and common orientation to the sacred is what produces solidarity among individuals, which in turn is what forms human society. Durkheim tended to associate the sacred with the lofty, collective practices that formed the moral community, and the profane with the mundane, pragmatic actions of individuals pursuing self-interest.

As Ann Warfield Rawls explains, magic for Durkheim "begins with individual instrumental action and involves the idea that a specific goal is to be achieved by either the individual or the collective performance of a rite";

there are no effects of magic that are purely social or collective.[48] This general idea had a long history in Enlightenment thought: "true religion" was a "'rational' belief system in a sovereign providence," writes Stanley Tambiah, whereas "magic" was a "class of acts ranging from sacramental ritualism to false manipulations of the supernatural and occult powers."[49] Thus magic and religion are contrary phenomena: magic is individualistic, and religion is based in the social group. As Durkheim put it, "religious beliefs proper" are always common to a definite group. They are not merely received individually by all the members of this group; they are something belonging to the group, and they make its unity.[50] Durkheim's equation of religion with a church means that magic does not have a church because it works by deception and thus can never be truly communal. And without true group unity (based on shared sentiment about the sacred) there is no moral force. He put a finer point on this distinction by stating that "magic takes a kind of professional pleasure in profaning holy things."[51] Given the way that Durkheim construed the "social," the "community," and the "individual" in relation to "religion"—as necessitating a particular kind of moral dimension—obeah will not fit within the category of "religion." Yet everything human beings do is "social," because we are collective, not solitary animals. Obeah, then, by definition is "social": it links persons to each other and to otherworldly, supernatural entities. The latter are in many cases vibrant interlocutors in the worlds of the living. Whether or not obeah, or Hosay, for that matter, has all the "isms"—standardized texts, established liturgy, community rituals—required to be "really religion" is an important question because, as we have seen, such determinations can be forceful weapons in the arsenals of power. But more than simply asserting (or denying) that obeah, or anything else, is or is not religion, it is important to unpack the epistemic habits that commonsensically contribute to those determinations. For example, what is the "individual" and how does it work ideologically, particularly in terms of the religionization of race and the racialization of religion? How was the concept of fraud and credulity, so useful in pointing to individual culpability and away from structural culpability, linked to the image of the individual? How were these abstractions objectified into evidence of the need to obliterate obeah and contain Hosay?

For the most part, we have long rested to one degree or another on some version of Durkheim: that religion is fundamentally social (with "social" enjoying a particular definition), which produces the moral community of a church (in the sense of an institutionalized body of thought and its be-

lievers), and where the "sacred" is clearly discernable from the "profane."
Durkheim's distinction between the "individual" and "society" is multilayered, but in relation to obeah in particular, his idea that the individual
magician has individual clientele rather than a church congregation is significant. "Between the magician and the individuals who consult him,"
Durkheim wrote, "there are no durable ties that make them members of a
single moral body. . . . The magician has a clientele, not a Church, and
his clients may have no mutual relations, and may even be unknown to
one another . . . the relations they have with him are . . . analogous to those
of a sick man with his doctor"—and thus they lack sociality. "That he functions in broad daylight does not join him in a more regular and lasting
manner with those who make use of his services."[52] Magic and mysteri-
ousness belong to the rogue individual, and as such they are the antithesis
of the community and its purpose, the common good.

## Occult Pornography

Writing about hookswinging in nineteenth-century British colonial India,
Nicholas Dirks observed that horror "has the uncanny capacity to obliterate
the quotidian."[53] In the context of the West Indies, horror shares this same
capacity, whether associated with the calculated resistance of subordinates
or the innate proclivities that establish identities and motivate actions.
Horror also is able to hyperbolize the quotidian—exaggerating, bloating
things out of proportion, making things seem unnatural, abnormal, ex-
ceeding the bounds of the mundane. The occult has long been a space of
horror: terror and titillation. As such, it can be viewed as what I call "occult pornography." Occult pornography is a kind of vernacular, a way of
stigmatizing a practice, a tradition, or an act (inclusive of but not limited
to sexuality) by taking it outside of civilized social community and con-
fining it within uncivilized, antisocial clusters. Like our conventional notion of sexual pornography, it is mimetic: it creates sensations out of context by using signifiers that are associated with the missing context; it arouses
desire and fear out of context. Occult pornography also titillates the senses
by means of the grotesque, or the malleable elaboration of something familiar so that it suggests the most disturbing aspects that can be associated with it. Occult pornography bloats, or exaggeratedly distorts, what is
familiar, what is socially permissible, to the absolute edge of acceptability
and tolerability, thus arousing or tapping into desire for either the indecent
or the tabooed. In these ways, occult pornography is also alienation—away

from what is "naturally" civil behavior toward what is "unnaturally" un-
civil behavior. For enthusiasts, the thrill is the indecency and the excess;
for critics, the indecency and the excess are the deficiency.

Throughout their respective histories and across their geographical locations, most religious traditions (Euro-Christianity included) allow some
version of the outward expression of sensations stimulated by communing
with the supernatural sphere or spiritual entities of various kinds—God,
deities, ancestors, saints. Even in the Old and New Testaments there are
those who deviate from the extant norm in demonstrating the presence
of supernatural inspiration, such as people identified as prophets, or who
receive visions. But these kinds of specialness, as it were, are not the kind
of excess to which colonial authority objected about the colonized. Channeled through the body, excess was the manifestation of forms of worship
that went beyond the bounds of proper, authorized worship, superabun-
dant in being an exaggeration of visible emotion. This representation of
hyperbole entwined race and religion together as the condition of the
savage—the dark, the underdeveloped, the unpredictable, the individual
gone rogue.

Of course we must bear in mind that the colonial voice was not homogeneous: there were intragroup squabbles, debates, and doubts; there were
tensions among various levels of regime officials and local missionaries,
who worked hand in hand and at cross-purposes. There were the governed
who concurred with the discourses of power, there were those who rejected
them, and there was everyone in between. The point of common sense
and its epistemic habits is not to imply uniformity in thought. Some assumed certainties are shed, others are preserved over time. As Foucault
argued, there is always change, but epistemic habits are tenacious. The
point is to identify what Anne Stoler calls the "easy to think": discourses
and representations that build up over time, creating points of reference or
discursive traditions that hold sway in guiding the ways people who share
them think about things.[54] Assumed certainties are revealed in the language used to convey them, the repeated concepts and images that evoke
charges meant to persuade, opinions meant to justify. Even in the sober
documents of imperial policing, disparaging adjectives color the texts and
suggest that greater fears, and excitements, lie below the explicit objections
and curtailments. Crises involving the proprieties of religion and the management of race entailed a mix of trepidation, profound condemnation,
and insistent captivation that produced an ethos of societal horror, repulsing

and attracting at the same time. As such, it was, one might say, mitigated "fun to think."

The fear was real, certainly, and when people were directly faced with it—not the least being from various kinds of retribution by enslaved or indentured subordinates—they likely did not perceive much else but terror. But when the horrors of lives and peoples gone awry were something that was learned about distant or only imagined others, a dimension of entertainment ensued. For example, in 1797, Bryan Edwards subtitled a work he wrote about Saint Domingue, soon to become known as Haiti, "A Narrative of the Calamities Which Have Desolated the Country Ever Since the Year 1789," suggesting a foretaste of his opinions about Haitian revolutionaries. He opens chapter VI with: "I am now to enter on the retrospect of scenes, the horrors of which imagination cannot adequately conceive nor pen describe. . . . Such a picture of human misery;—such a scene of woe, presents itself, as no other country, no former age has exhibited. Upwards of one hundred thousand savage people, habituated to the barbarities of Africa, avail themselves of the silence and obscurity of the night, and fall on the peaceful and unsuspicious planters, like so many famished tygers [*sic*] thirsting for human blood."[55] This imagined tableau is indeed horrifying, but there is also in the depiction a titillating allure that is as exciting to think about as it is alarming.

Edwards's portrayal of the Haitian Revolution can be read as pornographic through its imagery and the sensations that such imagery can stimulate, like the descriptions of hookswinging on mid-nineteenth-century British Guianese sugar plantations. Sexual innuendo is at work in the narativization of the "grotesque" rituals of the other precisely because of the evocations of primitiveness, passions shamelessly unleashed, bodies unconstrained by self-awareness—the Euro-Christian virtue of shame. Shame can be viewed as an evolutionary step forward in Enlightenment and post-Enlightenment thinking: Adam and Eve were evicted from Eden for gaining knowledge, but it was a certain kind of knowledge—self-consciousness through being ashamed of their nakedness. Various states of dress and undress of human groups reflect their evolutionary stage: the less body coverage, the closer to nature and to animals. Lacking shame, they miss the realization that Adam and Eve needed to perceive their human selves in relation to the natural world of Eden.

Other reportage lies between implicit and explicit suggestiveness. In his mid-nineteenth-century book *Trinidad and the Other West India Islands and Colonies,* Daniel Hart reported, "It is stated that on their arrival in the French colonies the Coolies are, previous to landing, made to attire themselves as civilized beings. For this purpose proper clothing is provided for them. . . . In Trinidad the eyes of the inhabitants, high and low, are compelled to behold these people almost in an entire state of nudity. . . . And are they not obliged to keep themselves clean? Surely then there could be no reason why they should not be told that they *must* clothe themselves as other people do. . . . Again, these people are without any true religion, and have, consequently, little to no regard for the laws of God or man."[56] Some pages later Hart informs readers that "Coolies generally are tractable" but become "violent . . . when their passions are aroused," at which point they have "little care for life or limb."[57] If we think of shame as, in part, a kind of self-censure or self-control, the naked coolie body aroused—in anger or in some other highly affective state—is as pornographic as bloodthirsty night prowlers or metal hooks in flesh. Readers may picture the scene as they like, and salivate in their disgust.

I am not suggesting that Edwards, Hart, and others who left such thoughts in print intended primarily for their imprints to be sexual. I am arguing, in fact, that given my expanded notion of pornography, unambiguous sexuality does not necessarily need to be present; pornography encompasses sexuality but is not limited to it. Part of the "magic" of evidence is the performance of shadows, of suggestion. Suggested proofs may be in the objects that are made to stand in for them. But suggested proof can also be the racialized behaviors associated with the antisociality of rogue individuals who enjoin the supernatural in the service of clients, or the uninhibited contortions and utterings of pseudoreligion, or the rogue individuals who defy the conditions of their indenture, allegedly through the suspect enactment of religious rituals historically "marked by awe-inspiring emotions" and the "passion inherent in the Indian character."[58] When religion, or the denial of religion, is a key part of the discourse, pornography and the occult dovetail.

Colonial concerns about the immorality and indecency of the lifeways of the so-called lower orders continued throughout the twentieth century. Key themes remained consistent, notably those involving the body and the bodily expressions of emotion that accompanied certain ritual practices. Depicted by objectors as excessive, these expressions at times generated in law, in popular discourse, and in social engineering debates about how "religious" they were, and thus what was the extent of their moral content and social acceptability.

## The "Generation of Independence" Tackles the Class of Race and Religion

Beginning about the time of the Great Depression of 1929, the West Indies were rife with social unrest. The 1930s saw massive unemployment, increasing immiseration of the poor and working classes, heightened labor union activity, and major labor rebellions throughout the region. This period saw the germination of anticolonial independence movements, many of which would eventually result in independent nation-states—for example, Trinidad and Tobago in 1962, Jamaica in 1962, Guyana in 1966, and Barbados in 1966. In particular, 1938 was a watershed moment, the events of which heralded a "political hurricane" that would sweep across the entire region.[59] That year inaugurated in Jamaica, for example, a "messy 'in-between' space," whose dimensions were comprised of both "the enclave of the colonial coloured family and the tumultuous world of black Jamaica."[60] This in-between space where race and class increasingly collided was manifest in the birth of the region's modern political culture, and also—in the related concerns among those who would govern—about the quality, value, and promise of the peoples who would be governed.

The situation prompted the British colonial office to establish a Social Services Department to investigate the causes of the disturbances. The authorities' acknowledgment of economic and infrastructural underdevelopment was couched in terms of social deficiencies and cultural deviance. At the time, and long thereafter, the prevailing scholarly and policy model of Caribbean social organization was that of shallow and unstable social institutions. Among the arenas under the most insistent scrutiny, which reflected some degree of puzzlement as well as genuine alarm, were the religious practices of the wayward communities of rural people and of poor and working-class urban people. These convictions, held by alarmed citizens and neutral analysts alike, focused on what was seen as the dysfunctional culture of the poor and working classes, which generated dysfunctional families and which was at the root of, essentially, their inability to become modern—defined according to a bourgeois template. This focus on "culture" and its injured ramifications drew attention away from the "profound crises,"[61] which had been mounting since long before the century began.

Adopting a model of what anthropologist Christine Barrow calls the "social pathology" approach to studying Caribbean families, observer-experts such as Thomas Simey and Lord Moyne (Walter Guinness) published, respectively, *Welfare and Planning in the West Indies* and the *West India Royal Commission Report*.[62] Simey argued that in aspects of their daily life other than religion, West Indians were prinicipally influenced by European traditions. According to the prevailing logic, Simey claimed that West Indian morals and manners were largely those of the slave master and "only continued repression of freedom has kept the Negro family from merging with that of the more fortunate whites."[63] While religion, from the point of view expressed by Simey and similar analysts, was evidently impervious to European influence, middle-class European family and household forms constituted the touchstone against which Caribbean families were deemed "deformed and malfunctioning," due to the dissolution effected by slavery and the plantation. They thus constituted a "threat to the social order."[64] For Simey and numerous others, including social worker and church representative contemporaries, the standards that needed to be met in order to have functioning and healthy Caribbean societies were Western, middle class, and Christian.

In November 1938, Jamaica's West India Royal Commission held its seventh session.[65] It was chaired by Lord Moyne and attended by ten others. All presumably were elites: three men were indicated as "Sir" and five as "Mr." There were two women, one listed as "Dr." and the other as "Dame." Also present were nine "Witnesses" from "the Christian Bodies," including, among others, the Church of England, the Roman Catholic Church, the Jamaica Baptist Union, and the Salvation Army. A Mr. Lewis, the only "witness" without "Rev." preceding his name (or in the case of the Salvation Army representative, "Col."), was there "to give evidence on obeah."[66] The meeting entailed an inquiry into the current (unfortunate) state of social conditions in Jamaica, a discussion, typed and filed for posterity, which consisted of sixty-three pages of questions posed by questioners (who are not always identified) to the "Witnesses," and the latter's responses. A major portion of the report was concerned with obeah and "peculiar cults," such as Myalism and Pocomania, treated as sharing a family resemblance.[67] Mr. Lewis refers to them as "tributaries of witchcraft."[68]

Mr. Lewis was asked about local laws pertaining to obeah, and to give "an outline as to what they may and may not do." He explained candidly: "Occasionally the police are informed that there is an obeah-man working, they set a trap for him and, very infrequently, they capture him. If they do, he is punished under the Obeah Law. I say 'infrequently' because the whole district knows at once, it is honeycombed with messengers of the obeah-man and all know what is happening. It is only in a town that they catch him—in the country it is difficult."[69] When Lewis was asked if the "quasi-religious cults" should be dealt with more leniently than obeah, he assented, saying that obeah "must have stronger measures" because it was so difficult to "catch the men who are doing the damage." He was asked whether he thought the reason was that the law was deficient or the administration was weak. Hedging a bit, Lewis said, "I do not think it is exactly deficient," because "there is something very fearful in the mind of the country person dealing with obeah and he will not betray, under any circumstances, the obeah-man." Obeah's antagonists always had asserted that fear of the obeah practitioner and their own lack of astuteness, or gullibility, robbed victims of their agency (free will). Active collusion among obeah practitioners and devotees was a worry to colonial authority and those charged with upholding its morals and mores; there is strength in shared ways of knowing. But characterizing people's unwillingness to help apprehend obeah practitioners as being active collusion implies that everyone is a villain and everyone (except the practitioner) is a victim. In this region's historical turning point from which "the generation of Independence"[70] emerged, the nation's obeah victims must be represented carefully. Whether with contempt, with pity, or some other characterization, ultimately the best message is one of populations having the potential to progress into this era's new world, even if they have a long way to go.

As the question-and-answer session continued, Lewis suggested that prosecuting obeah and thus driving it underground was futile. "You do not think you can deal with witchcraft by forcible measures, but that you must try to educate the people out of it?" he was asked. Lewis replied yes. In answer to a question about obeah and poverty, he said, "Definitely . . . obeah is a contributory factor to the poverty of the people" because of the exorbitant fees obeah practitioners charged. He also added a non sequitur, that obeah contributed to "immorality," but added nothing further. This spurred one of the committee members to shift seamlessly from obeah to the "peculiar cults," opining that they were "largely responsible for the breakdown in the relationship between man and woman which used to exist." Quoting from a Minister's Fraternity memorandum, Mr. Ward relayed that the sects "conduct noisy and exciting meetings, often carried on after midnight. These tend to wreck the nervous system of those attending, and the peace of the neighboring persons is seriously disturbed. Their influence on children is specially injurious, often leading to definite physical and mental harm. . . . A large proportion of the leaders of these sects are without mental balance and extremely ignorant."[71] Dysfunction in family and household were implied by the collapse of man-woman relationships and harmed children wrought by obeah, by cults—the conversation slides among unsavory folk traditions with little differentiation. "They [the sect meetings] are the most powerful agents in our Island for the maintenance of obeahism,"[72] Mr. Ward reiterated. A conviction shared by many, malformed culture was the culprit.

In one of the few more or less clear connections made between sects, or cults, and obeah, the late and noisy meetings were deemed the breeding grounds of—an undefined and otherwise unlocatable—"obeahism," where individuals hint at their occult powers and people think that spirits manifested themselves, including through being under the influence of ganja. But these sects were also inculcators of "disloyalty to the Crown"; they discouraged paying taxes, and—in the late 1930s cause for real alarm—they may have harbored "a Bolshevik element at work" among some of them; the meetings led to idleness and stealing crops and farm animals ("praedial larceny"). Most of the moral, social, and economic trouble "that affects large numbers of the lower classes of the people are due to their activities. There are many tens of thousands who attend meetings all over the country."[73] Is it "closely in contact with voodooism," someone asked, "or is it purely a Jamaican trouble?" One of the committee members answered, "It is related, since, being African in its origin, it comes from the same thing."[74]

The excerpts above, and what follows, suggest another kind of search for, and struggle with, evidence in the climate of the protracted colonial crisis. In the context of these "peculiar sects" or "cults," all roads led back to Africa, reinforcing the idea of atavistic African culture and the heritability of blackness passed down among rural people and the urban poor and working classes. This was an assumed connection; no evidence for it was given. Still, as "evidence" of the cultural deficiencies and social dysfunction propagated by these folk traditions, African origins were a distant source—proof without a solution. As this transcript proceeds, it is clear that there was real perplexity about how and why Jamaica (and its fellow colonies in the region) found itself in the disrupted and in some arenas backward condition it seemed to be in. A bit later in the document the questioners vacillate between "the levity with which the subject of obeah is treated" and a belief in its seriousness: obeah "certainly does exist"; it is "foolish" but it is also "wrong" and the "Government is against" it.[75] Switching gears, Lewis continued by confirming the committee's position that "belief of [sic] obeah is very deep-seated." His illustration was of a recent case where "a man was given nine months by the Government because he was caught practicing obeah," and upon his release, "his own people flogged him because they said he was an imposter," not "because the Government said he had done wrong."[76] Between the lines one can detect genuine incredulity that people would be upset about someone not being good at or unable to accomplish what was criminal, such as occult work. What looks today like absurd naiveté or bizarre denial was at the time exasperation and disgust with all parties concerned—charlatan and dupes both. At the twentieth century's almost halfway point, even the lowly were expected to be capable of some degree of rational thought, and when they apparently were not, it was perplexing.

The committee wondered whether "the better use of leisure time," such as participating in Boy Scouts and Girl Guides, would be a deterrent from obeah, especially among the youth. More adult education that would prepare them for "an elementary, simple type of occupation" was posed as being "a great help" in the anti-obeah campaign. Conflating obeah and the "peculiar cults," someone then elaborated, "I understand that they hold very big meetings in connection with obeah at which they get very excited. If you could get more music, dancing and singing into your elementary schools perhaps you would give them the opportunity of letting off the steam which is let off at the night meetings?" "There is a good deal of steam to let off," Bishop Sara replied.[77] It is unclear if that remark was meant as a wry comment about the current social unrest or a critique of the noisiness and bodily unrestraint that allegedly characterized these meetings. What does seem clear is that in the effort to figure out the causes of the trouble and ways to solve it, taming the rogue through proper socialization seemed an effective strategy. All manner of distasteful and injurious practices were, willy-nilly, lumped together, but there was a common denominator—heritage. The "Africa" lurking within indicated a blackness shared as a family resemblance irrespective of ancestral homeland.

Rev. Ward of the Presbyterian Church suggested coming up with a "five-year plan" to combat obeah. It should involve the churches, the schools, lecturers, the press, and pamphlets, because "there has never been a real united campaign against this thing [obeah]."[78] Someone asked if the united campaign should include a special enquiry by the Government. The response laid bare the fundamental contradiction that criminalizing obeah posed. Expert representatives were still wondering in 1938 whether, as raised by committee Vice Chairman Sir Edward Stubbs, there might be "a danger that if the Government attaches too much importance to a campaign, the effect would be exactly the contrary to what is hoped? People will say 'This matter is so serious that Government is 'afraid,'" which would increase the rogue power of the obeah man.[79] A "campaign of exposure" was suggested, exhibiting cases where obeah work was "absolutely disproved."[80] Showing obeah to be "folly" rather than a "danger," however, had its own pitfalls, for there were "a fair number of people of the intelligent class who have a sneaking belief in it and give it some support," observed Mr. Brown. Even "people of some education" support the reputed obeah-man, "actually visiting him." In this respect the press might be a problem too, Dame Rachel Crowdy thought. "They might say 'We dare not expose this because the people concerned with our paper and our readers, are many of them pro-obeah.'" This was the case despite the subsequent conversation about the difference between obeah, "vicious and pernicious," and primarily concerned with poisoning by herbs, and the unsavory but less problematic "quack doctor" to whom people flocked "in hundreds" to have spirits removed from them.[81] Obeah is not "merely superstition or imagination" because obeah practitioners "do poison!" It was conceded, however, that they also sometimes "prescribe genuine herbalist remedies." Akin to what "the bush" symbolized for British Guiana almost a century earlier—an untamed place of materials that are fashioned into the objects of untamed ritual practices like hookswinging—obeah's poisons "are not secured from the dispensers of the Island, they are growing in the bush. They are very, very dangerous."[82]

The report ends rather comically, and on as ambivalent a note as it began. The chairman, Lord Moyne, summed up the "Recommendations for the control of the religious cults," a paper that had been presented to the committee. It largely called for greater licensing—of buildings used for religious purposes, of all itinerant preachers, and of all religious bodies. Also suggested was a 9:00 p.m., rather than an 11:00 p.m., termination of "noisy assemblies." There ensued an argument about how to define "noisy assemblies," since these included local dances where people could be enjoying themselves. More discussion followed about limiting the rule to religious ceremonies—but how to identify the wrong as opposed to the right ones? Moyne added that the latter included, for example, the "excellent and legitimate open-air meetings such as the Salvation Army." Bishop Sara (Church of England) maintained that licensing would solve the problem "because the bush preachers have no headquarters and, therefore, they could not get licenses, whereas the Church of England has a certain organisation and would be licensed." Mr. Assheton, M.P., asked, "Would not that be rather dangerous? I can imagine that the early Christian Church would not have been given a license." The last word was Bishop Sara's: "No, but the early Christian Church was persecuted and came through. Perhaps the obeah-man will come through if he is persecuted—'Great is truth and it will prevail.'"[83] The commission then adjourned, having wrestled with a problem that ultimately was insoluble.

The commission's last exchange is, to say the least, unexpected, given all that historically had come before it: On the one hand, obeah is evil and causes societal dissolution, or at least retrogression; the obeah practitioner is dangerous, disingenuous in his or her methods and intentions; the seductions of obeah impede the realization of Western progress and modernity for all members of a society, not simply those who make use of it. On the other hand, obeah is compared to the early Christian Church and its own travails of persecution (a quite radical analogy, all things considered). In Euro-Christianity, persecution that produces martyrdom is the ultimate test of faith. The reward of martyrdom is God's grace, often in the form of sainthood. But there is another test: persecution that does not lead to martyrdom—that is, being persecuted and subsequently prevailing. To prevail is also an indication of God's endorsement or approval. These clergymen and other representatives of government were not looking to make martyrs of obeah practitioners. Nor was it likely that they were suggesting that if obeah practitioners survived persecution the "great truth" of their enterprise would be revealed. But it is striking (and almost surreal) that— among a small sample of clergy that nonetheless could not have been alone—persecution is the common denominator of early Christianity and obeah. The early Christians, these interlocutors seemed to be saying, were social rebels, rogues, too, after all. Still, that proposition can only go so far.

Perhaps reflecting the Zeitgeist of class, religious, and racial tensions that characterized this eve-of-world-war, rising anticolonialism moment, the clergy committee, "Leaders of Certain Christian Bodies in Jamaica," argued, "From a social standpoint, perhaps the worst is their [cult devotees] preaching of hatred. Openly, through the district, remarks are made to stir up hatred and fear that will lead to the employment of an obeah-man's services. When these leaders are visiting in the district, it is the usual thing at dead of night or at any time in the day to hear a powerful voice, crying out, 'Watch out for the coolie man.' 'What about that yellow snake.' Many other such vague references are made. These are remarks that among the people are meant to refer to the practice of obeah. They refer in particular instances to quarrels that have recently taken place in the district. They are calculated to instill fear in individuals so that they may be induced to seek help from these men." Contrary to the idea that these individuals and their practices are absurd and harmless, they constitute a serious danger among "the poorer people of Jamaica."[84] The work of alienation that fractures communities has become part of the routine job description of the obeah practitioner. Instigating the hostility and mistrust that allegedly are inherent reactions to racial difference (beware the coolie), rogue individuals apparently live for schism—literally to make their livelihood and figuratively as their evil calling.

The committee sought the compulsory registration of every denomination and sect on the island. As they pressed for a renewed effort to come up with a bill that would prohibit the activities of "peculiar cults," they acknowledged a "main difficulty." This difficulty was, perhaps not surprisingly despite the passage of a century and more, finding "a definition which will cover these harmful cults and yet do nothing to curtail a full religious liberty. A clear definition may be impossible to find but power might well be given to the Governor in Privy Council to declare that certain cults are 'peculiar' and therefore illegal."[85] The clergy's solution, even if only temporary, was to suggest that colonial authority be given blanket power, perhaps ad hoc, to decide which bodies were permissible and which were not.

As the committee of concerned clergy summarized, "The weakness of Jamaica along co-operative lines is largely due to the sway of obeah. It tends also to paralyze business and industry. Men have refused to improve their housing conditions, fearing that the evil eye of some one, fearing that a new house might mean a new grave."[86] The committee knitted together what was imagined about obeah's powers with what was imagined as being empirical evidence of sociological fact. Modernization, the "material and organizational features of world capitalism in specific locales," such as the growth of business and industry, are cramped by obeah's mystifications.[87]

Communal cooperation is dissuaded by obeah's emphasis on the rogue individual. The development of modern subjects and their capacity for individual agency is similarly jeopardized, with the stifling, for example, of such self-help (bootstrap) aspirations as those expressed in home improvement.

"Pockets of black consciousness" were "in the air" in Jamaica in the 1930s.[88] Contributing to this was the vernacular culture of poor, black Jamaicans, which drew attention to the issue of persisting "African elements" that were apparent in customs, folklore, folk religion, festivals and ceremonies, dancing, and drumming, and in "spirit superstitions" and "'black magic' customs" such as obeah.[89] These elements, along with the "Back to Africa" message and other expressions of black consciousness at the time, gained traction alongside a colonial education system that had "enshrined deep in their very purpose the 'enlightened' elements of the colonial project."[90] This project emphasized the production of the colonial subject, who could be taught to aspire to the idea of civilization promulgated by the educators.[91] Schools, among other institutional spaces, were a key site charged with the replication of an abiding Euro-colonial vision about certain ways of being in the world, including values, feelings, comportment, and ambitions.

Obeah and its related disquieting traditions among the unlettered and unabashed, which assemblages like the West India Royal Commission and similar committees of inquiry were concerned to eradicate or reform, were read through the optic of the kind of civilizing mission of which Stuart Hall speaks. The anxiety was real, the disgust palpable, the titillation conspicuous, and the performance of shadows quite alive. The reports that were generated from the intelligentsia and policing bodies of Jamaica and the rest of the region are clear indicators of colonial authority's and its various custodians' persistent fixation on religious misdirection, misappropriation, or mischief—and their racialized conductors. The records they left remain important barometers of the cultural construction of crisis and the racial and religious linchpins that fueled it. Although couched in this moment in paternalistic class terms rather than in the grosser racial terms of previous eras, there still remains something of the "savage" and "magical thinking" lurking in this discourse.

I argued earlier in this chapter, building on Stuart Hall and José Muñoz, that hookswinging, Hosay, and obeah each in their own way constitute a performance of shadows: purpose and consequence must be inferred from evidence; evidence is visible; visibility is "truth." Hosay's threatening

elusiveness was how its always-debated *un*-religiousness worked as a cata-
lyzing force in the secular domain, notably regarding labor unrest, and
how it exposed heritability in a human type that possessed the racial qualities of religious excess (Islamic heritage gone wrong) and the religious
qualities of a barbaric people (the atavistic "coolie"). The unseen of Hosay,
a necessarily public and viewed tradition, was cast as motive—a cover for
upending the social and moral order in the illegitimate name of workers'
rights. Equally if not more illegitimate, obeah's unseen is its power; motive
as well as method. Obeah's threatening elusiveness was how its always,
albeit differently debated, *un*-religiousness worked as a destructive force in
both secular and sacred domains, and how it exposed heritability in a
human type that possessed no religious qualities and the racial qualities
of a barbaric people (the atavistic "African"). In this sense, both obeah and
Hosay arguably were treated, explicitly or otherwise, as heritably "black,"
preserved by rogue individuals who would continue to dupe and terrify
despite the forces of modernity. As we will see in the next chapter, however,
modernity works hand in hand with these representations.

# 4

## THE TRIALS OF OBEAH TODAY

This chapter considers the nexus of race and religion in the mid-twentieth to the twenty-first centuries. Its focus is on the meeting ground of race and religion in obeah and its literal and figurative trials through popular culture, presenting three illustrative cases: a mid-twentieth-century theatrical play in Britain, a twenty-first-century live action series in the United States, and two twenty-first-century appellate court cases in Canada. Obeah's permeation into diasporic collective consciousness is an important confirmation that it does not simply manifest as varying ritual practices, which may or may not be labeled as "obeah."

For West Indians this contemporary moment is one of diaspora: outmigrations to the United Kingdom and North America, and homeland environments influenced by media's global circulations. Any discussion about the West Indies, and the Caribbean more generally, necessarily involves diaspora; with the exception of its Amerindian populations, all of the region's peoples and cultures hail from the Old World of Africa, Europe, Asia, and the Levant. The beliefs and practices they brought with them changed over time, implicated in varying relations of power—that is, they became "creolized," and in the process established new sorts of local traditions that can be viewed as indigenous. As numerous scholars have noted, the region is defined significantly by its diasporic constitution.[1] Obeah's imagery and its practices are part of these diasporic flows.

Obeah is inherently a diasporic phenomenon for a number of reasons. Its vast diffusions from Old World origins, primarily West and Central African, give it a traveling history. Absent a strictly standardized liturgy or doctrine, it can invite inclusions gathered throughout its travels. The appearance (empirical and imagined) of aspects of obeah in other religious traditions throughout the Americas—as in Vodou, for example—has carried it along, shaping and being shaped by them. The diaspora-shaping character of obeah is also evident in obeah's being variously, and sometimes contradictorily, identified as a firm and specified entity, properties under-scored by its mobility, and also as a fluid, unspecified, catch-all rubric, prop-erties resulting from its mobility. These factors make it challenging to pin down obeah ethnographically; each case may require distinct definition along with context-specific explanation. Another major reason why obeah is ethnographically elusive (in contrast to, say, studying it through legal arenas, official governing policies, and popular wisdom's suppositions) is the criminalization that historically drove obeah underground. Moreover, although in its North American and UK diasporas obeah does not suffer formal criminalization, the stigmatization that it still carries continues to make practitioners wary about their activities, and people in general reluctant to openly acknowledge obeah as part of their own religious beliefs and not simply that of others. In the process, obeah attains new associations yet retains familiar moralities and social messages. These moralities and mes-sages continue to distinguish obeah from other traditions once denounced but now reclaimed.

In numerous diasporic religious traditions, both practitioners and ob-servers engage in processes of selection and reduction that emphasize cer-tain aspects of a religion's repertoire and marginalize or deny others. In each of the three cases I explore below, artistic and legal representations produce portraits of obeah that promote a familiar story of obeah's dark powers but convey different social and political commentaries about their value. The racialization of religion and the religionization of race are pow-erfully reified; in obeah if only imagined.

### National Conscience and Consciousness:
### Checks, Balances, and Representation

There is a complex relationship between the contemporary, independent nation-state and the traditional pasts of those who comprise the nation and those who are governed by (or who govern) the state. This relationship is typically one of service, in the sense of the political harnessing of selected aspects of the past to the particular objectives of those presently in power. In the West Indies, some formerly stigmatized or marginalized traditions and practices have been embraced and valorized by newly independent regimes—for example, steelpan and calypso in the Republic of Trinidad and Tobago, reggae and Rastafari in Jamaica. More recently, in Trinidad and Tobago the historically much-maligned "Shouter" or Spiritual Baptists have enjoyed a shift in the commonsense view of their traditions, with enough broad approval to garner their own national holiday in 1996 (Spiritual Baptist Liberation Day), granted by the then-ruling United National Congress party.[2] This day of recognition (and one might say reconciliation) formally commemorates the 1951 repeal of the Shouters Prohibition ordinance of 1917. High-ranking officials weigh in annually with congratulatory salutations that are also a means of reinforcing liberalism's nationalist message. At the commemoration in 2015, for example, Trinidad's prime minister, Kamla Persad-Bissessar, was quoted in the *Daily Express* newspaper saying that "Shouter Baptists have come a long way, from having their religion prohibited to now being a 'colourful and vibrant part of our country's religious mosaic.'" "Like all others," she said, "this faith community enjoys protection under Trinidad and Tobago's 1976 Republican Constitution, which guarantees all citizens, 'freedom of conscience and religious belief and observance. . . . [The Spiritual Baptist faith] has managed to fuse the spontaneity and rhythms of Africa with the restrained, traditional tenets of Christianity to produce a religion that is vibrant, expressive and dynamic."[3]

In his own message of Spiritual Baptist support, opposition party leader Keith Rowley (and now, at the time of this writing, the prime minister) said rhetorically, "Imagine being forbidden to freely congregate for prayer and worship or being arrested for practising your religion. Picture being ridiculed, scorned and persecuted for your beliefs and having to flee to the hills, mountains and remote areas to escape the law, which prohibited your faith. . . . Far from the days when they were considered outlaws, the faith is now recognised for its positive contributions to our society."[4] The acting president, Reziah Ahmed, contributed this object lesson: the Prohibition Ordinance of 1917 is a signal reminder of how men and women are the possessors of hearts and minds that have capacity for injustice, intolerance, and persecution of innocent people."[5] Several corporate-sponsored full-page ads celebrated the day, such as Republic Bank's ad that year, which declared, "We are thankful for the freedom to praise God in our way. . . . Because joyful voices colour the fabric of our society. Let's celebrate the freedom to worship. Happy Spiritual Shouter Baptist Liberation Day!"[6]

Brought into the fold of the Republic of Trinidad and Tobago's multicultural "rainbow" nationalism, the Spiritual Baptist community these days is hailed by top government figures and corporations as a consummate example of nation-state tolerance, progress, and modernity. The same cannot be said for obeah, despite Trinidad and Tobago's obeah prohibition laws having been repealed. For example, a 2018 newspaper article about a man being arrested for the murder of a prison officer is titled, "Obeah Threats for Cops," and devotes the opening sentences to the suspect's relatives' threats of obeah retribution against the police for false arrest.[7] Nothing else about obeah is mentioned in the rest of the article, making it a headline grabber more than newsworthy itself. Nonetheless, obeah is clearly still part of the national-cultural consciousness, even if it no longer generates a culture of obeah in Trinidadian society. Perhaps more evocative of that culture of obeah which, to borrow a famous phrase from anthropologist Claude Levi-Strauss, made obeah "good to think" (with), is the charge made a few years earlier by Keith Rowley that a government contractor was the source of the television ads that portrayed Rowley "as an 'obeah' man." As the *Daily Express* reported, "Speaking at a public meeting . . . Rowley said: 'You have a situation in Trinidad and Tobago where a contractor on behalf of the Government could enter an election campaign and the contractor running ads. . . . Would you believe that? . . . Where is Trinidad and Tobago going? I told you that there is wickedness in high places,' he said."[8] "Wickedness in high places" implies that obeah is alive and well, even if, when pressed, the opposition party leader and others would dismiss obeah as, in local parlance, "foolishness" or "long time thinking," but still suggest that corruption, duplicity, and intentional injury permeate the most powerful levels of society, identified through the language of the occult. There is no rehabilitation afforded, at least not in these "high places."

The twentieth century's nationalist struggles in the West Indies involved calls for another version of emancipation: extrication from the yoke of political and economic control that kept these societies colonies rather than sovereign entities. But sovereignty also required new imagery that suitably represented independence. The nation should not be thought of in terms of Euro-colonial origins but rather in terms of the heritages and traditions of its peoples—African heritages and traditions in particular. These alternative, non-European heritages and traditions were meant to legitimate cultural-national foundations, yet, as Diana Paton notes, they were to do so without jeopardizing claims that the cultures of independence are "respectably modern and rational."[9] The tension between "modernity" and "tradition" is certainly not unique to obeah, or to the independence movements of the region. But given its particular history as an always enigmatic phenomenon, always multiple and singular at the same time, always fixed and fluid at the same time, obeah straddles both domains, traditional and modern, simultaneously, perhaps more steadfastly than other cultural symbols of past and present. Even as a symbol of an uncompromised (by Euro-colonialism) past, obeah has never entirely shed the retrograde associations that the "past" also possesses. During the twentieth century, Paton observes, obeah became both "a complex signifier of state support for African culture" and "a symbol of corrupt power," including among those who controlled the state.[10] In the latter vein, obeah came to be a national symbol put to work in the "ethnic politics" of the state; Paton gives as an example Guyana's former prime minister, Forbes Burnham, whose reported support of obeah "at a symbolic level" was indicative of his privileging of Afro-Guyanese concerns over those of Indo-Guyanese.[11] This "ethnic politics" of privilege throughout the West Indies is a significant mode of obeah's racialization, simultaneously centering obeah within an African sphere and decentering obeah from an Indian sphere. This is reinforced by the implied premise that "African" and "obeah" are mutually inclusive because "Indian" and "obeah" are mutually exclusive. In service of particular political projects, the universality of obeah (universal precisely because of its categorical pliability and thus the diverse populations whose traditions include it) becomes condensed, homogeneous, and heritable.

All consideration of obeah in former West Indian colonies takes place within the contexts of broader discursive traditions concerned with the place and value of Africa—a symbol to be celebrated, an empirical inheritance to be abjured, a part of the past that matters little, or one that matters much. All of these diverse constructions offer a representation of Africa as well as its valuation. Perhaps the most common and complicated of these representations are those produced in relation to Africa's presumed contrast, Europe. This contrast often is predicated on a distinction between European mind and African feeling or expressiveness. In writing about the mid-twentieth century's philosophical, artistic, and political movement known as "Negritude," for example, one of its principle figures, Leopold Senghor, celebrated the "Negro soul," contrasting the "'intuitive' nature of African reason" with "its 'analytical' European counterpart."[12] When Trinidad's former prime minister Persad-Bissessar described Shouter Baptists as being a fusion of the "spontaneity and rhythms of Africa" and the "restrained, traditional tenets of Christianity," she was drawing from a way of knowing the Caribbean, whose centuries-long history has entrenched it in an epistemic habit, a given part of the commonsense notion about the difference between "Africa" and "Europe."

In his classic 1970 work *Mirror, Mirror: Identity, Race, and Protest in Jamaica*, Rex Nettleford dedicated one of the chapters to the "melody of Europe" and the "rhythm of Africa," which, he explains, is "a phrase seeking to catch in language all too inadequate, the dynamic of the quavering existence that some people loosely label 'Jamaican.'"[13] Critiquing the putative social harmony of Jamaica's heterogeneous society, Nettleford argued that, officially, Jamaica "is committed to *multi-racialism* which is the latter-day attempt to describe the Jamaican ethos conceived as the occasion and outcome of the meeting of peoples with different racial-cultural memories who live in the society."[14] But in this metaphor for "Creole culture," things European attained ascriptive status, while things African were devalued; Europe took precedence over Africa, "melody over rhythm," which remains unchanged.[15] Today Jamaica "vacillates between exaggerated claims of a cultural consensus and exaggerated claims of a harmonious racial heterogeneity, the racial harmony being the result of the cultural consensus."[16] The "traditional carriers of Europe's melody" were "largely the brown biological and the black cultural hybrids."[17] Not surprisingly, continued Nettleford, "the black majority may find little cause to feel that multi-racialism has anything to do with them when 'multi-' conjures up a complex in which they hold an inferior position on grounds of class which in turn dovetails with race origin."[18] European elements were socially entrenched through institutions, while African elements "remained merely observable in such things as language, diet, folklore, family and kinship, property, marketing, medicine, magic and religion and some grass-root economic organizations."[19] Yet while Europe governs, Africa "rules in the sense of spiritual motivation."[20] And the "tenacity of the African rhythm / flavour was evident in the entire cultural complex," embedded in the albeit submerged forces of Africa from whence the majority of its members had in fact come.[21] Nettleford went on to elaborate on his metaphor of "rhythm" that represents Africa, whose "vibrations" challenge Europe's melody: "Sometimes the drum tones are deep, steady and haunting. At times they take on a rapid, breathless, frantic sequence of seemingly unstructured polyrhythms. At other times it is that dry, sustained and high-pitched sound called 'ciye' by the Haitian voodoo drummers"; but once the "lop-sided" privileging of white Creole culture is rectified, the fiction of harmony will become fact, and melody and rhythm "will no longer be regarded as mutually exclusive phenomena."[22] Nettleford's discussion is a perceptive critique of social inequality and its discursive masks. Yet he reiterated what is fundamentally a racial distinction, developed hundreds of years prior to his writings, between European mind and African body. Melody is thought; rhythm is feeling. This is a complex issue. It could be argued that all forms of oppression are visited upon the body; we have learned this from such diverse thinkers as, for example, Michel Foucault, Andrea Dworkin, and bell hooks. To reclaim the body as a site of creative production and rich signification, rather than its merely being an object of commodification and vulnerability, is an important act of resistance and consciousness re-formation. It remains a question, however, as to whether, and how, new or different uses of old ideas can reorient the latter toward contradictory, coun-terhegemonic messages.

Perhaps it is simply a matter of time and the changes in consciousness that time brings. In 2014 Kei Miller offered such a message in a commen-tary about African drums, using them as a literal and figurative reference to the attempts that colonial power makes to dominate, and the complicit acceptance to which the colonized may succumb. Miller equates the mid-eighteenth century official banning of drumming among Africans in the Caribbean as a banning of blackness. Laws across the Caribbean, he argues, "continued to ensure that whatever was associated with Africa, especially such things that might encourage black people to congregate in spaces away from white eyes or white control, spaces in which blackness might go unchecked . . . would continue to be banned and deemed evil." He includes among the criminalized practices those of "black religion," no-tably Spiritual Baptists and obeah. The prohibition of obeah was an effort to check "what was seen as an overt and dangerous expression of African-ness. . . . Many of us still fear the evil, backward, demonic and uncivilized spirits that might lurk in the barrel of those drums." The problem with unjust laws, Miller understands, is that the longer they stay on the books, the more their principles get "wired into the blood of [a] country, and for generations to come, we believe in the deep and terrible injustice that they promote." He laments, "On some deep level across the Caribbean we still believe that African religions are backward"; "alas, we do not need colo-nial laws to police our blackness. We police ourselves. We keep our black-ness in check."[23] Miller is decrying the misguided assumptions that can become so embedded and heritable as to become common sense, the epistemic habits of a colonial mentality. His is a call to be aware of such ways of knowing and the self-policing that is engendered. The fulcrum of his argument is that to deny obeah (or other Afro-Caribbean religious traditions) is to deny blackness, and vice versa. This is another mode of racializing obeah, though in the spirit of social justice and equality. In the process of this important message is the reiteration of obeah as both Africa-derived and an instantiation of blackness. It is a characterization of Africa/blackness that differs from Nettleford's, except that both imply the heritability of such deeply embedded identity.

### Arts and the "Windrush" Diaspora

In the tide of that watershed moment of 1938[24] of which I spoke in the previous chapter, a decade later, in 1948, the first of the "Windrush generation" of West Indians arrived in the United Kingdom. They were named after the ship they sailed on, the *Empire Windrush*. Initially called to the metropole because of postwar labor shortages, this "generation" continued its emigration until 1971. The decades-long stream of artists, intellectuals, workers, and students helped shape what was a changing local and transnational consciousness about race (blackness and whiteness) and religion (genuine and spurious) in the UK's postwar period of empire dismantling, mass migration, and colonies' independence struggles. Some of this discourse developed through the diasporic flow of obeah's practices and what people—the knowledgeable and the unfamiliar—thought about those practices. It was expressed in the everyday lives of the immigrants and their progeny, and in artistic representations of obeah that some of the Windrush generation produced—for example, in theater and in fiction. In diaspora the emphasis would shift away from obeah as a predominantly illegal, and culturally perverse, way of being in the world, to a test of the mettle of "enlightened democracy's" universalist agendas about protecting individual and civil liberties of various kinds. But there were also diasporic voices that mined hegemonic understandings of obeah, featuring its conventional unsavory depictions rather than recuperating them. In these various arenas, multiple publics produced particular representations of Caribbean history and culture in newly diasporic contexts and in numerous ways. Quotidian opinion, legal opinion, and the arts, all part of an encompassing Atlantic common sense, each diverged from and reiterated ways of knowing obeah in prior eras.

Among the first West Indian artists to have work produced in England was Barry Reckord, a Jamaican playwright who was part of the Windrush generation. Reckord worked at a time when black writing was being "discovered" in the UK; he was, some suggest, perhaps "the first of this small band to enter the scene."[25] *Adella* was his first play to be performed in London, in 1954, just six years after the first sailing of the Windrush generation and eight years before Jamaica's independence from Britain in 1962. Under the new title of *Flesh to a Tiger*, it was performed in 1958 at London's Royal Court Theatre.[26] Reckord saw himself as an activist-artist and in his work sought to tackle the "thorny issues of colonialism, race identity, and repression" that contributed to what would be a reevaluation of British theater in the postwar period.[27] *Flesh to a Tiger* has been described by scholars as a "detailed[,] melodically written examination of the hold which religion maintains over a population which has yet to seize true emancipation from the gravity of colonisation."[28] The play critiques the ways that power is abused through religious belief and fear by drawing attention to the destructive, collective impact of "religious superstition, poverty, corruption, and racial stratification in contemporary Jamaican society."[29] The "disenfranchised men and women of the area"—that is, Trench Town, Kingston, Jamaica—live in "the darkness of convenient if uncomfortable belief," from which the female protagonist, Della (Adella) wishes to lead them away, toward "the light of modernity."[30] The director, Cecil Antonio "Tony" Richardson, included calypso music and "reproduced 'voodoo' or obeah rites onstage, complete with a live goat,"[31] perhaps to add verisimilitude to the play's West Indies atmosphere, including its dark, occult mysteries.[32]

In *Flesh to a Tiger*, Reckord's perspective on the impact of racism and imperialism on "ordinary West Indians" could be construed as "elitist."[33] That Reckord was from a middle-class Kingston family, enjoyed a middle-class education there, and, once in England, attended Cambridge University,[34] likely was a shaping factor in his complex point of view. In this play he critiques the racial hierarchy that is part of the foundation of British colonialism in the Caribbean, but his story is ultimately one of enlightenment versus ignorance, modernity versus backwardness. The victims of religious superstition and imperial power (forces that work in concert) are dupes; backward and ignorant, they are not entirely sympathetic. Historian Amanda Bidnall writes that the lesson that *Flesh to a Tiger* drew "from its squalid Caribbean setting" was expressed by one contemporary critic as this: "White folk who get hot under the collar about the 'coloured' problem often thoughtlessly ask: 'Why don't the Jamaicans stay in their own country?' This fine play by a 30-year-old Jamaican playwright gives at least one clue."[35] This, however, does not seem like a very productive lesson to convey: that there are good reasons to flee one's unfortunate country in search of a better one, where the problems of the former have to do with the ills of backwardness and irrationality, and the benefits of the latter lie in their opposite. The writer seeks to praise, but in the attempt reinforces familiar dichotomies.

The play's action takes place in Trench Town, populated by the disfranchised, gullible, needy, and superstitious subordinated masses that are at the mercy of Shepherd Aaron. In Reckord's depiction, the Shepherd implies a combination of obeah man and Spiritual Baptist leader. He is a morally corrupt figure who preys on the deceived and intimidated residents who follow him, and fear him. About himself he says that he has "a thin skin and a vengeful heart."[36] Della, a resident of Trench Town, has removed her sick baby, Tata, from Shepherd Aaron's care, who has failed to cure the baby. She has taken up with a white doctor (who remains nameless but is called "White Wolf" by Shepherd Aaron), who also has not been able to cure the baby. There is sexual tension between Della and both medical practitioners; the power struggle between men, one black and one white, is implicitly more significant than either of their involvements with her. In this first scene, Della's son Joshie asks her friend Lal if she has heard that the "doctor say obeah is just silly black magic?"[37] But a bit later Lal challenges Della's explanation that she sought out the doctor out of desperation for her child's well-being: "You love the white man. It excite you to find a white man will mix with you."[38] Della admits that she would like the doctor to be her way out of Trench Town, although he has not made a decisive move in that direction (either by consummating the relationship or committing himself to it in some other way). Lal reminds her, "You're black, and white man would scorn you. . . . For black to white is flesh to a tiger. When they come 'cross it, they tear it."[39] There are multiple dynamics at play here: a woman, Della, trying to escape an oppressive relationship with the fearsome Shepherd Aaron, and, somewhat ambivalently, interested in a white, bourgeois man; a black Shepherd Aaron and a "White Wolf" doctor in a power struggle ostensibly over a woman but actually over a community and a worldview; the ineffectualness of the healing skills of both specialists; the moral turpitude of both men, one in the name of obeah (always and already tainted) and the other in the name of an excuse, charged by Lal, to keep visiting Della by not taking her baby to the hospital (where, it is implied, the baby could be cured).

As part of the doctor's dismissal of Shepherd Aaron's powers of obeah, he comforts Della: "Tata's all right. There's no charm on your baby. Calm Della, Shepherd has no power. . . . We want the whole balm-yard away from Shepherd. It's not only the jumping at the meetings, wearing themselves out night after night. It's the brutal stupidity and flourish of ignorance."[40] Reckord opens the second scene in Shepherd Aaron's room. The stage directions say that he "is going through obeah ritual, lighting a candle, blowing on the flame, until it flutters, then blowing it out. He does this several times, with great earnestness."[41] Shepherd Aaron chants, "Little wick, feeling the death wind, go mad with terror, then out. Out with Tata. . . . This morning I took the word death to Tata. Yet a baby can't catch the word, and hold it to his heart, flutter like this flame, then out. If Tata didn't hear the word, he can't conceive the fear, nor Della whisper to him her own fright. And without the word all the hundred elements of obeah at work come to nothing."[42] Shepherd Aaron has a problem: he wants to punish Della for leaving him and taking up with a white man–medical doctor by killing her baby. But how can this be accomplished when babies have no ability to reason (understand language and reflect on it)? He summons Lal, telling her that the "magic" he "sprinkled" on the baby from a distance "touch him, sicken him already as you know. But rightful obeah need not only magic but the word and how a baby to hear it?"[43] After admonishing Lal for visiting Della, breaking his command to the community to ostracize her (presumably as part of her terrorizing and punishment), he asks Lal, with a threat, to finish the obeah work and smother the baby. He reassures her that every night a deceased baby is buried in the "Trench Town heap." With Della's baby's death ostensibly due to Shepherd Aaron's obeah, she would return to revering him among "all the balm-yard."[44]

Lal does not want to kill the baby, so Shepherd Aaron underscores his need to reinforce his reputation in the balm yard, which is dwindling due to his age. "Those doctors can't do more than us, but they're out to mash up all obeah men's business to improve their own. They do mind cure, so do we, and better them because we do it from a distance. They use chemistry, we use herbs; and plenty who spend out money on them get cured by us."[45] Joshie, Della's son, sees things differently. In a later conversation with his mother, disappointed that she broke it off with the doctor, he says, "Mama, we must graft ourselves on to white people, for what we want they got—houses and fruitful land. We have candle and brushwood; they have science and make good light. They have history and learning. They had the strength to beat us up and bring us to this land."[46] But at the end of the final scene of the play, a man in the crowd (one of Shepherd Aaron's cronies) says, "The thing is to drag the woman Della here to preach white supremacy in Trench Town. That would bring the white man in to be Lord and God."[47] The tension between the cognizance of vulnerability and the aspiration to transcend it vacillates between the perspectives of these characters, all residents of Trench Town, a site that identifies them as poor and black. A significant factor in what holds them in the thrall of either fear or false consciousness is the obeah culture that permeates their lives, working in tandem with real material want. Lal cannot bring herself to kill Della's baby, but Shepherd Aaron is under the impression that the baby is dead. He demands that Della tell everyone gathered in the balm yard that it was obeah that killed the baby. She refuses. In the end Della herself smothers her baby and asks Lal to tell Trench Town that Shepherd Aaron is the murderer. They do not believe her; she grabs Shepherd Aaron's knife and stabs him to death. The police will soon arrive.

It would be hard to get more melodrama into a short play, but what ties together the tension and the tragedy is the tragedy of obeah itself. As Shepherd Aaron says to Della in the first scene of act 2 (the final act),

> I've got no more to fear from White-Wolf than from negro. All who come to the yard know two or three old herb women they believe in their heart are deadlier than me. They believe in old women; and all of them, even some of the children, believe in themselves. See them when the full moon come tie their heads with red cloth, see them in the early morning draw herbs. Or they believe in rings, or put Bible over water and read a dreadful psalm. Policemen are just dying to see me stumble because they tall like me, and carry guns and work for the Queen, yet don't possess my name and authority. But the joke is, Lord God, it's sweet, they afraid to arrest me. Most of them were born right in Trench Town here, where people have respect.[48]

Della challenges him on this: "Respect for what, Shepherd? Respect for spirits? That's what you teaching them: fear the spirits, fear this house, fear that neighbour, fear the evil eye; from the spirits come bad luck and sickness?" Shepherd Aaron's terse reply: "Yes. When I command them."[49] Shepherd Aaron does not fear blacks any more than he fears whites; everyone in the neighborhood knows a few old women who are reputed to be more dangerous in occult matters than even he. People also follow the dictates of their superstitions, wearing red hats when there is a full moon, picking medicinal garden herbs (which is apparently equivalent to sartorial decisions made according to astronomy), and subjecting the Bible to irrational acts in order to read a psalm. Even the police, who hate Shepherd Aaron, are afraid to arrest him because they too are products of the miasmic obeah culture of Trench Town and its balm yards. Ultimately, Della has no recourse at all, having been betrayed by both modern and traditional (backward) medicine, and their white and black male purveyors.

One could argue that the superstitiousness and gullibility of the duped masses symbolizes their underdevelopment, that they occupy a lower place on the evolutionary scale through not being able to think properly—that is, rationally, with reason. Reckord's obeah man moves between blackness (Shepherd Aaron is a black Jamaican) and Africanness (Shepherd Aaron refers to the provenience of the evil eye, wariness about spirits, and use of herbs). As Diana Paton indicates, into the early twentieth century in the Caribbean, African-derived elements were part of a worldview among ritual specialists more than they were part of an overt consciousness about Africa[50]; the latter would come later in the century. Reckord's obeah is both black and African; the two share a "family resemblance,"[51] but they are not synonymous. Whether with or against artistic intention, however, racialization is reinforced: a quality of mind is evidenced in the superstitiousness and gullibility of Trench Town (black) community members, reified and passed down through the generations. In this play we reencounter the rogue individual construed according to the disapproving eye of the playwright, whose characterization is not fine-grained. Still, Reckord's point of view about obeah was not simplistic; he used obeah as a device to deliver his message of social critique, even if that critique also was partly couched in hegemonic, Euro-colonial terms.

What is interesting, if also disappointing, about *Flesh to a Tiger* is Reckord's critique of social injustice through a reliance on hoary stereotypes about obeah, embodied in the person—persona, really—of Shepherd Aaron, which, according to theater director Yvonne Brewster, are in contrast to Reckord's ideas about obeah's opposites: emancipation from the mental slavery fostered by colonialism, development of political consciousness, achievement of modernity, and, more radically, escape from the opiate of religion.[52] Shepherd Aaron is a powerful character, but not particularly complex. One would wish that by the mid-twentieth century these kinds of monolithic depictions of obeah in the arts (and elsewhere) would have become anachronistic, but this is not yet the case even at the present writing, as we will see in the following section. What makes this ideological tenacity particularly striking is that, although they are rare, there are works by authors in previous centuries that portray obeah in a more nuanced light. Not surprisingly, perhaps, this is accomplished when obeah, through its practitioners, is given its own voice—even when that voice is ventriloquized by the imagination of an outside observer. One particularly important example will suffice: Cynric Williams's 1827 novel *Hamel, the Obeah Man,* about slavery and rebellion in Jamaica. Typical accounts of Caribbean obeah labeled it as evidence of Africans' ignorance and superstition; by contrast, "Western rationality . . . was the province of the enlightened white planter class."[53] However, in *Hamel,* described by Janelle Rodriques as "the first novel written in or about the West Indies to feature an obeah practitioner as protagonist and have that protagonist speak, at length, about himself and his beliefs," the Africanness of the obeah man is not counterposed against Enlightenment ideals.[54] Instead, Williams portrays African and European values and systems of beliefs about time, history, and culture as parallel rather than as hierarchically ranked.[55] Whether or not Williams was a particularly sophisticated and perceptive thinker, something in the cultural space of common sense in his social environment fostered this departure from the conventional.

### Diasporic Arts and Superheroes

In early twenty-first-century cultural spaces of common sense, there are a number of ways that obeah is imagined, reported, and interpreted, but still the predominant imagery recalls centuries-old ways of knowing, even if put to different ideological work. Let us take a look at one particularly apt example from late twentieth- and early twenty-first-century U.S. popular culture. In 1972, Marvel Comics introduced a new superhero created by Roy Thomas, Archie Goodwin, John Romita, and George Tuska. Luke Cage was the first black superhero to be the main character of his own, eponymous comic book. He fought crime in Harlem with his superhuman strength and an inability to be killed; he could withstand everything from fists to bullets. *Luke Cage* premiered on Netflix as a live action series in 2016 and was a popular program for its two seasons (despite some critics' lukewarm reviews).[56] The episodes were written by a range of different writers, all of whom seem to have shared a common notion of obeah and its purveyors. In its second season, released in 2018, Luke Cage's primary nemesis is "Bushmaster," the Jamaican leader of the "Yardie" crew in Brooklyn whose goal is to take over Harlem (heretofore watched over by Luke Cage). There are numerous characters important to the plot as it develops over this second season, including Luke's father, the Reverend James Lucas, and female leads, among them Mariah, an ambitious and amoral politician-cum-gangster-cum-philanthropist, who is knee-deep in foul play, and Tilda, her daughter, the physician–New Age healer–proprietor of a tony neighborhood botanica. Both, as it happens, are part of Bushmaster's extended family.

Most relevant for our purposes is that Bushmaster relies on occult practices (obeah) for his own supernatural powers: unusual strength, stamina, and bodily resistance to being vanquished. While Luke is apparently not particularly religious himself, Luke's father is a devoted reverend in a large neighborhood church, with beautiful stained-glass windows and polished wooden pews; it is the sanctioned space of a hallowed institution. Through consecutive or at times simultaneously alternating scenes, mostly dealing with Bushmaster or the reverend, viewers are inculcated with key binary oppositions in Western epistemology: good versus evil, magic versus science, tradition versus modernity. Another contrast is presented—that between African American and Afro-Caribbean communities, a demographic and cultural distinction that came to the fore in the United States about the middle of the twentieth century. This contrast is also depicted through the optic of Christianity versus obeah, respectively. In the process of this juxtaposition we can detect the religionization of race.

The second episode of season 2 finds Bushmaster in the botanica, shopping for items on a list he hands to the proprietor, Tilda. She scans the list and, with a look of concern, says, "This stuff is used for obeah."[57] The background music is mysterious and slightly creepy. Viewers do not see all the items she collects and bags for him except an odd, reddish, funguslike plant. As he pays for the items, she appears uncomfortable and a little afraid. Later, in episode 7, Tilda explains to her mother, Mariah, that she has "a feeling for healing people, and not just with medicine but by using the earth the way it was intended."[58] Two episodes later (episode 9) Tilda has a conversation with Reverend Lucas about Luke Cage's powers, observing, "They say that magic might just be science we haven't figured out yet." Then, later, talking with Luke Cage about her practice she explains: "I was a conventional doctor for a few years but . . . I became fascinated with holistic medicine and Mother Earth's unfiltered power. So I melded together ancient and modern medical practice, into Mother Nature's touch. Natural remedies for headaches, anxiety, fertility."[59] Luke asks her why Bushmaster came to her shop, and Tilda answers, "He really spooked me. Those items, they were so bizarre." She continues: "Some Old World practices, they use a flower called Nightshade heavily in some of their rituals . . . [for] power and a closeness to the gods." She muses that if she only had access to his bloodwork, she could truly understand what is affecting Bushmaster. "Then you could stop him," Luke says, hopefully. Tilda replies somewhat pensively that she does not know if she could. "I built this monster [i.e., Bushmaster]," she admits, with the Nightshade that she has helped him acquire, "and I don't know." . Back in episode 2, at the same time we have the botanica scene with Tilda and Bushmaster there is a scene with Reverend Lucas in his church, preaching, he informs the congregation, from Romans 12:19 (which is about leaving vengeance to God, not to humans). We also see, in alternating scenes, Bushmaster preparing the obeah items (powders, herbs, and the red fungus). Collected into a small pile, the items are ablaze from the lighted candle placed at its center; Bushmaster directs the smoke toward his face with his open palms. It has a powerful effect on him, notably the almost instant healing of some bullet wounds on his naked torso. The voice-over during this scene is Reverend Lucas's sermon to his congregation about the struggle between good and evil.

The reverend's preaching from the scriptures is juxtaposed with the assembling of obeah's objects and the performance of an obeah ritual and its intended effects, which enable the adversary, Bushmaster, to defy death and undertake (malicious) deeds. There is, on the one hand, Christianity: "good" religion symbolized by the church, the Bible-based sermon, the congregation. On the other hand, there is obeah: "bad" (anti-)religion, undertaken alone, symbolized by malevolent intentions and their accomplishment by means of specific objectives meant to have rapid results (which, as we have seen, are significant aspects of "magic" that help to stigmatize obeah). Tensions are not produced from relations between blacks and whites; rather, these various activities involve black communities and black agents. As Aisha Harris comments in her review of the series, "With Bushmaster's arrival as a new villain, he brings this facet of blackness that we didn't see much of in Season 1: Caribbean culture."[60] The result, intentional or otherwise, is the portrayal of different kinds of blackness, or black identity: African American / Christian and Afro-Jamaican / occult.

Obeah is represented through a combination of visual and sonic suggestion. In a key scene in episode 3, Bushmaster, with bare torso and tight pants, sits on the floor inside a circle of candles, mixing roots and powders in a mortar.[61] He throws handfuls of the mixture into a pile of burning materials. The soundtrack in the background is a reggae song whose refrain is, "I'm gonna put on iron shirt and chase Satan out of earth."[62] The implied analogy is between Bushmaster and Satan, not between Bushmaster and the one who rousts Satan. In the circle of lit candles, Bushmaster practices what looks like capoeira.[63] At the end of the scene, when he is fully saturated with his obeah infusion, his face briefly morphs into the faces of two other main characters. The supernatural and magic work as one.

In addition to its neatly arranged glass vessels and other items, Tilda's botanica has a shelf of books, their titles identifying them as medicinal healing texts. The shelf also displays the Jamaican flag, a marker identifying the texts.[64] Tilda is directing steam into her face, much like Bushmaster did in the previous episode with the smoke from burning obeah objects. Momentarily she opens an old trunk and takes out a book, looking for something. She says to herself, "Nightshade," evidently finding what she was looking for. Luke Cage comes into the shop, trying to locate Bushmaster. He asks about customers who recently may have bought certain (obeah) items. Conveying the unlikelihood of being able to ascertain this, Tilda replies that dried herbs are bought by half of her customers, who are Jamaican.[65] Her statement implicates all Jamaicans in obeah; so many customers are Jamaican, and their purchases are of things whose use one cannot be sure of.

While Tilda is in her botanica reading about Nightshade, in the Paradise Club in Harlem, the headquarters of Mariah and her henchmen, the band is playing B. B. King's "The Thrill Is Gone," repeating the song's refrain, "I'm free from your spell." Viewers soon hear another earlier blues classic, "I Put a Spell on You," by Screamin' Jay Hawkins. Inside the club Bushmaster assures Mariah that blues music constitutes "the ancestors, *they* remember." "You can't erase the past," he says, "you can't burn it away. That's the spell on you. That's magic, science in its purest form." The songs work as an obvious sonic reinforcement of the activity in the botanica. But along with Bushmaster's slightly menacing message, they also taint the positive impression viewers may have of obeah in the hands of Tilda, who represents the New Age potential of herbal medicine, obeah's benevolent alter ego. The source of herbal remedies, Mother Earth, also can be misused, turned into something dark. In one scene when Bushmaster fights Luke Cage mano a mano, he takes some powder out of his pocket and blows it into Luke's face, immobilizing him.[66] Bushmaster says, "You're paralyzed. Them have things that come from the earth, power you won't understand. Respect." The tension between good and evil runs through every dimension of the supernatural, divine or occult. Consequences depend on methods and goals, which can be either benevolent or malevolent. This tension also runs through every aspect of humanity's material heritage, Earth and its resources. Forces forever in conflict, good and evil can, respectively, make obeah palatable or toxic. If misused, there can be disastrous results. When Tilda offers Bushmaster "a secret weapon, a super shot of Nightshade" that can double his strength, it comes with a warning: "You'd need to be careful. Whatever you do, don't take it all at once. It can destroy your body and your mind."[67] The eventual destruction of mind and body that will come with overreliance on Nightshade, obeah's metonym, and here its principal object, is repeated a few times in various episodes, analogies drawn with the danger of steroid use. The obeah object can be denatured, further increasing its, essentially, "evil" results.

But Bushmaster says the risk of the "super shot" is worth it: "For me mother, for me father, . . . for me grandfather, all the people them. It's worth it."[68] Earlier, when it looks like Bushmaster might take over the Paradise Club, he is asked what his plans are for it. He replies that "it's all for the people and the pickney them, every dollar we make, every penny goes back home to the youth, to mash up the sufferation there."[69] Viewers can understand this sentiment because in another episode Bushmaster's sympathetic past is flashbacked.[70] He suffers childhood trauma from having seen his mother murdered in an arson-based fire in their home; two years later, while still young, he is shot. He is taken by a friend to the Blue Mountains and cured with Nightshade by an older woman. He asks her, "Mother, you sure this science thing going work?" She replies, "Just calm down . . . Nightshade no heal, Nightshade reveal," directing smoke from burning Nightshade into his face: "Come darling, breathe, breathe . . ." The bullet is ejected from his stomach, and he lives.

The Blue Mountains are the source of the pure, authentic Nightshade, not the synthetic product that Tilda makes for Bushmaster when the other runs out. The Blue Mountains are also a key symbol of Jamaica, which in turn signifies obeah. These kinds of homogenizing, and essentializing, characterizations of Jamaican blackness are tempered somewhat by alternative portrayals. In the next episode, for example, a young woman on the street in Harlem says to Luke Cage, "My cousin's getting smacked around by the cops because he has dreds. Every Jamaican ain't down with Bushmaster."[71] But this position is the exception to the rule that in *Luke Cage*, "Jamaican" and "obeah" are mutually constitutive. This message is conveyed in abbreviated terms, such as when Bushmaster's crony explains to him that growing Nightshade is going to "take some time. . . . It's totally different than ganja"—a gardening activity apparently familiar to most if not all Jamaicans.[72] It is also conveyed in more profound terms, such as when Bushmaster educates the police about Nanny, Jamaica's late seventeenth- and early eighteenth-century Maroon rebel leader. Nanny "kept the science alive," by which Bushmaster means obeah. She came to Jamaica "in chains," he continues, "but she never forgot who she was, she never forgot the old ways. . . . The maroons resisted. They broke their chains and they ran to the hills. In the Blue Mountains they live off the land, and Nanny, she would lead raids to the other plantations. . . . The British had the technology, but the maroons had the will, the determination, the magic. . . . That is the true birth of the real Jamaica. Resistance, independence, fire."[73] Here obeah is given a dignified provenance, a romanticized place in an admirable heritage. But it lends a kind of blackness, a black identity, that is exclusive and that, consequently, marks off a Jamaican other vis-à-vis African American (Christianity). Even when sympathetic—as a healing community-builder—obeah is contrary. And when obeah is unsympathetic—antisocial and opportunistic—it is deplorable. This tightrope of good and evil is walked only by Jamaicans; with the shield of Christianity, African Americans protect a different kind of blackness and black identity.

In the final scene of the second season's final episode, Rev. Lucas advises Luke, "Your strength is from God. . . . I have no doubt in my mind about that. But with that kind of power comes its share of pain. Science, magic, God—that power flows from within, from inside. What comes out when that pressure is heaviest, that's the *real* magic. That's what defines being a man. That's what defines being a hero."[74] These equivalences—science, magic, God—boil down to, and are encompassed by, Christianity, the real magic, from which the very definition of humanity derives. This again leaves obeah (non-Christian magic, bad magic) a religionized blackness that is unsavory, that creates an identity outside the boundaries of proper ways of knowing and of being. In this sense, "black magic" takes on a whole new meaning.

In their review of *Luke Cage*, Andray Domise and Sharine Taylor comment that "cinematic Jamaican culture is so often draped in occultism and mystery that it comes across as a kind of Afro-Orientalism."[75] Yet one could argue that the "Orient" is overshadowed by obeah's most common genealogy; as Domise and Taylor write, "Bushmaster's powers are catalyzed by his practice of 'Obeah' magic . . . the culture [being] derivative of the west African Vodun practices that become Voodoo in Haiti, Santeria in the Dominican Republic, and Candomblé in Brazil."[76] Another reviewer defined Bushmaster's obeah as "a system of Afro-Caribbean mysticism developed and practiced amongst the Maroons in the early 18th century."[77] Profoundly important in Caribbean peoples' history of autonomy and resistance, Maroons are also at times romanticized symbols in the discourse of scholars, activists, politicians, and ordinary people. "Orientalism" may add to what makes obeah seem exotic (foreign, alien, suspect), but its ideological association with Africa and/or blackness has a long and entrenched history. This history is further reinforced by the fact that obeah does have provenance in sub-Saharan Africa and was likely, in some fashion, part of many Maroon communities' religious traditions. But obeah's actual composition, at least in the West Indies, is from additive cultural streams—African, European, Asian, Levantine, and so on. Obeah is rightly argued to be too fluid to be precisely pinned down as a "unitary phenomenon," something it has never been,[78] and scholars often acknowledge its multiple historical antecedents and ethnographic practices. Yet at the same time, the centripetal force exerted by interpreting obeah in a particular way—whatever that way happens to be (supported, denigrated, etc.)—turns obeah into a unitary phenomenon whose reiteration, as common sense, keeps Africa and blackness not only a prime essence but also specifically racialized.

The depiction of Bushmaster as malevolent is somewhat rehabilitated by his sympathetic past and by his stated commitment to help his family and "all the people them."[79] Retribution and social justice make the "super shot" of Nightshade worth the risks to his body and mind that it poses. But obeah itself does not enjoy absolution. In connection with a physician's interest in holistic medicine, Mother Earth, Mother Nature, natural remedies, and the melding of ancient and modern healing practices, obeah gets some cosmetic surgery if you will; this is not a different way of being perceived, but the suggestion of improved possibilities. On its own, however, without such provisional modifiers as the innovative upgrades of modernity (science) and the purity of nature, obeah remains dark, occult, malevolent—if also effective. Obeah continues to be a homogeneous phenomenon rather than one comprised of different modus operandi. There is no echo, for example, of a more nuanced obeah that a friend of mine evoked when he explained to me about his own religious work as a santero (priest) in Santeria after a "reading" that I had with him in 2016.[80] "There is," he said, matter-of-factly, "good obeah and bad obeah. Bad is to destroy, hurt, do negative things. Good obeah is what we're doing right now. If we were in the islands they'd say what we're doing is 'obeah.' I'm a *good* obeah man. Good obeah is a 'science' too." Viewers of *Luke Cage* do not get treated to examples of possible "good obeah"; it is as if the obeah of Bushmaster, crucially facilitated by the Nightshade flower that Tilda, the botanica owner-physician, reproduces for him, has gone rogue. Its nefarious usage took Mother Nature into methods and objectives somehow unnatural, and therefore immoral. When used for good and not in "bizarre" combinations of items, "Old World practices" for reaching "closeness to the gods" do not create "monsters" like Bushmaster. In his own words, Bushmaster describes himself as "the stone the builders refused."[81] He does not elaborate on this characterization, but one can infer that it is a metaphor suggesting someone who is an outlier, marginal, or rejected—that no conventional use was made of his abilities or potential, so he turned them in another, unconventional (and unsavory) direction. Or he may be alluding to the biblical reference about the rejected stone becoming the cornerstone, or principle stone, thereby co-opting a Christian message.[82]

The personification of the rogue individual is a persistent aspect of obeah's constitution; it is fundamental to ideas about obeah's very nature. Whether the point of view is sympathetic or antagonistic toward obeah, the rogue individual is the flesh-and-blood maestro of obeah's designs as well as the emblem of obeah's counterhegemonic (or at least contrary) methods, and sometimes its objectives. Enlightenment and post-Enlightenment valorization of the reasoning, agentive individual and the human types who represented the developmental progression toward this state fed subsequent ideas about the individual in relation to community and society, notably in the modern study of religion. By the early twentieth century, aspects of the work of Emile Durkheim, among others, had helped shape

Western models of religion in collective terms that both produced and required a moral community and the common good to be legitimately "religion." This premise interprets individual members to be communicators of certain moral imperatives, who express a kind of agency that exhibits individual will but that also is checked by and subordinate to superior, divine will. Different expressions of individual will or different kinds of relationships with the supernatural tend to raise questions about social conformity and appropriate practical intentions among practitioners who express individual will or relationships with the supernatural in ways different from those groups who exercise the power to interpret and impose such normative standards.

In all religious traditions, engaging the spirit world, the supernatural, or the sacred in order to accomplish something is work. Characterizing a great deal of Western thought about religion is that when involvement with otherworldly powers has the objective of achieving immediate or rapid results, such expediency is suspect, smacking of magic or other spurious forms of involvement with otherworldly powers. This can be exacerbated by the distinction made in Western thought between asking God or other supernatural forces for something (human humility) and the belief that certain practices will compel supernatural forces to do what is being bidden (human hubris). Such perspectives call to mind Euro-colonialism's characterization of obeah, which was part of the ideological weaponry against it. Many religious traditions, including so-called world religions, have their own continuums along which the goals and promises of worship and belief run, from the immediate present at one end to the indefinite future at the other; not all efforts are delayed, nor are they all instantaneously realized. But this continuum in Christianity was left unacknowledged by Euro-colonials in their agendas of vilification of obeah and obeah practitioners, who were allegedly invested in immediate and practical returns—and allegedly malevolent ones, at that. In this way of thinking, expediency lends itself well to related infringements such as fraudulence, duplicity, and personal gain as opposed to the welfare of the common good.

### Diaspora on Trial: Obeah in Canada

Criminalization of practices or beliefs can take any form or rest on any justification that hegemonic power allows; the retaliatory consequences that are a response to those practices or beliefs are meted out by legal means that are devised and controlled by those who find them objectionable and have the power to exercise their objections. In addition to living with the perverse optic of the colonizer, however, is the very real precariousness of working with otherworldly forces, especially those who are for mortals difficult to persuade or impossible to control. The clients of a diviner, healer, or spirit-world mediator have expectations about their questions being answered and their problems being alleviated. Failure to produce results also can have consequences for the specialist—not the criminalization of colonial authority, certainly, but in varying degrees of social disapproval. Other specialists, known as therapists, physicians, and clergy, also must contend with their clients' expectations of success. But in Western traditions, each of these constituencies has a socially powerful, institutionalized structure that can provide explanation of and justification for failure. Clients may not be satisfied by these means at the disposal of specialists and may seek redress, but it must accord with the same institutionalized structures. Obeah specialists (and other Atlantic religious traditions) lack this kind of standardization that is part of the structure of their respective broader societies. Obeah specialists tend to be held to standards by the communities they serve, which if not met can end up stigmatizing and marginalizing the obeah man or woman among their community peers. In a kind of Catch-22, the image of the lone (rogue) individual is reinforced—not only through oppressive legal structures but also through the nature of the work itself as it is interpreted in societies, such as those in the West Indies, that are organized according to certain abiding philosophical principles about the nature, role, and agency of the individual.

Thus different forms of agency are at work, as all people who live with obeah, in whatever fashion, attempt to manage the activities, and the veracity, of those who undertake this otherworldly labor—either by denying obeah's curative or revelatory truths, or making sure these truths produce. These tensions have a long history in the West Indies. Historian Katherine Gerbner tells of how in mid-eighteenth-century Jamaica, for example, if an obeah man or woman failed to perform such tasks as "healing the sick; mediating affairs between masters and slaves or within the slave community; communicating with supernatural powers; and dealing in the symbolic worlds of death and dying," he or she was "at risk of losing his or her title and the community's respect."[83] Over two hundred years later, between 1970 and 1974, folklorist Jane Beck collected data on obeah in Grenada, the Windward Islands, Bequia, and Dominica. Not surprisingly, she found that obeah "is so fundamental to life in the West Indies that whether it is outlawed by the government or made legal by official decree matters little to the people who consider it not only an inalienable right, but a basic of life itself."[84] Beck understood one of obeah's primary functions to be "a mechanism which enforces social control at the level of the total community."[85] Extrapolating from the communities in which she studied to "West Indian society" in general, she argued that there are two kinds of obeah men. One is an "actual" obeah man, who is "acclaimed by his community" through his work with "both good and evil" to mediate between the natural and supernatural world on their behalf. The other kind of practitioner she identified as the "implied obeah man." The issue about "implied" is not that this person has no real mastery of obeah, but rather that he uses his specialized skills with the supernatural for "personal aggrandizement" and for himself alone rather than to help others. The "implied obeah man" thereby defies social convention, which causes him to be "despised," "hated," and "reviled" by the community in which he resides, who define him as "totally anti-social."[86] In other words, the "implied obeah man"—not the genuine obeah man—is a rogue individual, one who does not serve the social good, a valuation that is defined by residents of local communities steeped in obeah culture. Among them, obeah's "fraud" is not what is stigmatized, nor is the mere fact of practicing obeah a cause for marginalization or isolation. What is denounced is the selfish hoarding of obeah's successful results. The individualized methodology of obeah appears to be the same for these two figures, but the intentions and objectives of that methodology are in stark contrast. Nonetheless, the individual/community binary remains.

A different Caribbean diaspora gained momentum from the late 1960s on, when migrants from former and soon-to-be-former British colonies settled in Canada and the United States. Like their "Windrush" counterparts in the UK a generation before, they brought with them their understandings and practices of obeah. As in centuries past, at times obeah's critics, neutral observers, and devotees see it as having a "family resemblance" to religious traditions of the Afro-Atlantic, such as Vodou and Santeria. Whether as part of these belief systems or as a singular phenomenon, obeah is entangled in the religious precepts and racial thinking of U.S. and Canadian societies, which together enfold and inform the official, dual mission of "enlightened democracies": controlling individual freedoms while promoting religious pluralism. These entanglements also reflect obeah's own ambivalences: many of its devotees today think about it as a helpful means of solving personal problems, if only "privately."[87] This is not privacy in the sense of something sacred that is accessible only, for example, to the few who possess specialized knowledge. It is a privacy that keeps obeah under the criminalization radar of the law and away from the moral disapproval, at least outwardly, of one's community. Even when people turn to obeah men and women in order to alleviate difficulties they are facing, they do so within a common sense of representations of obeah that live in the popular diasporic imagination. Stigmatized or sanctioned, criminalized or protected—or, more accurately, stigmatized and sanctioned, criminalized and protected—obeah's practitioners, ritual practices, and popular imagery convey the messages of identity categories that are both tenacious and multipurpose.

In December 2005 the Court of Appeal for Ontario heard a case involving the conviction five years earlier of a defendant for the murder of a bank employee during the course of a bank robbery in Brampton, Ontario.[88] In December 2012 the Court of Appeal for Ontario heard another case, this one about the conviction of a reputed drug dealer in 2008 for the first-degree murder of one of his acquaintances, also in Brampton.[89] Falling within the Greater Toronto area, Brampton's more than 300,000 immigrants comprise slightly over half of its total population. According to the 2016 census, the top five countries of origin of Brampton's immigrants are, in descending order, India, Jamaica, Pakistan, the Philippines, and Guyana.[90] The demographics of these diasporas have given the city such alternate sobriquets as "Browntown," "Bramladesh," "Singhdale," or simply "ghetto."[91]

The arrests and convictions in the two court cases relied on strategies of entrapment, "sting" operations that had induced the Afro-Jamaican defendants to reveal to apparent "obeah men" their culpability in the crimes. In the first case, the bank robbery murder, an Afro-Jamaican "spiritualist" and "psychic counsellor" who practiced his craft at the back of his neighborhood botanica, cooperated with local police in their apprehension of the suspects by acting as a police agent. He allowed his telephone to be tapped and his shop to be installed with video- and audio-recording equipment, in order that his admittedly invented "obeah" rituals in the course of his consultations with the suspects would produce evidence and confessions for the prosecution. In the second case, the drug gang murder, an Afro-Jamaican police officer impersonated an obeah man as a means of extracting evidence and confessions from the suspects. Both of these entrapment strategies—involving would-be obeah man and ersatz obeah man, respectively—raised legal questions about the definition of religion, about the nature of belief, how much and what kind of belief is required to be deemed legitimately religious, and about the particular vulnerability of certain racial communities to state harassment and injustice—in other words, a link between "minority groups" and "less established religions," as it was phrased in the court documents of these cases. This link is based in part on the idea that racial identities are constituted significantly through religious practices (the religionization of race). Key to these appeals cases were the meaning, significance, and practice of obeah, which, ultimately, the attorneys presenting the appeal argued, was a matter of national importance—the legal protection of religion under the Canadian *Charter of Rights and Freedoms.*

As the documents on the bank robbery case have it, the neighborhood herbalist, spiritualist, and psychic counselor—whom I am calling the "would-be obeah man" for reasons that will become clear shortly—was taken by neighborhood residents to be a "'very religious man,' with mystical powers." His principal business was giving "psychic" or "spiritual" readings for clients from the Caribbean community.[92] In a room at the back of his shop he kept "an altar and a range of sacramental, occult and spiritual artifacts from different religious traditions." However, he denied practicing obeah, claimed little knowledge about Jamaican supernatural beliefs and traditions, and devised rituals based on materials that he had read.[93] He conceded that he had "no genuine spiritual powers and that he could be described as a 'con man and a charlatan,'" knowingly misleading his clients. Despite his awareness that the community thought of him as an obeah practitioner, he did not dissuade them from this impression.[94] (One would assume because it was a source of his livelihood.) Among his services was to provide "'spiritual protection' against apprehension" to people planning to commit crimes.[95] Some weeks before the robbery-murder, the appellant had asked him for protection from getting caught. He testified that he had refused.

Soon after the crime, on the day it took place, the would-be obeah man heard about it in the news media. He went to the police, telling them about his previous encounter with the appellant, who became known to him as the possible perpetrator through his conversation with another member of the community who frequently used the would-be obeah man's counseling services and who had been in contact with the suspects after the crime.

Up to that point, the police had very little information to go on except that the perpetrators "spoke with Jamaican accents."[96] He was then enlisted as a paid police agent, and by telephone he initiated a meeting with the appellant in his shop. In their conversation he asked the appellant if he truly believed in the things he did (obeah), and the appellant assented. The would-be obeah man instructed the appellant not to wear anything black to their meeting, and to put an egg in a black sock, knot the sock twice, and bring it with him.[97] The explanation for this, which he gave in his testimony, was that the instructions were to "make it seem real" to the appellant, that although they were not obeah practices, he assumed that the appellant believed that he practiced obeah. At the face-to-face meeting he wore "clerical vestments" (which he characterized as "props"), and prodded the appellant about whether he "believed in science and Obeah and those types of things," in order to reinforce to the appellant that he was an obeah practitioner with the "power to plug into the supernatural."[98] At their meeting he explained that in order to help the appellant, he needed a detailed recounting of events; the appellant admitted to the robbery, provided the names of the other participants, and identified himself as the shooter. He then asked for payment from the appellant, who put part of it on the table, and, at the would-be obeah man's instruction, placed a candle on top of the cash.[99]

The court documents describe the conversation between the appellant and the would-be obeah man at their meeting as "a blend of the spiritual, sacramental, superstitious and practical," where the appellant was warned that his "future well-being was threatened by the invasive spirit" of the murdered bank employee. At this point the document parenthetically instructs the reader that the "invasive spirit" is "known in Obeah practice as a 'duppy' [i.e., ghost or spirit]."[100] Earlier on, this document asserts that "expert evidence established that eggs and the colour black both have special significance in Obeah."[101] The appellant is also described as deferential to the would-be obeah man's "moral authority" and ritual instructions (which included reciting the addresses of his accomplices backward and taking a "reversible bath" with oils in order to "cleanse him of the sin" he had committed). This demeanor, the documents note, is "best appreciated by viewing the videos in conjunction with the transcript," both provided by the surveillance equipment.[102] Here, despite the would-be obeah man's admission of pretense, the idea is to establish the persuasiveness of the proceedings to the appellant. There is no suggestion of "gullibility" on his part, which could cast doubt on obeah itself. One is gullible when something is false; something true does not deceive. The point was to protect obeah as a valid religion while exposing the tainted interaction of these particular interlocutors.

Grounds for appeal of this case were numerous, but the one germane to my present discussion was the admissibility of the appellant's statement to the would-be obeah man during their conversations and meeting. The appellant's position at trial was that his statement was inadmissible because it was the result of a "dirty trick" ploy (in Canadian jurisprudence, extracting a confession through the manipulation of religious beliefs), which violates the Canadian *Charter of Rights and Freedoms*. Instead, the appellant argued, his communication should be protected by religious privilege.[103] In a "lengthy pre-trial motion," four expert witnesses gave evidence that the sessions conducted by the would-be obeah man were "in their essence, religious."[104] One was a Roman Catholic priest and professor of theology at a university in Toronto, who testified that the would-be obeah man's actions during the meeting with the appellant suggested a "syncretistic" religious rite of "undoing" the applicant's wrongs—"a kind of forgiveness of it."[105] He saw other parallels with Roman Catholic practice: the "exorcism of evil spirits," and, because the back room of the shop had an altar and religious artifacts, it constituted a "sacred space" akin to a chapel or small church.[106] There were, however, some contrasts that the priest noted in the cross-examination. Among these are the prohibitions against offering protection against arrest for past or future crimes ("You can never counsel someone to do evil"), assisting someone to flee the jurisdiction after committing a crime, and charging a fee for a sacrament. What was missing during their meeting also negated the parallel between Catholicism and obeah: there was "no articulable prayer or appeal to a deity" and insufficient "solemnity" associated with a Catholic confessional.[107]

Another of the expert witnesses was a religious studies professor at the same university who specialized in Caribbean religions. He echoed that the would-be obeah man was "purporting to practice a form of religion," one that is "syncretistic" and draws on "a cluster of phenomena" that also go by the name of "Santeria," "Orisha," and "Shango," among others. In his opinion, the rituals in the surveillance footage portrayed what is common to many religions: the effort to protect the living from the spirits of the dead. Moreover, the would-be obeah man voiced a "moral admonition" to the appellant that what he had done was "very, very wrong," which rendered the meeting "a religious phenomenon."[108] The third expert witness was also an expert scholar of Caribbean and African religions. In his opinion, obeah is not a "religion" but rather "a form of spirituality in which there is 'absolute belief in the world of spirits,'" including the "exorcism of 'duppies'—spirits capable of haunting a place or a person"—and where objects such as lit candles and oils, as well as baths, are common. Moreover, there is the expectation in obeah that clients must be completely truthful to the obeah man in order for the rituals to be effective, and that any revelation will be held in confidence.[109] On viewing the surveillance tape, he found that many of the would-be obeah man's actions "were consistent with Obeah practices, but that others resembled 'not so good theatre.'" The meeting could be deemed a "genuine Obeah session" if the "clients were sufficiently aware of the kind of things that are done commonly in Obeah." Then "they might well be taken in by it," which seemed to be the situation in this particular case, although the appellant had not expressed "remorse or a desire to be forgiven," nor was he encouraged to do so by the would-be obeah man.[110] In other words, obeah's authenticity (and hence handling as a protected religious right under the Canadian *Charter*) hinges in part on a devotee's knowledge of obeah and understanding about why he or she is pursuing it, and the sincere belief that is engendered by reason— rather than the gullibility of superstition. In cross-examination, this expert witness drew a distinction between this would-be obeah man and "legitimate Obeah practitioners."[111] In this perspective, obeah, a real religion, cannot be false or illegitimate; it is only made so by frauds. In this vein, the expert's language is interesting: even with knowledge of obeah's rites, devotees are "taken in," which implies, even against deliberate intention, being fooled.

The fourth expert witness was also an academic specialist in "Caribbean spiritual practices." She echoed the imperative of trust that is expected between client and obeah practitioner, and also that although the surveillance video did not show many "ritual behaviours," those that were captured in the footage "are consistent with the belief and practice of Obeah." Some of the genuine obeah practices that she identified included the would-be obeah man's rituals to "remove a duppy" from the appellant,[112] the "lavish use of oil and water," and the "reversing" of "bad influences."[113] Also key was the evident relationship between the client and the practitioner, which was "based on trust, confidentiality, and above all, faith in the efficacy of this belief system." Most significantly, the would-be obeah man's "primary assistance" came through "his special relationship with supernatural forces." She concluded that even if what was in the footage was "staged," it may be interpreted as "a form of behaviour that attempts to relate the natural and supernatural worlds."[114] This casts an even finer line between, on the one hand, a spurious performance ("staged") and, on the other hand, an authentic performance (knowledge of methods for relating natural and supernatural). Both sides of this case—the prosecution and the defense, along with their expert witnesses—relied on certain more or less random but repeated features of obeah in order to define and validate it. Obeah's objects, in particular—as curious, contingent, and diverse as they have always been throughout their history in the Americas—played an important role in this regard (for example, the eggs, oil, the color black, the color white, baths, duppies, overlapping natural and supernatural spheres). These repetitions of selected (reduced) features, ostensibly crucial to "real" obeah, consolidate obeah into a *thing* by standardizing it. But even with this concretization (this "thingness"), obeah's enactment, its conduct, defies a neat and steady distinction between "real" religion and what is "fraudulent," "outrageous," "totally profane," and "totally out of bounds," as the second expert in Caribbean and African religions put it, qualities, he said, that would "outrage most legitimate Obeah practitioners."[115] Another aspect of its thingness that obeah's objects and features conjure is obeah's race. Singly, none necessarily represents racial identity; a candle is a candle. However, in a cluster (the basis of obeah's animated energy), the power of obeah is projected in part through its ostensible blackness—occult, magical, mysterious.

The Applicant's Memorandum of Argument regarding this case identified a common feature that was shared by the trial judge's findings as well as the distinctions relied on by the Court of Appeal: both drew on what was "essentially a Judeo-Christian model of religion." "'Pastoral counseling,' 'repentance,' 'confession to sin,' 'divine forgiveness,' and 'spiritual cleansing' are 'all distinctly Christian concepts.'" But even Christian religions, it was pointed out, including in "contemporary, multi-cultural Canada," vary in terms of the way they interpret confession and God's forgiveness as "conferring earthly protection and benefits on the penitent."[116] In other words, seeking favorable consequences in the material world is not exclusive to "syncretistic" religions. The favorable comparison with Christianity continued with the charge that the basic premise of the ruling was that "if a person hopes a religious ritual will yield a temporal ('secular') benefit, his purpose is for that reason alone not 'religious' and the ritual is stripped entirely of its religious character." This premise rests on a false dichotomy because many "mainstream Christian denominations teach that ritual, combined with faith, will be efficacious in sparing believers from the deserved consequences of their actions" and can result in garnering blessings in their secular affairs.[117] But the primary issue was not determining if obeah could be categorized as a "religion"; under Canadian law, it is. Obeah's "truth," instead, lay in its practitioners: the way they approached obeah and what that said, or did not say, about their racial identity and its social consequences.

The cross-examination of the four experts stressed that the appellant had sought advance protection for future crimes, that he sought to escape legal punishment, and that he did not renounce his criminal behavior.[118] Although the experts' statements were ruled by the trial judge to be admissible, he underscored that the purpose of the meeting was neither repentance nor pastoral counseling, nor was their relationship that between penitent and religious practitioner.[119] Among other omissions, the judge said, the appellant "does not ask for absolution, he does not ask for forgiveness. . . . He does not even say he is sorry. This is not a religious experience at all."[120] "Money, escape, and protection," the judge continued, were what was on the appellant's mind.[121] The implied condemnation of such seemingly immediate, instrumentalist goals seems clear. The judge concluded that the police's entrapment measures "would not shock the conscience of the community and did not amount to a 'dirty trick.'"[122]

The Applicant's Memorandum of Argument stated that the trial record and the judgment of the Court of Appeal showed that this case had significant implications for the "meaning and scope of the *Charter's* protection against 'dirty tricks,'" and thus represented "an issue of significant national importance."[123] The posing of police as obeah practitioners in order to exploit the "spiritual beliefs of Jamaican Canadians" as a means of obtaining self-incriminating ("inculpatory") "evidence against them or their loved ones" is a technique, the argument concluded, that is both unconstitutional and, in being selectively employed "against an identifiable minority group," is "particularly odious and objectionable."[124] The crux of the matter was the extent to which entrapment can be a reasonable method of policing, based on consideration of such a method's uneven application and consequences. Vulnerable and at greatest risk, the logic went, communities of color, especially those whose religious or "spiritual" traditions are "syncretistic"—like Jamaicans' obeah—still must pass a kind of standards test in terms of criteria about belief: the nature of the belief, and to what ends they put it. That is, irrespective of whether or not an obeah practitioner is a "pretend" one, did the appellant truly believe in obeah and truly think of the would-be obeah man as a "real" one with actual supernatural powers, and therefore be unguarded in what he revealed?[125] If so, then the appellant's revelations during the meeting should enjoy the protections that other religions do. Or was this belief (allowing that it existed on the appellant's part in the first place) compromised by the wrong meanings and purposes?

In 2006 the appeal of this bank robbery–murder case involving the would-be obeah man was denied. The racial nature of this case and the marginal status of obeah as a religion is suggested when we try to imagine what the court would think if someone had impersonated a clergyperson from a so-called world religion in order to extract a confession. Yet obeah was protected as a religion, one that is genuinely believed in by many, at the same time that its practice (in this case) was critiqued as instrumental, material, and an insincere kind of performance. The legal harassment and social marginalization of "small church" religious traditions, the logic goes, cannot be separated from the diasporic communities of color who still are their majority constituents. Thus, seeking the Achilles heel of criminalized groups in their religious traditions smacks of racial profiling. When religion is a key identifier of race, there is a fine line between defending the religion, thus in turn defending the race (which keeps these identity categories intact and important) and presenting the (mis)use of a religious tradition to locate and prosecute crime. In this case, obeah is Jamaican and Jamaican is black; obeah under duress is racial discrimination. The religionization of race and the racialization of religion together are a problematic, double-edged sword.

The second murder case, with the ersatz obeah man, and its appeal differ in a number of ways from the first case of the would-be obeah man, seven years before.[126] But it also shares some important similarities with that earlier case. Notably, the prosecution shaped its arguments in large part on the previous appeal. Moreover, the undercover police officer in this case lured the suspects into an admission of guilt by posing as an obeah man. Although they were in many respects different, both cases involved first-degree murder convictions, failed appeals, social justice issues involving race, and obeah.

In connection with a gangland encounter in Brampton in 2004, a local drug dealer was killed.[127] Three Jamaican Canadian men were convicted of first-degree murder. As part of the police investigation of the crime, an officer, also a "black man of Caribbean ancestry," posed as an obeah spiritual adviser in order to extract information that would lead to solving the case.[128] He prepared for his supposed ritual performances of obeah by modeling them after those of the would-be obeah man, information he gleaned from the surveillance footage that had been videotaped in the would-be obeah man's shop.[129]

According to the *Toronto Star* newspaper and the defense's 2012 appeal of the conviction at the Court of Appeal for Ontario, at which I was present for the purpose of conducting ethnographic research, a significant part of the legal argument was whether the police engaged in permissible, criminal-apprehending "tricks" or perpetrated a "dirty tricks" ploy that "shocks the conscience of the community" by going beyond what is morally and socially tolerable.[130] The prosecution's position was that the conduct of the police was not sufficiently egregious to shock community conscience, and that societal interests would be served by allowing the prosecution to proceed despite police misconduct. The defense's arguments were multilayered, defending obeah yet describing it in conventionally religious, and racial, terms.

Not long after the crime, the local police department learned that the mother of two of the murder suspects was a believer in obeah.[131] They sent an undercover police officer to pose as an obeah man and persuade her that he possessed "spiritual powers" in order to exploit her spiritual beliefs as a means of procuring inculpatory evidence against the suspects—her children. The undercover ersatz obeah man told the suspects' mother that an evil spirit wished to do her family harm, and offered to rid her of it. For their initial meeting he told her to wear white and bring an egg in a black sock.[132] In a hotel room procured for this purpose, he held seventeen sessions, or consultations, with one of the suspects, sometimes with his mother or another of the suspects attending. The consultations were secretly videotaped and audiotaped. The defense claimed that the sting's ruse was aided by the occult authenticity that the ersatz obeah man's identity implied. A homicide officer, he "was Black, weighed 280 pounds and was 6'1". His family was of Caribbean ancestry. He spoke with a British accent. He'd been raised in an area of London with a Jamaican cultural presence and his relatives still spoke with a Jamaican accent. This neighborhood and family background had given him familiarity with patois and terms such as 'Babylon' and 'Beastman.' . . . He had also acquired some knowledge about *Obeah* and he had obtained professional experience with it"—by viewing the hidden camera footage from a previous case (of the would-be obeah man, discussed above), by researching Jamaican culture and obeah on the internet, and by listening to reggae music, notably Bob Marley.[133] These efforts were supplemented with "an English dictionary definition of *Obeah* and anecdotal comments by a few Black police officers."[134] Presumably he had to resort to this kind of homework because, as he explained to the jury, obeah is "a Caribbean belief system involving voodoo and witchcraft that wasn't practised in public."[135]

The defense argued that "the use of religious beliefs to gull credulous subjects into self-incrimination is deeply offensive to the constitution."[136] Yet the very foundation of religious practice is faith.[137] The assumption is that credulity is distinct from faith; in Judeo-Christian epistemology, we have faith in things that are true, and our credulity is defined by believing in that which is false. The defense went on to say that what happened in this case "smacks not only of exploitation but of discrimination" and is "an affront to the *Charter of Rights and Freedoms*," conclusions that would be drawn in any context other than a criminal trial.[138] The gulling of "credulous subjects" has been a centuries-long theme in the discursive tradition of obeah. Historically in the West Indies, such assessments of vulnerability were one weapon in the criminalization of obeah's mysteries and its allegedly unscrupulous, antisocial, rogue practitioners. Today, in another postcolonial society, one committed, at least in principle, to multicultural nationhood based on equality and justice for all, such assessments of vulnerability are weapons in the nullification of "rogue" authority rather than of "rogue" enclaves. Yet the image of weakness and simple-mindedness that credulity conveys has remained. Contrary to the good impulses behind obeah's protection, embedded in this image is a categorization of vulnerable (inferior) race: those individuals or groups whose genealogy passes down racial identity inherited through religion, and religious identity inherited through race. Indeed, in justifying the conduct of the police department in this case, the ersatz obeah man's superior officer testified that "Obeah seemed like a logical way to go because they [the defendants] were black and Jamaican," who tend to "believe in these practices."[139] Thus it is not surprising that the defense charged that the "police impersonation of an *Obeah* religious advisor was designed specifically to prey on the Appellants' religious beliefs rooted in their identity as Caribbean people of African descent."[140] The police "used *Obeah* as a gateway to exploit African Canadians' distrust of the police," which "dates back to slavery" and derives from their "experiences with discrimination" and "racist oppression."[141]

The performance of the undercover ersatz obeah man was based on a selective pastiche of racializing signifiers of obeah, or at least of those persons who presumably subscribe to it. He relied on a grab bag of obeah objects, but he also performed obeah, and thereby projected an embodied obeah persona, through casting the shadows of cultural emblems—sonic, textual, visual (and some clandestine)—that ostensibly identified a community of believers and, as the local police authorities maintained, a novel and effective methodology for apprehending criminals. Using these guidelines, the ersatz obeah man "donned a black robe and wore a head covering and chanted in a darkened room lit by candlelight." He feigned a trance.[142] To further exhibit his power over supernatural evil, "he had a dead crow placed on the [suspect's] family's front steps," and at the scene of the murder he cracked open an egg in which he had injected red dye that would look like blood. The ersatz obeah man engaged the defendants in such ostensible obeah rituals as taking special baths and chanting, with the use of such props as candles and white handkerchiefs, which he assured them would suppress the evil spirit. He also offered the defendants protection from the justice system, which he referred to in the negative as "Babylon," as well as from judges and police, whom he represented as the "Beast Man."[143] The suspect became increasingly concerned about the safety of his mother, and in the course of ascertaining from the ersatz obeah man how to protect her, he revealed his role in the murder.

The undercover ersatz obeah man was given wide latitude to exploit the suspects' spiritual beliefs as long as he tainted the role of spiritual adviser/clergy by offering to protect them from being apprehended or by requesting payment for his services. Doing so would show the illegitimacy of his representing any valid religion, obeah included: it would "corrupt" his ostensible relationship to religion, thus taking it outside the realm of legal protection. Anthropologist Kamari Clarke has written that the police department involved in this case proceeded as it did because it "did not believe Obeah qualified as an actual religion." Recorded in the *Toronto Star*, a detective-sergeant who testified at the trial stated that "the Obeah idea was his. Obeah is not a religion, he maintained, and he would not have infiltrated Catholics, Buddhists, Muslims, or Hindus."[144] At the same time, as Clarke also noted, obeah was indeed a "religion" in legal terms, with the protections that go with the category. She pinpointed the conundrum exposed by the case: the *Charter's* religious protections "only cover a believer's right to express their beliefs to their own satisfaction, regardless of the authenticity of the experience itself. In other words, as long as someone believes he's speaking with a priest, rabbi, or imam, it doesn't violate his Charter protections—even if that religious advisor was actually a police officer."[145] Without oversight of the regulating structure (in this case, the police department), the onus is on the devotee rather than the institution, which keeps the (im)balance of power intact.

The prosecution's position was the question of whether police conduct was sufficiently egregious as to "shock the conscience of the community" and whether societal interests would be served by allowing the prosecution to proceed despite police misconduct. The defense's arguments were multilayered, defending obeah yet describing it in conventionally religious terms. As I wrote in my field notes (taken in the courtroom over the course of the appeal), a member of the defense team stated that the line between acceptable and unacceptable is crossed when one goes outside of the spiritual world into the manifestation of things in the secular world—such as damaging the rights of others or physically harming them. A false spiritual adviser strikes at the very core of religious freedom and is antithetical to what religion is: a genuine, personal connection to the divine or spiritual; a communion with God. Religion, he said, ceases to be legitimate when its activities cause adherents to "do something in the physical world." The arguments went on to point out that obeah has no churches, synagogues, or mosques, and no written liturgy. There is no structure to these religions; they are fluid, less defined. They have no buildings.

Even compared to other of its family resemblance Atlantic religious traditions, obeah seems particularly fluid. For example, as scholars have noted about Santería, although generalizations can be made about its epistemology and its practices, it is difficult to identify a formally organized structure beyond its specialists, notably priests, and their formally recognized levels of expertise. Afro-Cuban religious traditions more generally do not have "hard and fast criteria for identifying a 'community of believers'" or methods to compel consensus among them. Yet these religious traditions, including Santeria, may still experience the efforts of different groups among its practitioners to standardize and codify it.[146] But without even such basics as a hierarchical structure that defines, legitimizes, and ranks priests; an institutionalized canon; and regulated material culture for its rituals, obeah's "magical" nature keeps it nebulous, or its nebulousness keeps it magical—difficult to define and a challenge to apprehend. At the same time, obeah's racial identity seems set: overdetermined and definitive.

Nonetheless, the defense team reaffirmed that it is clear that some religions cannot be deemed better than others. One attorney went on to say that this would never happen in a Catholic church; it is the unstructured, less-defined religions, such as those of Native Americans and Africans, that are the most vulnerable and therefore that most require legal protection because they are most susceptible to "dirty tricks" kinds of ploys. Another of the team argued similarly that when the state encourages people to believe that extraterrestrial beings will have material consequences on their lives, it is an instance of crossing the line—of community conscience.

Sincerity of belief was also a key element in the defense's argument in another sense. In order to make a case for the sanctity of revelations to clergy, it was important to establish that the appellants truly believed in obeah. As one of the attorneys rhetorically asked the court, what reason would the appellant have had to light candles, engage in chanting, and the like, "if he did not believe"?[147] The prosecutor later argued that freedom of religion must involve sincere belief; the appellants had a "tangential" connection to obeah. Moreover, although freedom of religion is a *Charter* right, she argued, religion can be used for negative purposes, which can override its social value. She conceded that all religions have violent histories, but the negative purposes to which any religion may be put to use is not what "we as a society" wish to protect in a religion. Perhaps one of the defense team put it best, although without obvious resolution: "Religious belief is a spectrum, not a threshold."[148] This spectrum was continuously tested throughout the trials. The test rested to a significant extent on racial thinking and the identities that race confers.

The undercover ersatz obeah man identified the evil spirit who allegedly had cursed the suspect's family as being that of the murdered man, a "white boy" who had led the police and the judiciary to the defendants.[149] Given the description of the murdered man's spirit as "white," we can assume he was probably not Afro-Jamaican, which would have been a stretch not likely convincing to the suspects. But from his photograph in the newspaper, at least, the racial identification as "white" is ambiguous. Assigning a historically antagonistic racial identity to the evil spirit and his curse may have been intended to instill even more fear, and thus compliance. On the first day of the appeals case (December 18, 2012), a member of the defense team offered that "Babylon" and "Beast" are ancient biblical terms used by African peoples oppressed by slavery and colonialism, thereby accentuating the linkage between racial identity and the obeah-believing suspects. In fact, it was argued that obeah necessarily involves race, color, and national or ethnic origins.

At the same time that obeah's racial constitution was affirmed, the misuse or abuse of race was pointed out. The defense contended that there were racial undertones throughout the meetings between the undercover ersatz obeah man and the suspects. Not least of these was the racial dichotomy that grouped undercover policeman and suspects together: the ersatz obeah man and the suspects belonged to the same racial group; the ersatz obeah man employed vocabulary and references from colonialism; and, as we have seen, he racialized the murdered man's spirit as "white." In short, the ersatz obeah man worked to establish a camaraderie based on "mutual color and history." He coerced the suspects by way of their religion, remarked another of the defense attorneys; the suspects had "ethnicity-based trust in their spiritual adviser." She added that obeah is associated with a historically disadvantaged group of practitioners who suffer discrimination directed against African communities and "ethnicity-based religions." One of the appellate court judges responded that obeah was targeted because it was the suspects' religion. What if they were white and Catholic?, the judge asked. Would that be religious discrimination? The defense attorney replied that it could very well be.[150] Race was not simply one way of identifying the living; race itself lingered—in this case as its own kind of malevolent (stigmatizing) force. The defense team underscored the racial implications of conviction, especially relevant, perhaps, in a situation where obeah's status as a religion could not be contested. As with the bank robbery–murder case discussed earlier, a built-in premise of this gangland-murder case was that obeah is comparable enough to other, unequivocally legitimate religions to garner legal protection. Obeah itself could not be on trial.

The legal criterion of whether an act or a strategy "shocks the conscience of the community" illustrates the importance of the premise that communities are, through consensus, moral arbiters. The right to privileged, confidential counsel between clergy and their parishioners also conveys this same premise; communities exercise a kind of gestalt force of moral imperatives, where certain rules about the conduct of belief must be met. One might relate this perspective to a kind of "rogue individual," which the undercover ersatz obeah man represents: he broke the bonds of trust and faith held by the religious community of local obeah believers, who included the appellant (former suspect) and his family. The language of "rogue individual" as I have described it did not figure into the legal concept of "dirty trick." Yet someone who manipulates others' religious beliefs for clandestine purposes that are contrary to the knowledge and objectives of the devotee—a "dirty trickster," so to speak—by this logic would be rogue, objectionable in terms of deception, fraud, and malice turned on the client and thus dishonoring their contract. The client may be deceived by the promises and claims of the obeah practitioner, but this is not the same kind of transgression as when malice is directed toward the client—in this case, for example, for the purpose of their entrapment. In this line of thinking, fraudulent obeah does not jeopardize the integrity of the obeah community; in fact, it can keep the community intact by keeping the tradition and its practices alive. Even the "implied" obeah practitioner is the exception that proves the rule;[151] he or she is simply ineffectual in carrying out the client's request rather than potentially destructive of the group. Malice used against the client threatens the community from within. Extending the perspective of the legal defense team, the law confirms the sanctity of community as part of the definition of religion, and it decries the breach of the social cohesion that is the basis of "religion" as opposed to, say, "magic," as Durkheim argued so influentially. For its own good, obeah must not look like magic.

As the defense team argued their appeal, the "rogue" was not obeah but rather the undercover ersatz obeah man. Working under the auspices of the broader law enforcement apparatus, he was in fact the criminal. A pivotal point was that there is no religion that does not have violence in its past or have its members pray to vanquish its enemies. Those are components of all religions, the defense argued, noting Christianity, Judaism, and Islam. The transgression is to go outside the spiritual world and manifest in the secular world—for example, damaging the rights of others or physically harming them. When the religious activity causes the devotee to do something in the physical world, that is when the religion ceases to be legitimate. The appellants, suspects at the time, never asked the undercover ersatz obeah man to do a physical act in the concrete world. It was he, a "fake religious adviser" corrupting the legal system (and by extension the moral community), who was encouraging criminal behavior, not obeah.[152] Ironically, this argument, which defended obeah as much as it did the appellants, rested on the notion of a clear separation between physical and intangible, secular and spiritual worlds, the overlap of which is morally and legally objectionable. In most if not all Atlantic world religious traditions, however, the material world and the incorporeal world, the world of the living and that of the dead, intersect; daily life is a matter of negotiating the intersections. In every defense there must be an alternative culprit. In this case, in order that the culprit not be (a) religion, the culprit must be the untenable use of religion by a breaker of rules, the moral codes which govern existential as well as civil laws. This particular "rogue" took immoral advantage of the racial identity that helped suggest to the authorities an effective methodology: entrapment by (religious) belief.

Despite the defense's insistence that "respect for and tolerance of the rights and practices of religious minorities is one of the hallmarks of an enlightened democracy,"[153] in 2013 the appeal of the case of the ersatz obeah man was also denied. As both of these court cases show, obeah still remains, as Kamari Clarke puts it, "religiously questionable,"[154] even in the face of its legally mandated protections under Canada's *Charter*, which the prosecution teams and appeal court judges asserted they were honoring. If societal standards dictate that "religion," however it may be defined, is unassailable, then its agents must be targeted. Even in enlightened, multicultural democracies, the actions of the individual can be (must be?) sacrificed for the ideals upon which the common good is predicated. The protection of hallowed, Enlightenment-derived expressions of agency (being "free," mobile, rational, self-determined) may require the excision of those who exercise the wrong—that is, nonconformist—kinds of agency. Individuals' noncompliance is a relative act, determined by the normative moral order of a given social formation. Its policing, certainly by the modern era, is through criminalization, in some form, that attempts to prohibit such acts. Ironically, perhaps, the individual is sacrificed for the sake of the Individual; in other words, the wrong kind, the rogue who stands for himself or herself and threatens "community" in the process, must be curtailed in order to preserve the right kind, the compliant, he or she who stands for the whole and thus upholds "community." Perhaps because oppressed peoples have greater investment in going rogue against a system set up for their subordination—and in the West Indies, those oppressed peoples predominantly have been of African and Indian descent—it has been convenient to locate religion's betrayers among these populations. But it was easy to locate the betrayers among these populations by their racial inheritance, a legacy that slanted them in a "criminal" direction from the beginning.

By the time of these two Ontario Court of Appeal cases, the twenty-first century's versions of nation and justice—built on calls, even if rhetorical, for the equal application of that justice across a racially and ethnically diverse nation—mean that racial identity and religious tradition ought, in theory at least, to be disarticulated. In practice their apparent articulation presented a rational basis for law enforcement strategy. Thus, determining where the lines that distinguish "religion" and its "agents" begin and end is not an easy navigation, since the work of religion—its meaning-making, its results—requires human agency. Navigating the ostensible lines between religion and agent is easier when a people (a type) is denied the possession of "religion," or is viewed as possessing inaccurate or insufficient knowledge and understanding of their religion, the latter being tantamount to not having it. This was the case, on a selective basis, for enslaved, indentured, and free persons in the West Indies until well into the twentieth century. Rogue agents can be persecuted, and prosecuted, without fear that this pursuit is committing moral hypocrisy if the morals under critique are themselves tainted. Protecting religion requires protecting the quality of society in which that religion resides. One option is to criminalize the agent practitioners, the rogues whose identities, as we have seen throughout this book, often play a significant role in their criminalization. Another option is to corrupt the process of engagement with religion by making sure that the ostensible clergy, or other sort of rogue practitioner, breaks just enough rules to render religion into something no longer sacred, but secular and unlawful, and somehow still naturally linked to the racial groups who are supposedly drawn to it.

# 5

## THE SPIRIT OF HOSAY TODAY

Like obeah, Hosay is fundamentally a product of diaspora. Its ancestral
origins in Muharram of the Persianate world, its dispersion throughout
the Indian subcontinent, and its presence wherever Indian indentured labor
settled—from South Africa to Fiji to the West Indies—make Hosay a
tradition that travels in space and time and that morphs along the way,
absorbing local beliefs and practices of diverse others. Unlike obeah,
however, Hosay's key features are its visibility as a public exhibition, its
communal organization, and its world religion–recognized template, Islam.
It is intended to be widely seen and heard, it is planned and prepared by
groups consisting of both religious devotees and participants not necessarily
religious, and it is drawn from Islamic doctrine and tradition meant to edify
Muslims and non-Muslims alike. As I suggested in chapter 1, whereas obeah
is the diffuse whole that defies precise or uniform definition, Hosay is a
compact part of a recognizable, larger whole. Hosay thus lends itself to ethnographic inquiry in ways that obeah can elude it. Yet at the same time,
despite its apparently greater internal consistency, Hosay is not the cultural
cornerstone of Caribbean, North American, and North Atlantic lifeworlds
that obeah is. Rather, Hosay's most vibrant existence in the western hemi-
sphere remains in the West Indies, confined, comparatively speaking, to a
calendrical cycle, a formal canon, and, most importantly, constituencies
who place great investment in defining personal and national identity in
part through ancestral traditions that represent precolonial or anticolonial
sentiments. This tells us something about the way we might look at diasporas—as processes that, despite their fluidity, have their own spatial and
temporal boundaries, shaped by the human (and ethereal) agents that constitute them within specific contexts.[1]

## Narratives of Nation, Tools of the State

The gradual transformation of Hosay from an obstreperous commemoration among indentured and other plantation laborers to "a major annual event on [Trinidad's] cultural calendar"[2] reflects a shift from its calculated rejection by colonial authority to its calculated embrace by the postindependence nation-state. What has not changed is the question of "*Whose* culture?," as one Indo-Trinidadian Hosay enthusiast rhetorically asked me in 2012 during our conversation about current government influence on the meaning of Hosay and its symbolization. "Whose culture?" is another way to claim cultural ownership: Who is drawn to Hosay and is most committed to it? These concerns reflect power struggles that historically and today reflect ideas about the heritability of religion—whether through the language of race, as in indenture plantation society, or through the language of culture, as in postindependence multicultural society. As the *Port of Spain Gazette* described Hosay in 1897, it included the *jharoo*, or broom dance; the *banaithe*, twirling long sticks on fire at both ends; *gatka*, the martial art of stick fighting; tassa drumming; and the "fire-pass," walking barefoot through hot coals.[3] In 1897 these practices would largely have been interpreted in racial terms, as evidence of the inherited, customary proclivities of certain human types. With the exception of tassa drumming, these traditions would not survive long into the twentieth century of Hosay commemoration, except as historical example or heritage nostalgia.

In the present day, commentators on Hosay recognize that there "are complex issues surrounding a festival like this," but they still tend to stay within the binary of sacred versus secular, religion versus culture. Although Hosay "arose out of Muslim religion and history," one newspaper article opined, it is not "a religious rite." Yet "the players of Hosay and the religious figures all address the division between devout Muslims and players of Hosay and the bastardization of the festival away from religious roots into fete-like festivities."[4] Here the author is outlining three constituencies: those who view Hosay in religious (Islamic) terms, those who *play* Hosay (perhaps drawing an analogy with "playing" mas' at Carnival) but do so with some sense of purpose or devotion, and those who hybridize and debase (bastardize) Hosay into a fete—the "crowds" of "'revellers' [who] treat the whole event as a major street party."[5] The depictions of Hosay's local color and meaning are based on choices made by writers of public media, of course, who make decisions about what to record and what to highlight.

But they do not create narratives out of whole cloth; they piece together prevailing common sentiments, typically taking them at face value, as other cultural analysts and scholars also do at times. In Clarendon Parish, Jamaica, for example, Hosay's "large, colourful floats" were "pushed along the road as dancing women, enthusiastic drummers and one excited bunch of party-goers participated in the annual Hussay Festival" of 2006.[6] "In the heat of the midday sun," this newspaper reporter continued, women "were dancing wildly to the sounds of drums being beaten by shirtless men." When the reporter asked one of the women what the celebration was about, she replied (in replicated patois, ostensibly for extra verisimilitude), "'Is Hussay, man! Afta it nuh got no meaning,' she said, still gyrating. 'Is just a party. Is what de people round here look forward to,' she added as she wiggled and dipped her way down the road.'" "Taking a sip from a green bottle," a local man who had built one of the tadjahs added another dominant rhetorical theme of Hosay across the West Indies: it "is a thing weh [that] bring everybody together. Black, white, Indian, and Chiney."[7] Despite that, as Guha Shankar writes, "Hussay in Jamaica has been identified as an 'Indian session' ever since it first made its appearance" there,[8] the egalitarianism of democracies that vociferously tolerate their demographic diversity is well symbolized, the local tadjah maker above suggests, by customs that bring every racial and ethnic group together. Another onlooker, a septuagenarian given the last word in this newspaper coverage, commented that "Hussay is di only thing me see bring people together so [like this]." This is an accomplishment that renders the ephemeral ("afta it nuh got no meaning") quality of a party or a procession—or a party-procession— irrelevant because the celebratory principle, the uplifting philosophy of unity and tolerance, is the sustained message of the modern nation-state. An "Indian session" is a racialized custom; an everybody session, so to speak, is not, at least in theory, racialized. But there is a difference between "antiracial" (against racial thinking and bias) and "multiracial," or in more delicate (evasive) terms, "multicultural" (inclusive admission into a space, however that space is defined). In the tolerance of "diversity," racial thinking is reiterated, not abjured. Thus there is compatibility, not contradiction, in an Indian session that brings people together.

The issues that remain debated in Hosay reflect contemporary political and social contexts; street party has replaced plantation protest as Hosay's focal point, with the street party's positive association as a unifier of diversity or negative association as the light-hearted contrast to solemn, deep

feeling. The theme of plantation protest may be revived as a general political rallying cry not to forget past oppression—notably colonial oppression. For example, in 2012 in St. James, Trinidad, on Hosay's final day, when
the tadjahs are set out to sea, a car with a loud speaker stopped by the
grounds where the tadjahs amass and final ritual prayers take place. A
man whom I thought to be an imam exhorted the crowd to "remember
1884, remember 1884! The British massacred the people down in San
Fernando, in Palmiste, in south, remember 1884, my brothers and sisters,
remember 1884! Imam Hussein! The king of the martyrs! The king of the
martyrs! The king of the martyrs!" He then cited the Bible and spoke of
its foretelling of Imam Hussein's being deprived of water at Kerbala, which
is one of the dimensions of his suffering that is commonly recounted in
the telling of the story of the Kerbala battle.

Other evocations of injustice and its resistance take a different kind of
performative turn. In 2009 the Jahaji Massacre Committee was formed as
part of an effort to commemorate what the organizers saw as a neglected
aspect of Hosay's history in Trinidad. The committee put out a call in the
newspaper inviting "all to join in a march" honoring the 125th anniversary
of "the Jahaji Massacre, also known as the Hosay Riots."[9] The march was
not part of the Hosay commemoration itself, nor has it become an annual
event. But on the day of the march, organizers reminded readers of the
importance of this kind of activity, as "many history books have neglected
to mention that dark day."[10] Selecting a moment in the political history of
colonial Trinidad—a moment of consciousness-raising and resistance
against domination—as a hallmark of Hosay suggested a symbolic thrust
to this ritual that, significantly, neither confirmed nor denied its religious
content or meaning. But it was a claim of ownership of the people's history, so to speak, that selected one, albeit momentous, occasion—the Hosay
massacre, or "riot," which unintentionally or not gave a particular slant to
a local tradition typically discussed within the frame of reference of "religion." In a letter to the editor in Trinidad's *Newsday* newspaper, poet and
cultural activist Eintou Springer wanted to "publicly support the call of the
Indian community for the re-enactment of the Hosay Riots [of 1884]. . . .
I feel it is critically important for the Hosay Riots to be staged; and for events
like these to be a strong part of our national consciousness." Referring to
the leaders of this call as "my brothers in culture and love of our landscape," she asserted her "commitment to our shared concepts of value for
our great ancient ethnic ancestries and our struggles for cultural retention

as cultural resistance in this space of our shared nationality. This I consider vital to our survival as a people even as we see the relegation of our culture to the highest bidder in the global marketplace, or shall we say to the modern day auction block. For that is the point to which our Carnival has regressed."[11] In both of these examples, the man exhorting the crowd to "remember 1884!" and the organized protest march commemorating the "Jahaji Massacre," Hosay's symbolic value has little to do with religious provenance but, instead, with the agency of the refusal of colonial and neocolonial domination. Both religion and dissent, diversely defined, are part of Hosay's heritage, and both are interpreted by many long-term devotees as deeply engrained within themselves.

Whether as staged protest, impromptu street party, or reflective ritual undertaking, the idea persists that Hosay is shaped and inspired by deeply engrained, essential qualities. These qualities ultimately are thought to be evidence of inherited proclivities that define human types. An editorial in the *Trinidad Guardian* newspaper from thirty years ago illustrates Hosay's multilayered and complicated messaging. It could have been written today, and is useful to quote at length. The "production of the glittering tadjahs," it begins, "may result from some vestigial zeal of a central few," but in spite or because of this expression of zeal, Hosay's "open and vigorous participation" is matched only by Carnival. Hosay's attractions notably include Trinidad's "rich treasury of artistic skills" and "the opportunity for a 'good lime' [recreational hanging out]." In the (unnamed) author's estimation, it "is fair to say that the event has evolved into a popular spectacle and celebration that holds no religious significance for the large crowd it annually attracts." But for the families who have kept it going over generations, "Hosay is a fervent religious compulsion handed down from their ancestors." The author concludes, quite rightly, that "the 'national' festival of Hosay, then, has different faces, different depths. Where the festival is going no one really knows." In "fun-loving cosmopolitan Trinidad," its "popularity and a multi-ethnic participation" lend it a prominent place on the national calendar. "Will the religious fervour that drives it eventually disintegrate?" the author asks. The answer is that "only time holds the key to this unique and exotic event."[12] This text reiterates familiar themes in contemporary discourse about Hosay: the tension (and, implicitly, untenable relationship) between religion ("religious zeal") and popular culture, the compulsion to express sacred or secular zeal ("religious fervour" versus "fun-loving" liming), and the "multiethnic participation" of a "cosmopolitan" national population. Or, put in another way, identity groups carry urges that may manifest as faith or festivity and that help define groups; religious compulsions such as the abiding continuation of Hosay derive from some intangible vestige of culture that is transmitted as race would be, persistently, through genealogical inheritance. The irresistible call of a good lime brings callaloo (heterogeneous, diverse) Trinidadians together; the irresistible call of ancestral impulses sets them apart, but not outside of the nation's rainbow mosaic.

Until about the mid-twentieth century's inception of the independence era of nation-building and state sovereignty in the West Indies, the principal issue about Hosay was whether or not it was a legitimate form of religion and what racial types its proponents represented. The core debate was tautological: racial type denoted capacity for religious expression (or propensity for unreligious expression), and capacity for religious expression denoted racial type. Commonsense understandings of the day about human groups and the cultures and societies they produced assumed race and religion to be essential, heritable qualities that in unison forged the internal, unseen identities and presented the external, visible identities that defined human groups. Receding from its salience as a major site of destructive social unrest during the indenture plantation era, Hosay emerged, particularly in Trinidad among Indo-Trinidadians (its main practitioners in the region), as an aspect of cultural heritage that merits state-dispensed resources and the national inclusion sought by all religio-racial constituencies, defined as such by the state. In the postindependence period, the principal issue about Hosay became whether or not it is a legitimate form of *Islam* rather than the older debates' broader emphasis on legitimate *religion*, notwithstanding that colonial authorities did on occasion resort to using what they knew about canonical Islam as a template in their critique and disciplining of Hosay. "Religion" has been subsumed under the litmus test of "Islam," rather than, as in the past, "Islam" being subsumed under the litmus test of "religion." The question of what racial types Hosay's proponents represent—who can lay claim to Hosay, and on what basis— remains, however, into the present day. A puzzle emerges, as much about Hosay as about obeah: On the one hand, we have religious traditions whose powers and participation are historically and presently empirically diverse. On the other hand, they are also symbolized, often implicitly, as homogeneous. Yet the advent of multiculturalism as the national narrative in former West Indian colonies, even in its most basic rhetorical mottos—"Out of many, one people" (Jamaica), "One people, one nation, one destiny" (Guyana), "Together we aspire, together we achieve" (Trinidad and Tobago)—made room for additional interpretations within commonsense views about racial groups and "their" religions, and religious traditions and "their" races.

The rhetorical strategy of multicultural nationalism promoted by recent, postindependence governments of Trinidad and Tobago also is shaped and promoted within the context of the country's tourism industry. According to one commentator, it was largely media attention that designated St. James, in the north of Trinidad, as the "home of Hosay."[13] Soon after independence in 1962, "the State [*sic*] began promoting Hosay as a tourist attraction." In 1971, Prime Minister Eric Williams visited St. James's tadjah-building yards to promote the idea of boosting the local economy through approaching Hosay as a commercial venture, emphasizing a "festive atmosphere" that would appeal to tourists.[14] The fruits of national belonging apply to locals, of course, in the form of various rights and privileges. But these fruits also come in other, ostensibly less politicized forms, such as an invitation to others, nonlocals, to enjoy, at least for a moment, all that diversity has to offer—with diversity's typical focus on the arts, cuisines, and traditional customs. In numbers and in regional popularity (including Caribbean diasporas in North America), Hosay cannot compare with other national cultural emblems, such as Carnival. Yet Hosay's reputed and, to some, problematic "carnivalization" is in part an unavoidable consequence of association with the multicultural nation's promotion of its "rainbow" of major events, where its cultural calendar includes religious "festivals" such as Hosay. In the indenture plantation era, the image of Hosay as a festival jeopardized its claims to religious legitimacy, given that the region's festivals (for example, Robert Dirks's "saturnalias"[15]) commonly connoted chaotic unruliness and worldliness, among both elites and subordinates, as opposed to specialized knowledge-based sacrality or rules-imposing orthodoxy. In the current nationalist-modern era, Hosay-as-festival also still generates local debate about its religious legitimacy, but, in addition, there is the question of what kind of character a "cultural" identity lends Hosay.

Multiculturalism and tourism share at least one common element: a self-congratulatory celebration of whatever aspect of diversity is being highlighted. Touted as an event that represents Trinidad's rainbow heritage and is thus worth preserving, Hosay in this context raises the major question, "What kind of culture?", rather than "Whose culture?" In other words, how can mourning, a cornerstone of Hosay, be made a celebratory event? In a conversation I had in 2012 with an Indo-Trinidadian, self-identified Sunni, taxi driver as we headed toward Cedros, southern Trinidad's center of Hosay, he expressed disapproval of Hosay as not legitimate Islam, as having no "proof from the Quran." He heatedly added that "the government supports Hosay, they funding it. But the government [is] only interested in culture and tourism. But what *culture* is it? The Indian community [is] separate, they have Muslim, Hindu, Pentecostal, and so on, so what culture you talking about?" His critique was insightful; when "culture" becomes a tool of the state as nationalist ideology, the equal celebration of *multi*cultures is unlikely to be more than a rhetorical strategy, in practice favoring one culture over others.

Moreover, if the state's emphasis on Hosay is in terms of Trinidadian culture—a traditional art form that represents national unity, harmony, and tolerance—must Hosay's presentation not then also communicate joy? Joy-ousness is difficult to separate from "carnivalization," and it is difficult to claim for national identity those aspects of history that are sorrowful. (In the United States, we see distancing and denial all the time in debates about how to commemorate the past.) The nation and its expressions of unity are to be rejoiced. Group-specific observances may maintain any profile, within legal limits, whether they ratify nationalist ideology or not. Thus, if Hosay remained associated exclusively with a particular sector of the population, the demands of inclusive culture—that is, the multicultural, diverse, het-erogeneous, "callaloo" nation—would not be an issue. In its association with the state's nationalist agendas of democracy and equality, which are realized in part through honoring "difference," inclusivity itself is some-thing to be celebrated, and, further, what is included cannot go against the grain of celebration. It is this celebratory, praising quality that brings, or at least fosters, the "fete," the carnival, to Hosay. When left to their own de-vices, when "everybody do it as their own," as Derek, a Hosay participant, told me in 2018, one can accommodate "both joy and sorrow in the cele-bration," as another long-time tadjah builder told me in Trinidad twenty-nine years earlier. The joy, he explained to me, is that "Islam survived; the sorrow is that Hussein died such a death." The relentless assertion of achievement through a particularly orchestrated tolerance can eclipse ideas or practices that seem anomalous or contradictory to its agenda. Moder-nity, democracy, and equality are the symbols and goals of multiculturalism as a nation-defining strategy of the state. As one journalist put it, "There are many more cultural anomalies in T&T [Trinidad and Tobago] that are dying out and being replaced by more modern concerns, just like Hosay."[16] But modernity, democracy, and equality are not open-ended; they have prescriptions for meeting those goals that can, and often do, undermine their own claims of an all-inclusive vision. Although Jameel Bisnath, then–general secretary of the St. James/Cocorite Hosay Association, was not speaking directly about the ironies and limitations of multiculturalism as a national credo and state project, his comment about the precariousness of annual government funding for Hosay is apt. He said that his association does not "depend on the Government to bring out Hosay because this is a religious thing. We spend our money to do our thing."[17] The popular cultural arts may be an expedient organ of state control, orchestrated as they are through government ministries, including tourism, but what many think of as a "religious thing" (variously defined) may have greater potential for self-expression when "everybody do it as their own." Hosay's exterior character is its art, for all in the public arena to see, and be inspired by. And as countless Hosay participants have long said, "You can't control the public" in terms of guarding the solemnity and religiosity of the commemoration. But the ways that people interpret Hosay's provenance and its significance are viewed by many to come out of personal orientation, and a motivation that in large part is inherited generationally. These aspects require nothing more than individual imagination and cooperation among community peers.

Coming to the fore in the message of multiculturalism are questions about what it means in the constructions of racial identity and, as importantly, racial harmony (the ideological, if aspirational, root of multiculturalism), questions about the provenience of Islam, and what that might mean for the definition of groups. The "cultures" of "ethnic groups" superseded "race" as the governing discourse about national belonging (as "group" has done vis-à-vis "type"). Multiculturalism discourages the language of race—being *racial*—which is an epistemic habit of colonialism, its historical legacy being rac*ism*. However, some of those epistemic habits of racial thinking were only submerged, made into covert references in public discourse rather than being abandoned as the assumed, inherited substratum of typological difference. Of course, overt reference to race in public discourse has another important signifier: the political critique of racism, whose racial thinking is counterhegemonic—a counter-epistemic habit, one might say. This is certainly the case, among a number of examples, in the Caribbean (and other) regions' Black Power movements. Yet however the concept of race is envisioned, valued, and deployed, in the broad West Indian popular imagination, race is never entirely disengaged from religion, nor are either fully removed from the perspective of heritability.

The still-familiar if now submerged commonsense, default explanation among British colonial authorities was that Afro-Caribbeans and rogue individual coolies—in the plantation context, in certain ways comparably black—originally brought religion-nullifying festivity to Hosay/Muharram. This narrative clung on into the postindependence era, a standard if certainly not always ratified accusation. The appearance and meaning of Hosay has transformed over time through its diverse participants (which includes sideline observers) and the changing historical and political contexts in which Hosay occurs. To maintain the logic of race across space and time is to reiterate Euro-colonial epistemology's logic of racial categorization and hierarchy, even in the ideological mission of the multicultural rainbow. Multiculturalism also rests on the premise of distinct groups (types) bounded by discernable and persistent markers, which are passed down from generation to generation. It is important to call attention to these shadows of Euro-colonial thought, which quietly sustain the idea that racialized carriers at best misconstrue Hosay and at worst commit infractions against it, or that, conversely, a "callaloo" spectrum confirms membership in the society and protects the right of (certain, appropriate) self-expression. But it is equally if not more important to take a step back and look more broadly at the ideological project that the arts can become when they are assigned a particular agenda—such as placing them under the rubric of "arts" in the first place. Hosay is located within an ideological agenda that supports the promise that diversity should be celebrated, not feared. This has had significant consequences for the ways that commonsense, quotidian ideas about race and religion are conscripted into the meaning of Hosay and the identities of its supporters.

### Hosay's Islamic Provenances

In the conventional Caribbean narrative, contemporary Indo-Caribbean Muslims predominantly are born Muslims. There is, of course, the possibility of conversion, which does occur, but the common image is one of an uninterrupted genealogical history of Islam. Many would say that Indo-Caribbean Islam has a "traditional," culturally inflected early history in the region, which may encourage noncanonical or "innovative" practices like Hosay. But it is an inheritance that sustains their Muslim identity claims—even in the face of challenges to those claims, including from other Muslims. Contemporary Afro-Caribbean Muslims may consider themselves "returnees" to Islam. But their historically interrupted and thus not as easily traceable genealogy, compounded by the vastly greater numbers of Afro-Caribbeans who follow other religious traditions, helps key rituals in Islam, such as Hosay, to remain "Indian," even while Hosay also can represent governments' rhetorical strategy of Trinidad and Tobago's multicultural nationalism's multicultural/multiethnic "rainbow," with its Muslim, Hindu, and Christian, Indo-Trinidadian and Afro-Trinidadian participants. These distinctions connote racial divisions, just as the racial divisions suggest different religions, ones that typically (although not necessarily) correspond with a particular race. The significant historical as well as contemporary participation of Hindus in Hosay certainly also helps maintain its association as "Indian"—that is, not exclusively "Muslim." The position espoused by some devotees that Hosay is not about religion at all may have the similar effect of racializing Hosay—"Indian" becomes the racial representative, so to speak, in Trinidad's rainbow of multiples. These multiples are not primarily couched in terms of religious participation but rather in terms of "cultural" or "ethnic" (cautious codes for "racial") constituencies. The emphasis on Hosay's various diversities does not deracinate it; its participating religious traditions always carry connotations of racial belonging, and its participating "ethnic" groups always carry connotations of religious belonging. This carrying is also a carrying *over*, channeled through the heritability of racial and religious identities. But the debated Muslim provenance of Hosay is more nuanced; these contentions are not only an argument about what is legitimate religion or authentic Islam. They also illustrate the relationship between contested meanings of Hosay and the effort to establish one's identity in a particularly configured and a particularly fraught world.

During several of my ethnographic research trips to Trinidad over the years, I have had numerous conversations with the "pumpkin vine kin" (extended family) and community members who yearly build tadjahs and participate in the other rites connected to Hosay. My visits to the remaining locales in Trinidad where Hosay is observed today—the "yards" in St. James and the "camps" in Cedros (sites of tadjah design and construction, and ritual preparation)—began in 1988; my most recent visit was in 2018. I have had the privilege of talking to some of the same people over a quarter of a century, seeing their children grow up and dedicate themselves in turn to what they view as a family tradition, and of noting the vicissitudes of broader economic and political contexts and their impact on people's commitment to what they see as their art, their cooperative labor, their expression of spirituality, and their insistent self-realization. Our exchanges allow deeper probing under the surface of Hosay's debates about whether or not it is "religion," whether or not it is "Islam," and whether it represents the multiculturalism of Trinidad's "rainbow" society (in the form of a fete or otherwise). A more complex story emerges, one that raises questions about these very organizing principles—"religion," "Islam," "multicultural"—that categorize and interpret Hosay today.

In Trinidad the basic objections to Hosay have been that it is sacrilege to undertake Hosay the wrong way (that is, party rather than piety), and that it is sacrilege to hold Hosay altogether, that it is un-Islamic. The former position is espoused by Hosay's devotees; the latter position is espoused by certain Muslim constituencies, often characterized by scholars and local media as "orthodox" or, at times, as "Sunni." The characterization of Hosay by both its devotees and its detractors as a specifically Shi'a practice is largely a relatively recent phenomenon. The issue of Hosay's Shi'a identity has been less clearly delineated in contemporary as well as historical times. In their published field notes from 1960s Trinidad, for example, Colin and Gillian Clarke record information they were given by their interlocutors. "There are some Shia followers here [in the town of San Fernando], but they cannot reveal themselves."[18] The Clarkes go on to say, "Orthodox Sunni Muslims do not recognize Hosay. . . . It is an annual fete, introduced by Shias when they came from India. Now all *tadjah*-makers are Sunni, and no one in Trinidad will admit to being Shia."[19] They do not elaborate on these claims, so it cannot be certain what their interlocutors meant. But what can be inferred is that at least from some perspectives, Shi'a identity was at the time, as in the past and more current present, contested or denied as well as acknowledged.

As I have discussed in previous chapters, part of the reason for this ambiguity is that knowing exactly who among the indentured immigrants and their progeny were Shi'a is difficult, if not impossible, to determine. Moreover, Hosay devotees are largely not Muslim, which makes these identity stakes perhaps less crucial. As Roop, a self-defined "Hindu christened in the Catholic Church," with whom I spoke in 2012 about his fifty years of involvement in Hosay, told me, "In our [yard] we have Catholics, Hindus,

Muslims, Christians. Is only now the Shi'a issue is coming up; we go by tradition. In any case," he said with a puzzled shrug, "the Shi'a community here is so small." He added, "In this yard, you might find only *one* Muslim. . . . And the one Muslim may not be a *proper* Muslim, in any case." Twenty-three years earlier, in that same yard, another man, an Indo-Trinidadian Muslim octogenarian, Abdul, speculated that "people feel Shi'ite is sort of out of the way, they are only in the country areas. Maybe in India they were Shi'ite, but here maybe they throw it off. Here they celebrate the festival [Hosay] because it is a religious heritage. It has nothing to do with Shi'ite now."

The debate about the Shi'a aspects or roots of Hosay is ultimately insoluble. Scholars and others who affirm this identity for Hosay often are making an effort to limn origins and thus historicize diasporas in particular ways. This is often an interesting agenda but can obfuscate the ways that symbols and semantics are produced from lived experience and the exigent factors that shape that experience. "Shi'a," I am suggesting with respect to Hosay, is much larger than a precise, traceable school of religious thought. Other narratives allow Hosay's genealogical inheritance to remain in place but shorn of the conventional and reductive either/or contentions about Islam per se—its authenticity, its appropriations.

This Shi'a reference point has increased over the years as devotees seek to further legitimate and protect it, and as scholars seek to explain it as a tradition ensconced within Islam whose Hindu aspects do not undermine its Islamic provenance. The indenture plantation era was a time of colonial authority's effort to profile Hosay as non-Islamic and therefore not "religion" that could enjoy the protections of imperial modernity and largesse. Among other ostensible shortcomings were the dubious influences of Hosay's majority Hindu practitioners. Today the objection to Hindu influence—or as Imam Amin, an Afro-Caribbean imam who leads the rites of Hosay, put it to me during my last visit in 2018, "the Ganesh ethic"—is greatly diminished. For one thing, for countries interested in their international image, cultural, religious, and ethnic (racial) combinations of populations living together harmoniously are useful symbols of a nation-state's embrace of diversity and thus its proof of modernity: Hindus, Muslims, Christians, and people from other religious traditions interacting together peacefully and creatively holds great symbolic capital for Trinidad. On the ground there is the social fact of generations of pumpkin vine kin families created by intermarriages between Hindus and Muslims.[20] These wide-ranging consanguineal and affinal "vines" also generate loyalties that are not kinship-based but that also sustain the hybrid quality of Hosay, and thus Hosay's pliable meanings and significance—its " sliding signifier"-like symbolization. For example, Janee, an octogenarian acquaintance of mine, a woman who has been involved with Hosay her entire life, was, as I learned in 2012, "born in Hindu" and "raised a Catholic." For the last three days of Hosay each year, she invites an imam (an Indo-Trinidadian) to her home to conduct what she calls a "puja": "make niaj [pray] over the melida [sweets]" and other food, including the chicken he had "halal'd" that morning. This particular imam happens also to openly disapprove of Hosay, calling it "un-Islamic." His explanation for continuing to conduct these rites for this devotee and her family is that he has been doing it for them "for years and years," that it is part of his long-term relationship with them. Here, in sum, is an imam who frowns on Hosay, yet conducts Hosay-related prayer sessions for a lifelong devotee who was "born in Hindu" and raised Catholic, who refers to these prayer sessions as "pujas," and who hosts them in a living room decorated with Hindu murtis, while those present hold their hands up to pray in the Muslim prayer gesture (upturned palms, elbows bent, arms up). Other sorts of dedication, to friends and to family—and to what becomes a more generalized conceptualization of religion—supersede concerns about identity boundaries that accept or reject Hosay as both customary practice and as social institution.

In 1989 I was in a Hosay yard and asked one of the men there, an Indo-Trinidadian Muslim, why he thought non-Muslims get involved in Hosay. He explained, "They realize the religious aspect of it all, they realize it is something good. And due to their friendship with the Muslims, they will participate. The majority of Hindus and Christians participating know the story [of Hosay] so they know it is a religious tradition, so it is something good." In other words, Hosay necessarily includes various participants, and it ultimately constitutes religion; religion belongs to everyone, which it should because in general religion is something that enhances one's life. Theorizing from a different but equally unperturbed perspective, Imam Amin explained to me that "in order to exist, Hosay acquired some aspects of Hinduism. It's a balance between Hinduism and Islam. Hosay is shrouded in some aspects of Hinduism in order to survive in India." Symbolizing the contemporary "rainbow" nation, forming families and households in plantations, towns, and villages without great heed to religious differences, working with a generic concept of religion that is universally beneficial, and interpreting what amounts to "creolization" (although the imam did not use this word) in terms of cultural transformation and insistent survival has contributed to today's diminished critique of Hosay's relationship with Hinduism.

## Making Art: Fellowship and the Moral Good

The expansive kinds of meaning and significance that Hosay's practitioners attribute to it challenge more reductive boundary-maintenance approaches that focus on "religion" versus "culture" and other binaries that have served as Hosay's explanatory frameworks. I am not arguing that these sorts of dualisms should be entirely discounted, only that we bear in mind that commonsense knowledge is not composed of what everybody thinks, but of certain ways of knowing that predominate. One way that predominance works is when the plethora of points of view that are in discursive play at any given moment are congealed (reduced) into what are ostensibly the most salient few. One way that predominance can be nuanced (or challenged) is to think about the connections between, for example, religion and culture, rather than their seemingly built-in opposition as dimensions of everyday life. As I have observed elsewhere, even the most entrenched rhetorical strategies about the purity and distinctiveness of identities tend to be far more intersected in lived experience.[21]

These intersections derive from what people see as their personal, individual commitments to a greater moral good, which they articulate in religious terms that are piecemeal and overlapping. These kinds of articulations transcend the strict, doctrine-based limits that define and segregate the categorical boundaries that create exclusive religious and other "isms," and also illustrate the work of agency as people decide for themselves—albeit within the contours of abiding epistemic principles—what comprises religious belief, commitment, and intentions. Thus we are able to see "religion" as a kind of summarizing symbol; a more capacious, more fluid category incorporating not only multiple religious dimensions but also varied sorts of mundane and ostensibly nonreligious influences and experiences. In the process, some hegemonic categories, such as religion, are diminished in their policing power, and others, such as race, remain resonant.

During a long conversation I had in 2018 with Imam Amin about his deep dedication to Hosay, he explained that "Imam Hussein [martyred grandson of the Prophet Mohammed] did not stand for any 'ism.'" His examples of the danger of "isms" were ISIS and Boko Haram, which he said are "not conscious Islamic movements" but are "only used to confuse young men." He continued: "Imam Hussein stands only for the truth. Followers of Imam Hussein cannot stand for any 'ism'; we have to conscientiously keep the pristine truth going. This is the road of truth." A bit later in our conversation he explained, "The tadjah only represents Hassan and Hussein. Itself, it's not ultimately important. The physical aspect is not as important as the spiritual aspect. The soul does not die, it lives with us here. The attitude should be toward spirituality more than the physical. The [tadjah's] paper is going to finish [biodegrade]. But the spiritual realm is remembered." That said, he continued that "if you cannot see Imam Hussein in the beauty of the tadjah, you have lost the plot." I asked him to clarify for me what the plot was. "You have gone into your personal mental construct of desires of what *you* want, not the desires of Imam Hussein, which is to establish truth in everything that you do. Building a tadjah is about truth, the Creator's truth." We might characterize his perspective as evoking individuality without selfishness.

This idea of a higher calling that allows freedom from the imposed barriers of dogma were expressed to me in a number of ways. I hesitate to use the word "spiritual" in place of "religion," because over the decades that I have been talking with people in Trinidad about Hosay, this word does not typically come up. But it is not uncommon for people to circumvent the freighted commands and expectations of "religion" by referring to Hosay as a "memorial" or a "remembrance." Over the decades I have heard many echoes of the remark made several years ago by a Hosay devotee to a newspaper reporter: "Hosay is not necessarily a religious festival but is a memorial for the grandsons of Prophet Mohammed."[22] Some make the contrast between "religion" and a "memorial" unequivocally. One well-known Hosay camp leader, Arvind, told me during my last visit in 2018 that his maternal great-grandmother was a Muslim, though the rest of his family line is Hindu. He was firm in his position: "Hosay is not about religion; it is a *memorial*. I love it because whether it right or it wrong, you must respect a person who stood up for what he *believes* in. Imam Hussein died for what he believed in. Hosay memorializes that kind of commitment and standing up for what you believe in so much you are willing to die for it. Hosay is not a religious thing. In the holy Quran, is there any mention of Hussein? You must do the *research* to know [if it] is religion. The fact that it's Muslim prayers that are made for Hosay is connected to Hosay's history of battle and sacrifice."

"It's like you still remember the good guy," Derek said during this same visit. "Hassan and Hussein were the good people, and they were the grandsons of the Prophet Mohammed. Even my grandmother on my mother's side, she would make promises [during the ten days of Ashura]. She had land and cattle. She said [pledged] she will do it for a couple of years to give thanks for what she had and also for her grandson's health. Hosay is a remembrance; everybody do it as their own." He had begun by telling me that he does not think of Hosay as "a 'tradition,' because we change, we improvise, like our materials and tools." In addition to describing Hosay as a "memorial," people frequently made reference to the act of "making promises" during Ashura, or to Hussein, or to the tadjahs directly. One tadjah-builder, a man in his sixties, told me in 2012 that his grandparents had a "tradition of making promises to get a boy child, get good health, and so I carry on their tradition with the Hosay. Big Hosay night is when we make our promises." Speaking the language of tolerance and inclusiveness, a key Muslim family member of a Hosay yard noted to me in 1989 that "people make a promise to do something, ask Allah for something, or the God of their choice." "Not every man in a topi is a Muslim," he said. "It's worn as a mark of respect." He added that every evening he reminds the gathering at the yard that their "imam says if you don't understand Arabic or are not Muslim, pray in your own way."

These practicalities of devotion are means to loftier ends and, as the thinking goes, should not be confused with the rogue individualism that seeks immediate gratification of self-centered objectives, such as that purportedly of obeah, or magic in general. Being able to see Imam Hussein and truth in the beauty of the tadjah, for example, allows truth and beauty to be the definitive qualities of such allegedly borderline superstitious practices as making promises in order to have requests granted, or revering the tadjahs as objects by tossing flowers, coins, and perfume at them in procession, or by praying to Hassan and Hussein through them. But truth and beauty in Hosay also comes in what may seem more mundane acts. A "semi-retired," as he put it, Hindu tadjah builder who works with two Hosay camps told me with real emotion in 2018 that he feels his "gift to these younger generations is to show them about the beauty of this [Hosay] and to teach them about it, with all the skills they learn [in the process], like carpentry, drafting, masonry. And their gift to me is to show me what they can do. I feel good to pass this [knowledge] along." This "good" feeling is not casual; it has to do with a person's gratification at being recognized as having something valuable to contribute that has immediate and long-term benefits. And in the service of beauty, that contribution is all the more uplifting, in both the sense of preparing one's livelihood and the enrichment of intangible reward.

Many people comment on the artistry involved in designing and constructing the tadjahs: the pleasure, skill, mental absorption, purposefulness, and joint efforts that are both required and sought. Derek told me during this same visit that he was a designer of Carnival mas' bands as well as of tadjahs. He looks forward to "the public's enjoyment of Hosay," who "look for the designs of the tadjahs and compare them." He noted with some resignation that "the less funds you have, the more simple your design must be." Part of his own satisfaction derives from the local community's participation in the "artistic side of Hosay, by commenting and judging the tadjahs. They congratulate you or suggest changes, give you a thumbs up and things like that." Prayer is also part of his art; prayer "shows you what you can do and what you can't do" artistically. "I gain experience from it, trials and errors of creativity. Who could draw, who could design, who could decorate [will do so]. You foresee what you have in your brain before it's on paper. You visualize and make it a reality. When Muharram time is coming up, you get dreams: you have to do this, you have to do that— building, preparations, all that." Hosay is the "cooperative teamwork of an art project [with] a religious aspect—everybody come together. . . . You try to be spiritual." Based on our conversation, I asked Derek about the connections he made between art and religion associated with Hosay. He replied, "You must be in the religious part to be in the artistic part, to get through the artistic part. The meaning of the art comes from the religion. The art shows the religious story. And on the street the public asks you plenty questions and you have to be able to answer them. You must have the knowledge, or you can ask the imam if you can't answer on the spur [of the moment]. These boys [who work on the tadjahs] are voluntary. If you do good, you shall be good. You do good to be good." I asked him what he thinks keeps Hosay alive, especially given what I had heard, including from him, about the current financial and labor shortages that make it a challenge to keep it going. In his opinion, what keeps Hosay alive is "togetherness with the villagers," and that "all prayer is good." In a reverie about Hosay, my elderly friend Pearl, a lifelong Hindu devotee of Hosay, said to me in 2012 with real joy, "*That* is the most amazing thing. *All* the people is united, everybody, Hindu, Muslim, Christian. All the people is united for Hosay." Toward the end of my conversation with Derek I said that I was hearing five themes from what he had been telling me: art, religion, community, teamwork, and knowledge possession. I asked him if he agreed with these themes and, if so, how he might rank them in order of importance. "You start with teamwork," he replied, "then everybody come together with all their knowledge, [next] the priest do the prayers, then comes the designs, and then the community support." In his estimation, the teamwork, the fellowship of Hosay, was foremost in its rewards; religion comes in the form of ritual expertise. As it is for so many others, Hosay is for him a multilayered project, bigger than simply its ritual undertaking or its mission to memorialize, where the difference between sacred and worldly are in practice indistinct.

Of course ritual and memorialization are undeniably important aspects of Hosay. But they are only a part of what Hosay means on the ground. Many factors contribute to the multilayered project that is Hosay. However, an aspiration to engage a moral good (fulfill it, benefit from it) motivates many, perhaps most participants. This moral good exceeds this-worldly, quotidian affairs, but at the same time the worldly and quotidian lead to that good. There is beauty and truth in protraction, as there is in pedagogy and in honoring "the good people," whether Hassan and Hussein or one's grandparents. Multiple, simultaneous infusions inform this aspiration to engage a moral good, which ought not to be condensed into and metonymized as "ritual" and "memorial." Making promises, giving thanks, honoring one's forebears, drawing from what is most familiar, and contributing to the welfare and longevity of one's community are inseparable, equal channels toward this end. These channels are kept in motion over time as particular practices. But they are also kept in motion over time as embodied forces. A constant refrain one hears from those dedicated to Hosay is that "it is in our blood." This conviction is also held by those who have no relationship to Hosay. My friend Kamala, who has lived in Trinidad her entire life and had never witnessed Hosay firsthand, recently told me a story about a Hindu family from Cedros who had moved to another locale after a number of years. "The teenage son," she recounted, "always ran back down to Cedros for Hosay every year. His family was not in it, but he had to go; it was in his blood. His grandfather [had] remained in Cedros; he played the tassa [drum] during Hosay." The mother was vexed with her son, but my friend counseled her to "leave him [alone]; it's in his blood. When you grow up in something, it becomes part of you." Kamala was talking about enculturation, the process through which we learn and assimilate (and question) the norms, beliefs, and practices of the culture and society in which we grow up. These norms, beliefs, and practices are passed down generationally. Like most other people, she would be able to identify specific features of culture that are learned and transmitted. But she, like others, also materializes the habits or compulsions that make people unable to resist the call, the inexorable appeal of participation in something we hold dear, as "part of you," in the blood.

## The Spirit in the Blood

The blood is that of the ancestral generations (grandparents, great-grandparents), and, as Imam Amin put it, "Blood is a spirit," the "spirit of truth" through which Hosay lives on. It would be most unlikely that anyone would expressly connect blood or spirit with a specific racial identity, in terms of Hosay's provenance or otherwise. But race finds its way into people's understandings of their identities, imagined through the necessarily politicized reference points of group history, defense of heritage, and, in at least one case that I discuss below, scientific models of genetics and heredity—all of which lend credence to ideas about heritability, racial thinking's common sense, even if not invoking "race" directly.

Indo-Caribbeans and Afro-Caribbeans share a plantation heritage. Although they certainly understand the differences between enslavement and indenture, it is not unusual for people, including Trinidadians, to draw analogies between these two pasts, particularly in terms of the working and living conditions endured by coerced laborers. The plantation is a historical icon whose slaves and coolies were the backbone of these respective systems of production. Among Indo-Caribbean people, the plantation looms large as a heritage symbol, recent enough to remain fresh in family genealogies, if no longer in the firsthand memories of living people. In my own experience over the decades with Indo-Trinidadians in Trinidad and in the diaspora, the plantation frequently comes up in conversation. More times than is anomalous or idiosyncratic, my interlocutors have used the term "slaves" or "indentured slaves" to refer to their forebears. Derek saw involvement with Hosay as the conduit through which this flow, what is in the blood, was passed down, through his great-grandfather's, grandfather's, and father's abiding commitment. "On the estates [indenture plantations]," he explained, "all the slaves used to come together to do it [Hosay]. They did it on the estates so that everybody could come together." Here, Hosay is a means of unity and of joy, sustained for well over a century. In this scenario, like so many others that see Hosay "in the blood," it is not solely the continuation of the practice of Hosay—its specialized knowledge of art, craft, and ritual—although Hosay's practice certainly includes these. It is also something sublime, beyond words, made more palpable when translated, so to speak, into sensation: the desire to be worthy, to honor and show gratitude, to have something to offer others that has value. "It was real emotional," Derek commented about his late father's striving to "be spiritual" when singing *marsiyahs*, Muharram's songs of mourning about the martyred brothers. Blood, at least as a metaphor, contains, preserves, and transmits into feelings what is otherwise not seen; feelings can be envisaged through one's consciousness of their effects and through the practices they drive. Thus the immaterial is made material, but it is a kind of materiality that is not precisely tangible because blood is both an empirical, viscous substance that one can hold in one's hand, and it is something much more, which cannot be held but can be felt.

The shared heritage of the indenture plantation also produces rhetorical strategies that people can deploy in defense of Hosay against its critics. These rebuttals are also couched in terms of a group's identity, one that challenges religion with (what amounts to) race. This ostensibly nonreligious identity is the category "Indian," which can be marshaled to override or negate boundaries between "Muslim" and "Hindu." Indicating the diyas—teacup-shaped clay, oil-burning (or wax-burning) lamps that are lit and used as part of the ritual accoutrements—a member of a Hosay yard pointed out to me during one of my visits to the yards in 1989 that "diyas aren't Hindu; they're *Indian*, from India." He was Indo-Trinidadian, from a Muslim family who were longtime builders and marchers of tadjahs. It was apparently not important for him to assert the Islamic provenance of Hosay as much as it was to claim it for "Indians," whose religion in this context was irrelevant. His (unspoken) key interlocutors were Trinidadian Muslim critics of Hosay, who, as we have seen, charge that Hosay is not Islamic in part because it has been inscribed with Hindu tradition and interpretation. But all Muslims from the subcontinent would be considered "Indian"; in principle, "Indian" stretches to cover everyone in Trinidad from that part of the world. In Trinidad's postindependence political parsing of its multicultural populations, "Indian" is the racial correlate of "African." According to this man's logic, one can stay legitimately Muslim and be Indian at the same time—both Hindus and Muslims left the subcontinent for indenture plantations. The only other contrast at the same level of inclusion is "African"; "Hindu" and "Muslim" are subsets or kinds of "Indian." In a different context, notably in certain portraits of national unity, the most-encompassing identity, "Trinidadian," might subsume "Indian" and "African" (although maintaining their respective racial distinctiveness rather than blending them together). But vis-à-vis Hosay and the competition for both its ownership and its survival, race, as "Indian," provides a common ground for those claims and struggles.

Disentangling Hosay from "religion" subjects it to the logic of racialization. This logic may be expressed in terms of a lexicon of ethnicity or of color, but racial identity remains the subtext. As Arvind asserted, "The tadjah is not built by Muslims or Hindus but by *Indians*. There is a melting pot! The animosity between Hindus and Muslims did not exist during indentureship. I believe when the tadjah is immersed in the ocean, [it] is a Hindu thing. But it didn't start out as a Hindu thing." In his view, what (rightly) divests Hosay from being thought of as "religion" is to identify it as "Indian." The melting pot renders Hindu-Muslim distinctions irrelevant when it comes to Hosay, but identifying what kind of *thing* it is still requires a label; "Indian" groups them together, indicating shared ancestry while minimizing religious differences. The work of the melting pot can be imagined in other ways, with a similar implicit message. For example, in an article written for Trinidad's *Express* newspaper in 1993, Kim Johnson observed about Hosay that today "most of the crowd in St. James would be hard pressed to distinguish Hindu from Muslim, far less Shi'ite from Sunni Islam. People of all ages and races mingled—rum-faced old men, burly youths in baggy jeans, girls in short shorts or body suits, middle-aged men [with] their daughters on their shoulders, tourists who spoke in Spanish. The night turned everyone dark brown except the foreign 'anthropologists.'"[23] In this free-for-all, religion becomes indistinct and color terminology evoking race comes to the fore. All of this mingling of heterogeneity congeals into one "dark brown" type, except, curiously, the "foreign anthropologists," who, perhaps being outsiders even more than the Spanish-speaking tourists, are immune to the unity of sameness that Hosay affords. Yet this sameness is predicated on a shared color term associated with racial categories.

In another of my conversations in 2012, Breds, an elderly Hosay aficionado, took a different tack about Hindu influence while still invoking his Indian essence. He had voluntarily brought up the criticism levied by other

Muslims about Hosay. His tone was adamant when he said, "I'm no scholar but I *read*. The Muslims only occupy India for a short space of time. All our Muslim ancestors were originally Hindu." Addressing Muslim critics of Hosay in absentia, he continued, "If you're not here, don't give your mouth liberty to say wrong things about how [there] is drinkin', winin'.[24] I is a *Indian!* Why the Sunni doing niaj?" he asked rhetorically.[25] "Is same thing, same idea." That is, niaj is a practice that is not found in the Quran or the Hadith, he contends, and thus is not a strict observance in Islamic doctrine. So, he argues, do not charge us with or blame us for any inappropriate, objectionable behavior during the Hosay period because not only are we unable to control the public (commonly said by Hosay's devotees), but you self-ascribed authentic, legitimate Muslims also have aspects of your worship that are subject to the same kind of criticism. He gave me another example of what he saw as a stark double standard: "You go to Mecca and you want to kiss the Kaba. But they say we worship the tadjah. You're making dua [praying] for all those sick and passed away. Just so we are making dua for ten days [of Ashura], all the time for him [Hussein]." Breds's logic was clear: there is a double standard operative, and all people have analogous practices in common. His insistence that he is an *Indian*, interjected in the midst of his analysis, conveys the message that his Indian identity confers legitimate claims to Hosay and is ingrained and strong enough to withstand sideline misbehavior.

None of the people who used "Indian" as an identifying rubric for Hosay said they are "Indo-Trinidadian." Locals do not use this term much, and they understand this categorizing of population to be a heuristic device connected to the national image, state distribution of resources, and the postindependence organization of universal suffrage. (It is arguably also an influence of Trinidad's North American diaspora.) To be "Indian" in this context draws from the heritability of race, traced from India and its original Hindu ancestors, through the diaspora, landing in the Caribbean having preserved the essential, ancestral characteristics that give credence to identity claims. Although Breds did not use the word "blood" in our conversation, an implicit notion of essence is there. Essence is transmitted through cultural knowledge (of customs, of language, etc.), but essence is also inherited from birth, passed down from original subcontinental Hindus who later became Muslims but still remained "Indian." This man did not outline what he thought the common core might be, but in raising the problem of double standards and similarities he was implying the work of an engrained characteristic or set of characteristics that allow "Indian" to transcend time and space.

That same night, in a different yard, a middle-aged Indo-Trinidadian man was taking a break from working on that yard's tadjah. We sat on folding chairs outside the imambara and discussed the provenance and thus, implicitly, the legitimacy of Hosay.[26] The second rhetorical question I heard that night was posed when he asked, "The *slave* didn't bring Hosay? How you know they did not, how you know that?" He offered some evidence. "They [African Muslims] talk about the Prophet. The Africans are also Muslim." There is no historical evidence of which I am aware that Hosay was observed in the Caribbean prior to Indian indenture. But I think the point he was making is an important one. I interpret his suggestion about Hosay being traced back to African Muslims' presence in the Caribbean as his way to establish Hosay more firmly as a legitimately *Muslim* practice, since Trinidadians are aware that early Africans to the region included Muslims. It was likely also to establish Hosay more firmly as something indubitably belonging to Trinidad and to the Caribbean. This was another kind of racializing of Hosay. In his historiography, African Muslims transported Hosay to the region. But this channel does not make Hosay an African, or black, commemoration; it solidifies Hosay's Muslim identity. Rather than religion ultimately verifying race, as in the previous examples, here race is in service of religion. Religion, in the form of Hosay, is the stable essence that, embodied in more than one racial group, affirms Islamic foundations in the face of all-too-familiar criticisms of inadequate religious authenticity. In the Caribbean, the roots of Islam are African (and Iberian), but for this interlocutor, the relevance is only to establish Hosay's original devotees, Africans, thus making the incursions of Hinduism by way of indentured Indians insignificant.

My final example of the ways that current ideas about race and religion form the provenance and thus the legitimacy of Hosay is of someone whom we have already met: Imam Amin, whose journey into devotion to Hosay took another kind of path, one that began with his growing political consciousness about racial hierarchies and developed into his own scientific model of genetics and heredity, which he combines with his understandings of the spirit world. In his theorizing, blood becomes yet another kind of draw toward Hosay.

Born into a Roman Catholic home, Imam Amin as a young boy was an acolyte in the Roman Catholic Church in his West Indies hometown. One day during Mass, he was particularly struck by the priest's intonation of this message to the congregation: "The pews you sit on are not your own." Imam Amin said that even at that age he reflected on the political implications of this lesson: "It come like [was akin to] slavery. For 450 years we couldn't go into a church. So now we are in there but even the pews, that piece of wood, is not ours? How do you tell that to my mother and grandmother sitting on those pews? My father supported me in this [critique], but he said I was on my own. So I tried to find the unity of Godhead." I asked him what he meant by "Godhead." He explained that it is "establishing intrinsically who this being is. It's not Jesus because he prays to another, higher entity, God. Don't play with the intellect, man! [i.e., do not try to promote stories that are false]. The Godhead was established from Abraham to Hussein. A portal was opened at that juncture. And I never look back. Right after that my sister gave me a book on Malcolm X, the biography of Malcolm X. I used to walk with it in my back pocket. He [Malcolm X] was like the catalyst, then, at that time. He was fundamental in that [in Imam Amin's changing worldview]. I was looking for truth." He could not find the truth in a Euro-Christian message that seemed to reiterate the deprivations of centuries of enslavement in the name of rejecting worldly preoccupations. Later in his life he could not find truth in the initial puzzlement and doubt he discerned among other Muslims from various parts of the world, who saw "a black man knowing so much" about Islam.

Imam Amin found truth in the human spirit, which flowed "from Karbala to India to indenture here [Trinidad]. The spirit resonates in people, creating a community. The spirit immersed itself in people and reached here." Perhaps he viewed Karbala as the source of the spirit of truth. As the site of battle, Karbala represents for many Hosay devotees standing up for what one believes in, resistance embodied in Hussein's struggle—doing good to be good, as Derek had put it. Imam Amin continued that this spirit of truth can be thought of as blood: "not literal blood, but the true spirit of God that emanates in you. The spirit can be seen to be transferred in a similar way as blood." He continued that this spirit has DNA, "not [a] physical property but in the sense of mapping, a prescription whereby this thing [something] should exist and follow. DNA is a yardstick for explaining the spirit. Take the DNA of a spirit and use it as a yardstick to explain itself." I was fascinated and asked him to elaborate so that I could understand better. "The external cannot explain the internal. The breeze has its own DNA internally. We can only see the breeze's external realities, but it has internal realities we can't see. Externally we breathe in oxygen, but once it is inside us, only the internal organs can understand the intrinsic DNA of the breeze. What we inhale is not the same thing as what we use to transport our nutrients, et cetera. Internally it becomes something else: oxygen. The potential of the breeze's life force becomes something else within us." "So," he concluded, "blood is a spirit. If it wasn't a spirit, its life-giving force wouldn't be able to help you. Because the DNA is a life force with potentialities. DNA is a spirit or else it couldn't become a life force. External and internal realms are two realms connected but at different levels, at different rates of vibrations." The spirit is a sustaining energy that in people becomes materialized as blood; it courses across time and space, carrying biogenetic properties as well as "potentialities" for moral good and community building. Imam Amin does not speak entirely in terms of mysteries; his explanatory model of the workings of spirit employs genetics and heredity. If spirit also retains an ineffable quality that is not entirely reducible to Western science models, it works through what we might think of as heritability: whether seen or unseen, external or internal, something essential stays with us and is inevitably passed down. Imam Amin would not be likely to envision his notion of spirit in racialized terms. But the epistemic habits of racial thinking remain embedded in what some might call our "spiritual" and others might call our "religious" constitution.

There are also nonhuman, tangible conveyances of this essential spirit. According to Imam Amin, "The tadjah is the presence of Imam Hussein. Imam Hussein is present in the form of a being that we cannot see. Imam Hussein exists in a spiritual realm that we cannot traverse, so we only see the physical aspects of the flag or the tadjah." This air of mystery, forces that lie beyond the ken of human comprehension and control, fits comfortably within Western epistemological models of the relationship that mortals in this world have with otherworldly ethereal agents and the objects that serve as conduits or bridges between them. Some see other mysterious forces pervading Hosay in ways that are not necessarily captured by notions of the "spiritual" or the "religious," and may perhaps suggest more the workings of the supernatural than the holy. As the taxi driver mentioned earlier, who criticized the government's imbalanced representation of "culture," added in his disapproval of Hosay, "Even the sighting of the moon, all that is simi-dimi." As I have discussed elsewhere, "simi-dimi" is local parlance roughly equivalent to the concept of superstition. Or magic.[27]

Again in 2012, on another of my journeys, this time in a different taxi, the driver and his four passengers, including me, were talking about Hosay (given that the camps in Cedros were my destination). My fellow passengers were carefully noncommittal, but the driver said about Hosay, "It is a *secret* thing; you must treat it *properly*. This Hosay now[adays] is *serious* thing; you must do all the ritual correctly; you must know what you doing. It have strict thing behind it, and if you don't *know* what you doing, well, things could *happen* to you." This warning reflects a concern that I have heard many times before. When there seems not to be precise doctrine that can properly guide ritual actions, there is potential danger in error. When one is not sure what one is dealing with, the chance for misfortune to occur is all the more likely. In the Western tradition, malevolence may be unleashed by conducting a rite in reverse or in some other way that is deliberately contrary to the proper, sanctioned mode of undertaking it. Satan may be conjured this way; the dark forces of obeah as well, through obeah's odd assortment of perplexingly mundane or unappealing objects—far from the votive objects associated with "good" and "proper" religious worship and faith. This concern about secrets, doing things properly, and unnamed possible bad consequences is exacerbated with reference to religious traditions that have histories in the Caribbean as being suspect: too syncretic and thus ambiguous, too non-Western and thus occupying some variation of the "savage slot," those that are not "religion" in the first place, depending on perspective—such as obeah and Hosay.[28]

Yet similar understandings about mysterious forces can confirm a practice's place within the category of legitimate religion rather than render it dubiously so. I first met Mr. Ramlaya in 1988. We had many long and interesting conversations about his lifetime of dedication to Hosay as a Hindu Indo-Trinidadian, by which he carried on his family's multiple-generation tradition of commemoration. As virtually everyone does at some point in talking about Hosay, he brought up the problem of the public's "drinkin' rum and winin' up" that mars the gravitas of the contemporary observance. "In the old days," he said, "if you do any wrong thing near the Hosay [i.e., the tadjah], you get sick, you catch a fit. And they have to pray over you. So [Hosay] was more religious [than today]." To Mr. Ramlaya, prayer and punishment together gave Hosay of the old days more stable claims to being a truly religious phenomenon. He was not sure what could account for the retribution (in the form of catching a fit), but he viewed it in the same terms as he viewed prayer. Enigmatic energies surround the time during which the tadjahs are built. Mr. Ramlaya shared another example to illustrate his point. Two years earlier (in 1986), his niece, who lived abroad, telephoned him to say that she had had a dream in which "somebody appeared and said something [was] radically wrong with the tadjah, somebody was unclean [i.e., not following the rules of fasting during the month of Muharram]." Even before his niece called, Mr. Ramlaya said he had been "feeling a vibration," a kind of sign that something was amiss with the tadjah construction and that needed correction. These kinds of experiences— ethereal, supernatural, mysterious—are not necessarily at odds with Islamic religious philosophy. And they are certainly part of the human-spirit lifeworlds that in the Caribbean overlap in time and space, with no necessary cleavages separating them.[29] In fact, Mr. Ramlaya made no effort to interpret the dream as within or outside of Islam, Hinduism, or other religious tradition. He accepted both dream and vibration as guarding the sacredness of the tadjah and the tradition the tadjah sustains.

At one point during my 1991 research trip to Trinidad, one of my acquaintances, Frieda, an Indo-Trinidadian Muslim woman and lifetime participant in Hosay, related to me "a very serious, true story" about an experience she had had years before with the unseen powers that are associated with this event. One evening her husband came home after work bringing a fish for dinner. He accidently put it on the *taria*, or brass plate that was intended for the *melida*, or ritual sweets, that would be prayed over by the imam and distributed to everyone present. Frieda said, "[I] didn't know, and I took the taria to the chowk. I fell down in a faint on the chowk."[30] The imam prayed over her on the chowk, and she was carried back to her father's house near the sugar plantation. "When my father found out [about the ritual pollution from the fish], he made a promise for me that for five years I would return to the chowk. From this [incident], I always keep up the fasting for the ten days. Hosay is a very sensible thing. Hassan and Hussein, two brothers, lost their life. People have to be careful. You cannot be all how [any which way, careless, willy nilly]. It is a very dangerous thing."[31] At a different moment during that same trip, I was talking with a Hindu woman, Shalini, about her dedication to Hosay. In the course of our conversation she echoed Frieda's caution: "Hosay is a very dangerous thing. It is alive." She meant this in an entirely approving way, affirming Hosay's importance and value. She also meant that the tadjahs are animated with a kind of spiritual energy that makes them more than inanimate objects.

The distinction between what is mysterious and what is magic is one that can exalt or stigmatize. As people have described them to me, Hosay's mysteries are nothing they would derogate as "superstition" or as akin to "magic." Instead, they understand the forces that they cannot always explain in this-worldly terms as part of a larger moral universe, one informed by the positive values of striving, of giving, and of prevailing under duress. When people speak of danger, they are not expressing irrational fears which belong to minds that are not modern or not inclined toward rational thought. Concerns about treating others properly, whether ethereal or mortal, and about conducting one's ritual actions correctly, whether toward corporeal objects or intangible phenomena, is another way of approaching respect for power. Power is generative as well as destructive; its potential danger lies in its abuse, a disrespect that can upset in perilous ways what is unseen and not entirely explainable in empirical terms—but what is indubitably present and at work.

That there is today a shrinking of Hosay's public face does not go without comment. One tadjah builder lamented to me in 2012 that "people don't even know it [is] Hosay until they hear the drums. Hosay not properly advertised. Back around 1956 there used to be twenty thousand, thirty thousand people [observing]. Now on Flag Night you could lie down in the road and a car wouldn't run you down." Six years later, in 2018, Trinidad's CNC3 television station had a brief interview on "Big Hosay Night" with a local official in Cedros. He commented that this was the third year Hosay had gone without government funding. He felt particularly disappointed because, as he pointed out, Hosay is supposed to be an international tourist attraction. Another person told me that in his opinion "Hosay is shrinking today because the spirituality is being ignored. People have stepped off the path." It is true that the impact of labor and funding shortages have resulted in the diminution of Hosay as an event that is widely attended and broadly acknowledged. It is a national symbol, but one among a number of examples of Trinidad's multicultural callaloo; none, however, on the level of Carnival. Its news media coverage is slim; it is, much against its intentions, viewed by many as a three-night street party with revelers whose numbers have dwindled. Yet precisely because Hosay far exceeds the boundaries of its formal definition as an authentic or inauthentic feature of Islam, or as legitimately "religion" or not, I see no reason why it should not persist in some form and expression, irrespective of the vicissitudes of the economy and political culture.

From a parallax view, Hosay resides at the multiple perspective crossroads of local common sense: religion, festival, heresy, piety, sacred, sacrilegious—each of these characterizations contains further layers of meaning among participants and observers, who themselves can be subdivided into numerous points of view. As we have seen, people's reflections about Hosay, whether or not they are involved with it, show it to be a springboard to much broader existential concerns than simply a religious ritual. It is a vehicle through which participants work toward self-fulfillment and cooperative unity that is not confined to a specific space or time. It is a vehicle through which nonparticipants, either in praise or critique, can imagine the modernity and cooperative unity of the nation. And it is a vehicle through which the forces of spirit foster, through blood, air, and feeling, the identities of heritage.

# 6

## IDENTIFICATIONS

In his best-selling book *Between the World and Me,* Ta-Nehisi Coates writes that "race is the child of racism, not the father."[1] This is a profound and elegant way of affirming something that I have tried to capture in this book: What kinds of conditions and practices create the thing that is named? If we begin with race as is, there is the chance of it remaining viewed as inevitable, something to be unpacked and perhaps reorganized, but not discarded. When race is the starting point, it more easily appears to be a *thing,* stable and essential. But race is as much a process as is racism, being generated, as Coates comments, by being put into action (the "-ism" in race); the process creates the named thing. The same can be said of religion: its particular meanings (across time and place) give it the sense of stability and essence—*thingness.* But as with race, the production of meaning in relation to religion is a process—religionization. If race is the child of racism, then this identity category cannot be entirely shorn of its destructive pedigree. If the same were the case with religion (if religion were the child of religionism), then the same would hold. But these two identity categories, race and religion, are not identical, insofar as the concept of race primarily refers to human-to-human relations, and the concept of religion primarily refers to human-to-spirit/divine/cosmos/otherworld relations. In these respects, they are different kinds of existential projects. Yet as identity categories that arose from Western epistemological premises about human type and development, race and religion are intersected, embedded within the other, defining the other.

This analytical perspective of intersectionality, however, also coexists with one of a different register, in which identity categories, including race and religion, are conceptually disaggregated and function independently of each other. Both of these approaches to identity—as intersected or disaggregated—are investments in explanations about the ways that individuals and groups are socially constituted within unequal relations of power.

At its broadest, my contention in this book is that a parallax view productively discourages the examination of identities according to the conventional conceptual boundaries that define them, treating boundaries as given; or that these categories can somehow work independently of each other, each projecting its exclusive, inherent meanings and significance. While in this twenty-first-century moment in the Americas this premise may seem obvious to some, such a perspective has not reached the level of common sense; identity categories such as race and religion, for example, are still taken to be "obviously" separate, which is why theoretical-political interventions like intersectionality arise and are important. A focus on the varied ways and situations in which race and religion work intersectionally directs attention to the relations of power that enable stakeholders, empowered and subordinate alike, to configure and reconfigure models of human types, their proclivities and capabilities, in order to defend their agendas and projects. Euro-colonial authorities viewed the racial and religious identities of those whom they saw as perpetuating obeah and Hosay as aspects of personhood that reinforced each other or were in conflict with each other, which are in play alternately and also simultaneously. Race and religion thus produced, and "proved," particular kinds of persons.

Over the course of roughly 180 years (1838–present), obeah and Hosay went from being broadly characterized as racially uniform ("African" or "black," "Indian") false religion, to, in increasing quarters, racially diverse legitimate religion. In both cases, however, different heritage groups could be analogized in the same or similar racial terms. These perspectives about racial uniformity or differences, and religious authenticity or spuriousness, have been held across the West Indian social landscape of race, religion, and class. The shift in characterizations includes attempts at redemption: erasure of stigma and intolerance, for various and often quite different reasons. Yet in no version of which I am aware does the representation of obeah and Hosay negate their respective racialization; race plays a role in discourses of both their denigration and their defense. A parallax view of obeah suggests that its religious validation in large part draws it closer to racially specific roots that reinforce race, whether or not intentionally, as a key feature of human identity. This can be a problematic reinforcement, as race remains so freighted with the epistemological baggage of Euro-colonial, Enlightenment-derived presuppositions and models. A parallax view of Hosay suggests that its religious validation in large part attenuates it from racially specific roots, but race is nonetheless reinforced as a key feature of human identity because race remains an important reference point. For the same reasons as with obeah, this also can be a problematic reinforcement. At the same time, however, I want to acknowledge that epistemological baggage can be purposefully "lost" or reclaimed in another way.

When something is repeated enough to acquire "the timbre of truth, the way that statements uttered over and over or made in print again and again tend to do," writes historian Matthew Restall, it attains "confirmation bias."[2] The respective confirmation biases of obeah and Hosay are not narratives of a particular event and its spin. They entrench something more diffuse: an era's common sense, fashioned in transatlantic space, about the nature of identity and the deployment of identity's component parts in service of a colonial-capitalist labor scheme, one that reaped its profits by reaping a primitive grass (sugar cane)—sown, harvested, and processed by coerced labor transported across thousands of miles, Old World to New, from the seventeenth to the early twentieth century. "Confirmation bias" was built into the very organization of plantation production just as it was embedded within an epistemology about identity—different human types, propensities, capabilities, accomplishments—which ostensibly explained that production system. Both justification and critique had at their root a set of shared, Enlightenment- and post-Enlightenment-derived premises about liberty, individual agency, and reason-based worldviews, heritable and manifest in body as well as in mind.

Long after the plantation was essential to the existence of the societies that were made by it, and to the identity categorizations that both shaped and were shaped by it, the plantation's reverberations lingered in the commonsense understandings of the races and religions of its societies' constituent populations. The sovereign states and nationalist ideologies that political independence produced opened up other spaces for interpreting obeah and Hosay. Yet, although some of those interpretations reworked the valorization and critique of obeah and Hosay, none to date has dismantled the racial and religious thinking—the racialization of religion and the religionization of race—that seems to be an inevitable cornerstone of Western identity construction. But the "-ization" should not be taken to mean that one, race or religion, comes before the other, that one is a modifier of the other, an original condition of being. The intersectionality of race and religion is always a simultaneous process; one may be foregrounded in a particular historical or social context (as with any category of identity), but they are always and necessarily in a state of mutual definition, even as it is variously construed.

In contemporary times, and in particular this very troubled moment of racism, brutality, and death in the United States at the time of this writing (spring-summer 2020), race is a necessary part of our consciousness and our vocabulary. It is a lexical political tool that gives a condemning name to the rac*ism* that brought it into being and that sought to demean and erase those identified as being of certain races, and it is a lexical political tool that also can voice challenges, alternatives, and affirmations. Holding onto the concept of race and its work in identifying ourselves and others is a stark way of demanding attention to unequal relations of power that are often denied, hidden, or misrecognized. "Race" tells it like it is. But in doing so, does it also necessarily reiterate in some fashion something of its fundamental "-ism"? "Religion" is an explanatory framework for the everyday (and institutionalized) search for solace, inspiration, and elucidation. Unlike "race," whose meaning references human types and their ostensibly inherent hierarchies, the basic object of "religion" is not inferior or superior humans; it is otherworldly beings or forces (benevolent, malevolent, superior, or, perhaps, flawed in some way). But when "religion" is treated as an identity, it necessarily becomes entangled with other categories of identity (what "intersectional," at its broadest, means) and thus appertains to the unequal power relations that organize and maintain types of persons significantly through epistemic habits and common sense.

I began the journey that led to this book in my ponderings about why obeah retains its association with blackness and / or with Africa even while lay and scholarly perspectives recognize obeah, in addition to its undeniable African provenance, as a diffuse mosaic of many cultural traditions hailing from various parts of the world during different historical moments. Similarly, I contemplated why Hosay retains its association with Indianness and / or with Islam even while lay and scholarly perspectives recognize that Hosay, in addition to its undeniable South Asian provenance, is a palimpsest of persons of heterogeneous ancestries and devotions variously deemed religious or cultural or both. I wondered whether these apparent contradictions were actually not contradictions at all but perhaps more reasonably represented the conjugated work of racial and religious identities—that is, the ways that their relationship to each other in lived experience suggests their appearance as phenomenologically separate and distinct as well as intersected and mutually constitutive.

Pursuing these questions took me away from a book directly about obeah and Hosay per se that might lock them down into traced trajectories and telescoped synopses. Instead, I was drawn to thinking about race and religion, or racialization-religionization, examined through a parallax view that would suggest what obeah and Hosay together, as vehicles of race's and religion's intersectionality, could reveal about the historical and social processes that make them meaningful cultural things. Perhaps counterintuitively, how to understand them requires looking past and around them into the vicinity of their social relations and forces at particular moments in time, because understanding them calls for awareness of what they emerged from and what variously gives them meaning. The principal foundational components they share are their criminalization and their association with social disorder generated by labor unrest, whether slavery or indenture. Both were feared as tools of, or at least expressions of, unified resistance to colonial oppression on the part of the "lower races." Once particular racial and religious forms are imagined as dangers, they become dangerous. These climates of crisis brought Hosay as well as obeah into being as particularly marked *things* of West Indian colonial societies and their postindependence diasporas. Decriminalized or nationalized, so to speak, they could be domesticated at home as proper, or more or less proper, examples of local, indigenous culture. I hope that throughout the book it has been clear that my aim is not to equate obeah and Hosay; although I have engaged in a comparative exercise, they are obviously different phenomena. More interesting is to think about how their differences work conjunctively to communicate ideas and ideologies about what types of people may be assumed to be carriers of what types of behaviors and practices, and how differences produce or reflect commonly shared foundational features.

My aim also was not to present obeah and Hosay solely in terms of the still-abiding conventional wisdom about them. Obeah is much more than its reputation as a malevolent trafficking with the occult, and if and when it is accepted as such by some practitioners, there are layers of nuance even in this way of knowing obeah that also complicate this particular frame of reference. Hosay is much more than its reputation as an acceptable or unacceptable aspect of Islam; both sides of this way of knowing Hosay contain layers of nuance that point to other frames of reference and concerns. My interest has been to explore, through a parallax view, these frames of reference and concerns, which allow us to better understand how two cultural phenomena are distinct as well as comparable, through inquiring into the ways that their origins and development in the West Indies have come to be what they seem to be. Again, I am not arguing that obeah and Hosay are identical, or that their very real differences are insignificant. On the contrary, I think that inquiring into the epistemic habits that, over time, inform these two cultural phenomena and fashion them into certain kinds of things reveals how they have been represented into being, one might say, in lived experience. Such inquiry also reveals the kinds of stories these representations, embedded into common sense, tell about the broader relations of power that generate ways of knowing and the practices that give them impact and consequence. For obeah and Hosay, these relations of power have been expressed in their criminalization, racialization, and religionization.

In Western epistemology the concept of race generally includes attitudes and behaviors, and the concept of religion generally includes dimensions of experience that are beyond human comprehension. But race and religion are also embodied, materializing what otherwise are, respectively, taken to be difficult to discern or predict, or impossible to fully grasp. By this logic, bodies both reveal and substantiate categorical typologies: bodies are empirically observable, and what is observed can be interpreted to serve predominant perspectives and agendas. Moreover, through the social organization (typologizing) of bodies within particular relations of power, the body-as-carrier preserves and transmits types, or aspects of types (since "mixed" as opposed to "pure" races may be seen to hold only partial features of an identity). Preservation and transmission occur by means of heritability, the process by which identities—even if evanescent or intangible, such as some aspects of "religion"—are passed down generation by generation. Heritability can demonstrate that racial and religious identities are separable and inimical or mutually defining and reinforcing, depending on context and its stakes. In this way of thinking, certain races have reached certain stages of religious development, and other races have reached other stages. These stages, as we have seen, are rarely lateral and equivalent but, rather, are hierarchically ranked to indicate various examples of moral and technological achievement, which in turn identify the race(s) that express, and thus "belong" to those levels of achievement.

We should not yet be ready to eschew identification of self and other according to race, religion, or other identity categories, however, because that would render us putatively inadequate or invisible men and women, and thus with few to no ways of challenging the structures of inequality that prevail. We can challenge their premises by adding categories that expand the options and thus perhaps represent better how we see ourselves. "Bicultural," "biracial," and "trans" come to mind. But it is hard to even imagine how we might define and represent ourselves through identities based on options not somehow drawn from the usual suspects, not the least of which are race and religion. For now, however, we can remind ourselves that the concept of identity itself is not essential—in either sense of inherent or necessary. Further, we can treat identity more in terms of an open-ended question than a final answer.[3]

Just as race and religion are only *things* because of the processes that make them seem so, we assume that identity, like its subsets (race, religion, etc.), is something that people always already have, which is then put to use as they move through the world. Existential questions are universal to all peoples, but what is not a human universal is to think of oneself as an individual whose self-awareness expresses an identity, embedded at the core of consciousness. Instead, "identity" is what we call our existential questions; "identity" is the idea through which we make sense of this search to understand ourselves, to find ourselves in relation to the earth and to the cosmos, to locate ourselves as beings in the world made by our social interactions. Identity and individuality are interlinked aspects of the Western notion of personhood; the idea of the individual is predicated on the possession of a singular identity, a self that is distinct from that of the collective, which is comprised of an aggregate of individuals. The individual understands herself or himself through categories that are based on selected, intersecting features (phenotypical, cultural, biological, behavioral) through which she or he is both self-aware and socially recognized. Certainly since the beginning of the post-Colombian era in the Americas, social recognition has always included ranked valuations of persons, and self-awareness necessarily has included cognizance of one's ostensible social value. Because they are epistemologically connected, it might be assumed that one's identity is as sovereign as one's individuality is imagined to be; that identity, as the fundamental basis of one's self, is as much a possession to be claimed and owned as individualism is a possession to be claimed and owned. From the perspective of Enlightenment and post-Enlightenment thinking, both may appear to be inalienable and yet also subject to our free will. But, in fact, one's identity and the kind of individual that identity creates are not fully subject to free will (one's decisions about who one is, or others' decisions about who one is) when they are heritable, produced within specific relations of power whose concomitant common sense assumes that identities are visible in and on the body, passed down over time according to models of materialized heritability.

The connection between the concepts of identity and the individual has a long and complex history in Western thought. Michel Foucault saw this connection in terms of the working of the modern liberal state, whose power consists of "both an individualizing and a totalizing form of power."[4] He thought that we should not "consider the 'modern state' as an entity which was developed above individuals, ignoring what they are and even their very existence, but on the contrary as a very sophisticated structure, in which individuals can be integrated, under one condition: that this individuality would be shaped in a new form, and submitted to a set of very specific patterns."[5] This form and its patterns reflect what Foucault saw as the liberal state's presumption that, as Judith Butler writes, pressing for "rights and claims to entitlement can only be made on the basis of a singular and injured identity."[6] What seems to exist is a kind of Catch-22. Butler argues that what allows us to occupy this "discursive site of injury" is that "called by an injurious name," we are called into "social being"; we form an attachment to "any term that confers existence," and thus we are "led to embrace the terms that injure" us because they constitute us socially. Paradoxically, "only by occupying—being occupied by—that injurious term" can we resist and oppose it.[7] The possibility for "resignification" of an identity, however, can "rework and unsettle" such that an identity need not remain "always and forever rooted in its injury"—in other words, imposing new meanings that can remedy injuries.[8] As Foucault and Butler argue, the state produces and relies on the damaged identities of its individuated citizens. That said, our aim, according to Foucault, should not be "to try to liberate the individual from the state, and from the state's institutions, but to liberate us both from the state and from the type of individualization which is linked to the state. We have to promote new forms of subjectivity through the refusal of this kind of individuality which has been imposed on us for several centuries," back, in fact, to Enlightenment thought.[9] Liberation from the state and finding a new type of self-identification that eschews a notion of the individual that is concomitant with the state are tall orders, ones I have not called for in this book. But what I do want to draw attention to, in part with the points made in the works above, is the ways that the individual—proper or "rogue"—has contributed to identity types that are necessarily linked to the nation-state and that reinforce that entity's agendas.

Despite its asserted aspirations to the contrary, the contemporary nation-state requires, or certainly encourages, investment in racial thinking, often couched in terms of the "culture" of "ethnic groups" and politicized as "multiculturalism" and "diversity." Contemporary scholars, including myself, work with these kinds of classifications. But as Asad Haider reminds us, "Our political agency through identity is exactly what locks us into the state, what ensures our continued subjection."[10] "Clearly 'identity' is a real phenomenon," he continues. "It corresponds to the way the state parcels us out into individuals, and the way we form our selfhood in response to a wide range of social relations. But it is nevertheless an abstraction, one that doesn't tell us about the specific social relations that have constituted it."[11] We can "bring this abstraction back to earth" by focusing on the factors "that have put it in our heads." Haider writes that "in order to do that, we have to reject 'identity' as a foundation for thinking about identity politics."[12] While I agree with this in principle, it too is a tall order, given, as I note above, the paucity of alternative conceptual frameworks that we have presently to define ourselves, and thus the danger of diminishment or erasure.

In a recent book, Kwame Anthony Appiah probes the concept of identity, arguing that while there is "no dispensing with identities," we need to understand them better in order to reconfigure and reform them, in order to "free ourselves from mistakes about them that are often a couple of hundred years old."[13] He argues that identities make demands on us; they work by commanding us, "speaking to us as an inner voice" that other people also respond to as we present ourselves to each other according to that inner voice.[14] In this way, identities are "forms of confinement, conceptual mistakes underwriting moral ones," and also the "contours to our freedom" that aggregate groups and communities, fostering potential unity with a sense of (shared) purpose.[15] Defining the contours of freedom as somehow shared and capacious, identities bring into communication the familiar with the unfamiliar, the immediate with the distant, the microscale with the macroscale. As Appiah concludes, predicated on "lies," identities also "bind" us together. Here is another case for holding onto identity as an organizing principle with which to navigate our lives and our social relations. Again, I would say that currently we have little choice in the matter if we want to strive toward being better bound to each other. Given

Appiah's call to reform identities to emphasize their social work, so to speak, perhaps a useful place to begin is a critical look at identities as an "inner voice." Although not likely Appiah's intent, arguably this metaphor accentuates the figure of the individual, inherently defined by an essential self. We certainly need to have some way of describing how consciousness becomes self, but perhaps there are ways to envision identities without the notion of the individual in this translation. Alternate representations would not (and should not) make the concept of identity apolitical (neutral), but they might redirect the kind of individual-predicated identity politics that Foucault, Butler, and Haider are concerned about.

At least for the New World's last half-millennium, any identity is political in some way, and identity politics comes in many versions. In their own ways, obeah and Hosay are engaged with the politics of identity, the intersectionality of race and religion, as those who are determined either to contain or to encourage them struggle over their definition, meaning, practice, and valorization. But as a number of my interlocutors voiced about Hosay, state patronage of a "callaloo" (multicultural) nation is both a means of its survival and a means of its disappearance—as unrecognizable transformation or as demise. Obeah's individual practitioners have been either "rogue" individuals criminalized by the state and rejected by the nation (that is, not capitalized on), or decriminalized and held at arm's length within national belonging (that is, accepted hesitatingly, represented ambivalently).

Ordinary people work these divisions as well, as much to their own advantage as they can. But how much noncompliance is possible from within the system itself? I think the possibilities for dismantling are contingent, based on the ways those tools can be deployed—for example, reappropriations of words or concepts that insist on a different meaning or usage. This is a question of power; it is also another aspect of the argument that the Caribbean region, or Atlantic world, is not a dual system of Euro-modernity and Other-tradition; it is, instead, a simultaneous system, the locus of where modernity emerged from an integrated, mutually defining, encompassing web of intimate global histories.[16] This representation of the Caribbean seeks in part to correct the presumption that non-European histories and cultures were subordinate or nonexistent partners in this geohistorical space of what some have called "Atlantic Modernity."[17] In this space, Stuart Hall observes, "the West and the Rest became two sides of a single coin."[18] As C. L. R. James, Sidney Mintz, and Michel-Rolph Trouillot, among others, have variously argued, the region's colonized peoples cannot be reduced to merely the historical handmaidens of colonizer imprints; there is an indigenizing process whereby all forms (traditions, practices, aspirations) matter, and meld into each other, albeit unevenly.[19] The unevenness is the inequality of power at work; some ways of knowing and being prevail over others, at least for a time. This prevalence is captured and preserved, for a time, in a particular moment's common sense, what can be called an Atlantic Common Sense insofar as particular themes and premises and reference points recur, fueling the ways we define and interpret ourselves and others—that is, our identities and theirs. Therefore, when we acknowledge (and celebrate) the joint production that is the Caribbean, we must also consider how this synergism also rehearses ways of living in the world and ways of understanding it that reiterate some of the very cornerstones of inequality and injustice that we struggle against.

Earlier Euro-colonial understandings of racial type ("savage," "coolie") and religious impulse ("rational," "ecstatic") both have drawn together and divided population "types." As Foucault understood, fields of common knowledge are expressed through discursive practices that are ways of representing things and hence create meaning, setting the terms for how things are thought and talked about.[20] At the same time, Foucault was well aware that the commonsense foundations of historical moments are not static. Pre- and post-independence periods, for example, have significant differences. Nonetheless, both fall under colonialism's long shadow—current forms of governance that bear, in Brackette Williams's apt characterization, the ghosts of hegemonic dominance.[21] Within these shadows, people exercise varied forms of agency. Among those who have the power of representation and hence the formation of posterity's archive, including colonizers and some scholars, it is tempting to interpret agency in binary terms, as domination or resistance, however each may be nuanced. The agendas and consequences of domination often seem clear, either at the time or in hindsight. Resistance is easily assumed to be the explanation for responses to that domination, at least as a feature of individuals' will. In the West the understanding of the exercise of power seems obvious; it is rational that people would push back against what they see as curtailing their self-realization. For nineteenth- and twentieth-century British colonizers, that pushback was inadvisable, to say the least—objectionable because it shook the architectures of inequality that had been developed out of the basic political-economic realities. Today, for others without those vested interests, that pushback is a normative, healthy expression of selfhood, or individual identity. Colonizers and colonial elites also saw resistance and compliance in terms of individual will, either properly socialized toward conformity to the natural laws guiding the common good, or perversely rogue, or, in the case of abject "savages," absent altogether. More challenging to understand, and to establish through evidence, are the forms of noncompliance, or resistance, that agency may take other than what seems unequivocal, blatant rejection, and what significance is imputed to these forms by the actors themselves.

Not only is "confrontation" a multilayered manifestation of agency, but it has multiple meanings. Among the subordinated in the context of slave and indenture plantation society, motives—and the forms of consciousness that informed those motives—may be infered through recorded documents (although these were not often produced by the subordinated populations) and through retrospective surmise, which, by definition, is not beyond doubt. Thus, although it is certain that obeah played an important role as inspiration to participants in slave insurrections throughout the Caribbean, what kind of agency obeah itself expresses, as a practice or tradition, is harder to pin down. And although it is certain that indentured laborers posed strikes, sought legal redress, and on occasion amassed in protest groups that marshaled the mobility and religious mantle that was a part of Hosay, that service performed is not synonymous with the kind of agency that Hosay itself expresses as its own practice or tradition. The question is this: What do obeah and Hosay look like outside of the context of gross repression protected by law? Obeah in the West Indies consists of acts, imagery, and discourses that comprise a veritable obeah culture, which in one way or another is participated in by all residents of colonial society and which remains a significant factor in the way present-day, postindependence peoples in the West Indies and in its diasporas address existential questions about their well-being, their relationship to the world of spirits, and the shape of their futures. Hosay, too, consists of acts, imagery, and discourses that, in conjunction with both slave and indenture plantation society, shaped its own colonial moment. This moment did not engender a Hosay culture in the West Indies comparable to obeah, however. This is largely because the indenture system was only about eight decades long, and once Hosay ceased to be associated with labor unrest, it was enveloped into the cultural and religious backstory; it did not involve the majority of the populations of indenture colonies (and none of the Caribbean colonies that did not engage "bound coolie" laborers); and although it certainly contributed to the climates of crisis in these societies, it was not a quotidian frame of reference or habitus in them, both of which are needed in the production of cultural formations. As Jerome Handler and Kenneth Bilby point out, obeah has never been "a unitary phenomenon," and the term "obeah" has "carried multiple meanings and connotations, some of them contradictory, across both time and space."[22] Although no phenomenon is unitary, Handler and Bilby's point is well taken. Obeah's particular fluidity helps fashion it into the suffusive sliding signifier that established a regional obeah culture in the West Indies and in diaspora. Hosay also is not a unitary phenomenon; thus, in spite of its more boundaried temporal and spatial presence, it shares with obeah an important lineage of categorical race and religion.

Both obeah and Hosay in the West Indies were created, in the sense of being reified into things, significantly through their criminalization and stigmatization. Both are diasporic collections of beliefs and practices that have long been the targets of the tool kits of oppression, but they are also what people engage with in order to gain some control over their lives. Each in its own way is a moving vehicle of race and religion, establishing and confirming the intersectionality of these interpretive categories and their heritable transmission. Both are prime optics through which we may better grasp when, and why, something may or may not be legitimated as religion, and when something may or may not have a single racial constitution. Both molded and were molded by an abiding common sense about types of human beings: past baggage, present legacies, future potential. Both are heritable identities through their respective channels of race and religion—the former made evanescent in this genealogy, as the latter is materialized. Obeah and Hosay are what we might call religions-in-law, through a "family resemblance" caused by being creations of a shared Euro-colonial epistemology,[23] which haunts the present, shaping the ways Western common sense continues to treat race, religion, and the group identities that race and religion substantiate. As such, obeah and Hosay require us to understand "race" and "religion" as complex forms of agency that orient modes of identification (of ourselves and others) rather than as identities that are stable and predictable. However, people's investments in the presumed stability and indelibility of their identities are not necessarily evidence of internalized oppression or false consciousness; they are simply other forms of agency that race and religion take. How much of a break has there been, from colonial to "postcolonial" or "neocolonial" eras? As Foucault and many others have understood, the Enlightenment has played a key role in determining what we are, how we think, and what we do today.[24] Obeah and Hosay attained certain meanings throughout West Indian social formations that were projected from every vantage point, empowered and otherwise, within the broader context of coerced labor and imperial agendas that characterized the colonial-capitalist venture in the region. And obeah and Hosay have been given certain meanings in the context of late colonial transnational diasporas and the endeavors of the postindependence nation-state.

Today obeah remains illegal in much of the West Indies and censured by some sectors of all societies in which it is practiced or thought to be practiced. No longer criminalized in its West Indian localities, Hosay continues to be censured by some sectors of Muslim communities, and relegated to an auxiliary contribution to national culture. Both obeah and Hosay could be said to represent the "miracle of creolization," the heterogeneity of cultures in mutual encounter,[25] or to represent the distinct heritages of their ancestral origins, either as a mark of their legitimacy or their illegitimacy, depending upon the point of view. Perhaps identities could not exist altogether without a language of criminalization to stigmatize them into being, just as perhaps identities could not exist altogether without a language of validation to justify them into being. All are categorical political positions. And all, in some fashion, reinforce the habit of approaching cultural practice through the optic of identity. Identity is a category of experience, of personhood, whose ontological status, at least in contemporary Western thought, continues to lie between some kind of deeply engrained natural origin point and being socially constructed through storied histories.[26] This dual model raises questions about the grounds upon which people can make claims about, and with, identity categories. After all, writes John Kirkpatrick, "The history of identities is not the history of a group but of the changing passwords that grant access to social life."[27] Does what "we" or "they" *do* necessarily have to refer back to who we or they *are*? Self-affirmation seems obviously, commonsensically to be the consequence of our actions and our beliefs. But in this way of thinking, our selves still remain, fundamentally, as types defined by placement ahead or behind along that ideologically enduring developmental line of progression from past, to present, to future.[28] The racialization of religion and the religionization of race, perceived through the histories and cultural construction of obeah and Hosay, suggest that identities, even in acts of self-empowerment, reiterate their own epistemological limitations.

In reference to the cultural history of the New World, V. S. Naipaul remarked, "We were not given a proper history of the New World itself. . . . One didn't begin with knowledge. One wrote oneself into knowledge."[29] Anyone who is looking, as Naipaul did, and as scholars and activists do, can feel this absence: knowledge groping to find its way through a history that is clogged with certain kinds of common sense based on unequal and unjust relations of power. The silence of which Naipaul speaks is acutely evident in the archival record, which is limited by the absent voices of the enslaved, the indentured, and other subalterns. There are of course exceptions—for example, slave narratives (such as those by Mary Prince and Olaudah Equiano), "coolie" testimonies, such as in *The Cuba Commission Report*, and letters to the editor in colonial and postindependence West Indian newspapers.[30] There are also the approximations of those voices, with varying and likely often unreliable degrees of verisimilitude, portrayed in novels and other writings, from Edward Jenkins's *Lutchmee and Dilloo* to Harriet Beecher Stowe's *Uncle Tom's Cabin*.[31] On its face, I am not in agreement with Naipaul's view that New World peoples did not begin with knowledge. But the kind of knowledge they possessed was certainly not knowledge according to the hegemonic, authorized view of what "knowledge" should consist of. In that sense, then, New World peoples did not begin with knowledge. Greater ability to "write oneself into knowledge" would come later, but it is a power that is still too scarce even today among all subaltern peoples everywhere, not just in the New World.

In the story about the concept of identity—its development, its deployments, and its dead ends—that I want this book to tell, my interest is not, strictly speaking, in capturing the voices of the silenced and the marginalized. But my interest is in considering some ways of thinking about power and personhood—specifically, racial and religious constitutions—in a place and over a period of time that, ideally, requires the mustering of many voices. Most of those voices, the ones that can be retrieved, reflect the power of their owners to be heard and, in a sense, preserved. But in drawing from them I have also tried to read between the lines for both subtext and context; to extrapolate, with care and a parallax view, what history's unvoiced or little recorded may have been thinking as well as doing—as represented through the expressed thoughts of the empowered. In short, it takes a village to make and maintain common sense.

In the mid-twentieth century this "village" was increasingly expanding its voices, articulated through familiar channels—educational institutions, literary and performing arts, political activism—and typically with a fundamentally similar, implicit message about Caribbean obeah and Hosay: that they become *things* through the racialization of religion and the religionization of race, and criminalized through a model of embodied heritability that is both biological and social, interwoven such that neither is entirely conceptually distinct from the other. Obeah and Hosay share a family resemblance that, perhaps counterintuitively, perpetuates basic messages about human difference, otherness, and the mutual exclusivity of types that are reinforced by the alleged rogue behaviors that refuse to conform.

Yet this does not mean that "a proper history of the New World" cannot be reached. "Proper," to my mind, means being more fine-grained, more nuanced, and always more skeptical rather than comfortably situated within one particular stance. Ultimately my conclusions about the social justice–producing potential of the concept of identity, drawn from my exploration of obeah and Hosay, do not lean toward optimism. But I intend my analysis to suggest openness rather than foreclosure, inviting wider conversations about what kind of power tool, so to speak, "identity" is in lived experience. Throughout this book I have argued that, for better or for worse, this power continues to lie in the heritability of racial and religious identities and their conjunctive, intersectional work in creating, explaining, and perpetuating human types—the rogues and the proper—and their hierarchies.

# NOTES

## 1. A Parallax View

1. "Apprenticeship" was "a half-way covenant," as Thomas Holt describes it in Jamaica—the transition period from slave to free society during which time former slaves would be "reeducated as wage laborers and resocialized as citizens." Thomas Holt, *The Problem of Freedom: Race, Labor, and Politics in Jamaica and Britain 1832–1938* (Baltimore: Johns Hopkins University Press, 1992), 56–57.
2. In the early years of this labor scheme, other immigrants were also indentured, notably Chinese, Madeirans, and West Africans. But the majority population, those who came to characterize indenture, were from India.
3. Robert Orsi, *History and Presence* (Cambridge: Harvard University Press, 2016), 3.
4. Martin Heidegger argued that a "thing" is the "existing bearer of many existing yet changeable properties." The question itself, he said, is a historical one that requires attention to the historical character of both the question and the act of questioning. In other words, apparently self-evident definitions are never "natural'; the question already expresses a preliminary opinion about the thingness of the thing. "History already speaks through the type of question." Martin Heidegger, *What Is a Thing?*, trans. W. B. Barton Jr. and Vera Deutsch (Chicago: H. Regnery Co., 1967), 54, 39–40, 43.
5. Rev. H. V. P. Bronkhurst, *The Colony of British Guiana and Its Laboring Population* (London: T. Woolmer, 1883), 364.
6. Jerome Handler and Kenneth Bilby, *Enacting Power: The Criminalization of Obeah in the Anglophone Caribbean, 1760–2011* (Kingston, Jamaica: University of the West Indies Press, 2012), 4; Diana Paton, "Obeah Acts: Producing and Policing the Boundaries of Religion in the Caribbean," *Small Axe* 13, no. 1 (2009): 1–2.
7. Michel-Rolph Trouillot, *Silencing the Past: Power and the Production of History* (Boston: Beacon Press, 1995), xix.
8. Diana Paton, "The Racist History of Jamaica's Obeah Act," *The Gleaner*, October 8, 2019, http://jamaica-gleaner.com/article/news/20190616/.

9. Simone Morgan-Lindo, "Big Retirement Party Planned for Obeah Man," *The Star* (Jamaica), November 19, 2018, http://jamaica-star.com/article/news /20181119/.

10. Diana Paton, "The Racist History of Jamaica's Obeah Act," *The Gleaner*, June 16, 2019, http://jamaica-gleaner.com/article/news/20190616/.

11. Carlton Robert Ottley, *A Historical Account of the Trinidad and Tobago Police Force from the Earliest Times* (Port of Spain: published by the author, "Compiled on a special assignment from the Government of Trinidad and Tobago," 1964), 31.

12. Bridget Brereton, *Race Relations in Colonial Trinidad 1870–1900* (Cambridge: Cambridge University Press, 1979), 184.

13. Brereton, *Race Relations in Colonial Trinidad*, 184.

14. David Trotman, *Crime in Trinidad: Conflict and Control in a Plantation Society 1838–1900* (Baltimore: Johns Hopkins University Press, 1986), 101.

15. Trotman, *Crime in Trinidad*, 270.

16. In addition, identity categories such as race and religion, and their designated carriers, such as obeah and Hosay, being *things* in Heidegger's sense, work within a matrix produced by a kinship of ideas and the language that communicates ideas—what Ludwig Wittgenstein called "family resemblances." Wittgenstein argued that connections among things need not be based on a single common feature that draws them together, but rather on a series of overlapping similarities that relate them to each other in numerous ways. Ludwig Wittgenstein, *Philosophical Investigations*, ed. G. E. M. Anscombe and R. Rhees, trans. G. E. M. Anscombe (1953; repr., Englewood Cliffs, NJ: Prentice Hall, 1958).

17. "Varieties," *Mascot*, February 19, 1898, quoted in Laura Putnam, "Rites of Power and Rumors of Race: The Circulation of Supernatural Knowledge in the Greater Caribbean, 1890–1940," in *Obeah and Other Powers: The Politics of Caribbean Religion and Healing*, ed. Diana Paton and Maarit Forde (Durham, NC: Duke University Press, 2012), 251.

18. Constructions of type and ways of knowing oneself are mutually constitutive: through structures of power relations, individuals and the groups into which they are formed animate and embody these constructions and self-knowledge in combination, producing the intersections through which they are connected. There is always an entanglement between the ways people are defined by dominant classificatory systems and the ways they define themselves. These entanglements produce diverse messages and consequences. For good examples, see the well-known 1923 Supreme Court case *United States v. Bhagat Singh Thind* and Judith Weisenfeld's exploration of "religio-racial identity" in the early twentieth-century United States among black religious movements (Judith Weisenfeld, *New World a'Coming: Black*

*Religion and Racial Identity during the Great Migration* (New York: NYU Press, 2016).

19. Jurgen Habermas, *The Structural Transformation of the Public Sphere: An Inquiry into a Category of Bourgeois Society,* trans. Thomas Burger (repr; 1962, Cambridge, MA: MIT Press, 1989. Dorinda Outram, *The Enlightenment* (Cambridge: Cambridge University Press, 2005), 11; Larry Wolff, "Discovering Cultural Perspective: The Intellectual History of Anthropological Thought in the Age of Enlightenment," in *The Anthropology of the Enlightenment,* ed. Larry Wolff and Marco Cipolloni (Palo Alto, CA: Stanford University Press, 2007), 30.

20. Bronkhurst, *Colony of British Guiana,* 361.

21. Bronkhurst, 357–358.

22. Bronkhurst, 359–360.

23. Bronkhurst, 362–363.

24. Bronkhurst, 364.

25. Stuart Hall, *The Fateful Triangle: Race, Ethnicity, Nation* (Cambridge, MA: Harvard University Press, 2017), 32.

26. Stuart Hall, with Bill Schwartz, *Familiar Stranger: A Life between Two Islands* (Durham, NC: Duke University Press, 2017), 92, 96.

27. Diana Paton, *The Cultural Politics of Obeah: Religion, Colonialism, and Modernity in the Caribbean World* (Cambridge: Cambridge University Press, 2015), 315.

28. "https://dictionary.cambridge.org/us/dictionary/english/parallax.

29. Aram Yengoyan, "Introduction: On the Issue of Comparison," in *Modes of Comparison: Theory and Practice,* ed. Aram Yengoyan (Ann Arbor: University of Michigan Press, 2006), 4.

30. While this book was in production, historian Kris Manjapra's use of the notion of a parallax view was brought to my attention (many thanks to David Ludden). Similar to my own approach, Manjapra defines "parallactic understanding" as a "multiplied perspective, . . . the awareness that balances the many interrelated, yet different, perspectives on shared social experience." In contrast to my focus on two cultural phenomena in one region (the Atlantic world), he looks at five hundred years of different forms of colonialism in Europe, Asia, Africa, and the Americas. Kris Manjapra, *Colonialism in Global Perspective* (Cambridge: Cambridge University Press, 2020), 7.

31. Kimberlé Crenshaw, "Demarginalizing the Intersection of Race and Sex: A Black Feminist Critique of Antidiscrimination Doctrine, Feminist Theory, and Antiracist Politics," *University of Chicago Legal Forum* 140 (1989), 139.

32. Interview with Adolph Reed, "How Did Essentialism Lead to Intersectionality?," *The Michael Brooks Show,* May 17, 2020, https://youtu.be/4FngeEwsVLU.

Sociologist Rogers Brubaker has a similar critique of what he calls "groupism," which he defines as "the tendency to take discrete, bounded groups as basic constituents of social life, chief protagonists of social conflicts, and fundamental units of social analysis." Rogers Brubaker, *Ethnicity without Groups* (Cambridge, MA: Harvard University Press, 2004), 8.

33. Adolph Reed Jr., "Socialism and the Argument against Race Reductionism," *New Labor Forum* 29, no. 2 (2020): 36.

34. Robert Borofsky, Laura Nader, Matt Candea, and Jonathan Friedman, "Where Have All the Comparisons Gone?," https://www.publicanthropology.org/where -have-all-the-comparisons-gone/.

35. Sarah Pulliam Bailey, "Franklin Graham: Obama Born a Muslim, a Christian Now," *Gleanings*, 8/20/2010, https://www.christianitytoday.com/gleanings/2010 /august/franklin-graham-obama-born-muslim-christian-now.

36. Ania Loomba, "Race and the Possibilities of Comparative Critique," *New Literary History* 40, no. 3 (2009): 503.

37. Rebecca Goetz, *The Baptism of Early Virginia* (Baltimore: Johns Hopkins University Press, 2012), 5; see also Maria Elena Martinez, *Genealogical Fictions: Limpieza de Sangre, Religion, and Gender in Colonial Mexico* (Palo Alto, CA: Stanford University Press, 2008).

38. Diane Austin-Broos, "Race/Class: Jamaica's Discourse of Heritable Identity," *New West Indian Guide* 68, no. 3–4 (1994): 220. Goetz, *Baptism of Early Virginia*, 12.

39. Staffan Müller-Wille and Hans-Jörg Rheinberger, "Heredity—the Formation of an Epistemic Space," in *Heredity Produced*, ed. Staffan Müller-Wille and Hans-Jörg Rheinberger (Cambridge, MA: MIT Press, 2007), 7–9.

40. Ian Hacking, *Historical Ontology* (Cambridge, MA: Harvard University Press, 2002), 100.

41. Stuart Hall, *Formations of Modernity* (Cambridge: Polity Press, 1992). 314.

42. As I was developing my ideas about the rogue individual, Michel Foucault's reflections on four key figures in the Victorian social order were brought to my attention (thanks are due Bruce Grant). Foucault identified the hysterical woman, the Malthusian couple, the perverse adult, and the masturbating child as at the heart of debates about proper social behavior. Michel Foucault, *History of Sexuality*, vol. 1, *An Introduction* (New York: Pantheon Books, 1978), 105. My notion of rogue individual conveys a similar sense of social danger and disruption.

43. There have been similar ideas in the anthropological literature. Notable is Charles Nuckolls's "social cynosure," public figures and literary characters whose attributes, either appealing or offensive, reveal the "values that are most salient to the formation of cultural identity" in a society and who serve "as a benchmark against which people judge their conformity to accepted ideals."

Charles W. Nuckolls, *Culture: A Problem That Cannot Be Solved* (Madison: University of Wisconsin Press, 1998), 80. My notion of the rogue individual differs from social cynosure in that the West Indies rogue, certainly in the context of obeah and Hosay, is inflected toward the ambivalently admirable and generally not someone to emulate.

44. Charles Taylor, "The Politics of Recognition," in *Multiculturalism: Examining the Politics of Recognition*, ed. Amy Gutmann (Princeton, NJ: Princeton University Press, 1994), 28.

45. Ann Laura Stoler, *Along the Archival Grain: Epistemic Anxieties and Colonial Common Sense* (Princeton, NJ: Princeton University Press, 2009), 97.

46. Alan Richardson, "Romantic Voodoo: Obeah and British Culture, 1797–1807," in *Sacred Possessions: Vodou, Santeria, Obeah, and the Caribbean*, ed. Margarite Fernandez Olmos and Lizabeth Paravisini-Gebert (New Brunswick, NJ: Rutgers University Press, 1997), 171–194.

47. *Report of the Committee: Emigration from India to the Crown Colonies and Protectorates*, 1910, Part III. (London: His Majesty's Stationary Office).

48. Hesketh J. Bell, Obeah: *Witchcraft in the West Indies*, vol. 1 (London: Sampson Low, Marston & Company, 1893), 5–6.

49. Bell, *Obeah*, 9.

50. Bronkhurst, *Colony of British Guiana*, 382.

51. Michel Foucault, *The Order of Things: An Archaeology of the Human Sciences* (New York: Vintage Books, 1994).

52. Ann Laura Stoler, *Along the Archival Grain: Epistemic Anxieties and Colonial Common Sense* (Princeton, NJ: Princeton University Press, 2009), 39.

53. Trouillot, *Silencing the Past*.

54. Antonio Gramsci, *Selections from the Prison Notebooks of Antonio Gramsci*, ed. Quintin Hoare and Geoffrey Nowell Smith (London: Lawrence and Wishart, 1971).

55. Kate Crehan, *Gramsci's Common Sense: Inequality and Its Narratives* (Durham, NC: Duke University Press), 2016.

56. Keyy Wisecup and Toni Wall Jaudon, "On Knowing and Not Knowing about Obeah," *Atlantic Studies* 12, no. 2 (2015): 136.

57. John Campbell, *Obeah, Yes or No? A Study of Obeah and Spiritualism in Guyana* (published by author, Alma Jordan Library, University of the West Indies, St. Augustine, 1977), 5.

58. Campbell, *Obeah, Yes or No?*, 5.

59. Hindi: "bakara"; Urdu: "bakri."

60. Campbell, *Obeah, Yes or No?*, 5.

61. Campbell, *Obeah, Yes or No?*, 7.

62. See, for example, de Laurence's *Book of Magical Art, Hindu Magic, and East Indian Occultism*, published in 1915 (noted in Vijay Prashad, *Everybody Was*

*Kung Fu Fighting: Afro-Asian Connections and the Myth of Cultural Purity* [Boston: Beacon Press, 2001], 90).

63. Diana Paton, *The Cultural Politics of Obeah: Religion, Colonialism, and Modernity in the Caribbean World* (Cambridge: Cambridge University Press, 2015).

64. The student was Levonne Williams, and the course was Histories of the Caribbean, spring semester 2019, New York University.

65. Georg Simmel, "The Sociology of Secrecy and of Secret Societies," *American Journal of Sociology* 11, no. 4 (1906): 463.

66. John and Jean Comaroff, *Ethnography and the Historical Imagination* (Boulder, CO: Westview Press, 1992), 35.

67. Comaroff, *Ethnography and the Historical Imagination*, 11, 34.

68. Stephen Greenblatt, *Learning to Curse: Essays in Early Modern Culture* (New York: Routledge, 1990), 14.

69. Eric R. Wolf, *Europe and the People without History* (Berkeley: University of California Press, 1982).

70. John L. Comaroff, "Dialectical Systems, History, and Anthropology: Units of Study and Questions of Theory," *Journal of Southern African Studies* 8 (1982): 144.

71. These forms of association, or co-constructions, combined colonial categories of race and religion into "savage" and "coolie" identities cemented as heritable essences that defined inferior types and their customary traditions—such as obeah and Hosay. Heritable essence remained ostensibly fixed, while the racializing-religionizing boundaries around them shifted. Let me note that colonials' co-constructions are not akin to the concept of intersectionality. In the colonial perspective, co-constructed identities are composed of heritable traits and are unequal, inevitable, and inescapable. In a causal tautology, racial traits are expressed through bodies that exhibit either religious, areligious, or antireligious practices and worldviews, that, in turn, confirm the race of their practitioners. The dynamics of power are at issue only insofar as discrimination requires justification, not dismantling.

72. The primary themes in Hosay scholarship have been concerned with three areas of inquiry. One is describing and documenting Hosay (see, for example, Satnarine Balkaransingh, *The Shaping of Culture: Rituals and Festivals in Trinidad Compared with Selected Counterparts in India, 1900–2011* [Hertforshire, UK: Hansib Publications, 2016]; Frank Korom, *Hosay Trinidad* [Philadelphia: University of Pennsylvania Press, 2003]; Gustav Thaiss, "Contested Meanings and the Politics of Authenticity," in *Islam, Globalization, and Postmodernity*, ed. A. S. Ahmad and H. Donnan [London: Routledge, 1994], 38–62; Martha Warren Beckwith, *The Hussay Festival in Jamaica* [Poughkeepsie, NY: Vassar College, 1924]). The second is exploring Hosay's relationship to the labor struggles of indentured Indians on plantations (see, for example, Kelvin Singh, *Bloodstained*

*Tombs* [London: Macmillan, 1988]; Prabhu Mohapatra, "The Hosay Massacre of 1884: Class and Community among Indian Labourers in Trinidad," in *Work and Social Change in South Asia,* ed. Marcel van der Linden and Arvind N. Das [New Delhi: Manohar CSH, 2002]; Basdeo Mangru, *Indenture and Abolition* [Toronto: TSAR, 1993]; Vijay Prashad, *Everybody Was Kung Fu Fighting* [Boston: Beacon Press, 2001]). The third is analyzing postcolonial subjectivity (see, for example, Ajai and Lakshmi Mansingh, "Indian Heritage in Jamaica," *Jamaica Journal* 10, no. 2–4 [1976]: 10–19; Shalini Puri, *The Caribbean Postcolonial* [New York: Palgrave Macmillan, 2004]).

73. There is foundational ethnographic work by mid-twentieth-century scholars of the West Indies addressing the interlacing of Africans' and Indians' beliefs and practices, particularly those related to magical powers and the spirit world. See, as notable examples, Morton Klass, *East Indians in Trinidad* (New York: Columbia University Press, 1961); Arthur and Juanita Niehoff, *East Indians in the West Indies* (Milwaukee: Milwaukee Public Museum Publications in Anthropology, 1960). More recent work on the relationship between Afro-Trinidadian and Indo-Trinidadian religious traditions includes Keith McNeal (*Trance and Modernity in the Southern Caribbean* (Gainesville: University Press of Florida, 2011).

74. Among the numerous and very helpful works on or related to obeah's identification and meanings not specifically cited in this book include Maarit Forde, "Governing Death in Trinidad and Tobago," in *Passages and Afterworlds: Anthropological Perspectives on Death in the Caribbean,* ed. Maarit Forde and Yanique Hume (Durham, NC: Duke University Press, 2018), 176–198; Dianne M. Stewart, *Three Eyes for the Journey: African Dimensions of the Jamaican Religious Experience* (New York: Oxford University Press, 2005); and Janelle Rodriques, *Narratives of Obeah in West Indian Literature: Moving Through the Margins* (New York: Routledge, 2019). Work that came out as this book was in production includes J. Brent Crosson, *Experiments with Power: Obeah and the Remaking of Religion in Trinidad* (Chicago: University of Chicago Press, 2020).

75. Robert Borofsky, Laura Nader, Matt Candea, and Jonathan Friedman, "Where Have All the Comparisons Gone?," https://www.publicanthropology.org/where-have-all-the-comparisons-gone/.

## 2. Plantations and Climates of Crisis

1. I borrow "long shadow" from Michelle Johnson and Brian Moore, *Neither Led nor Driven: Contesting British Cultural Imperialism in Jamaica 1865–1920* (Kingston, Jamaica: University of the West Indies Press, 2004), 271.

2. Matthew Mulcahy, *Hurricanes and Society in the British Greater Caribbean, 1624–1783* (Baltimore: Johns Hopkins University Press, 2006).

3. Vincent Brown, *Tacky's Revolt: The Story of an Atlantic Slave War* (Cambridge, MA: Harvard University Press, 2020), 4.

4. Gaiutra Bahadur, *Coolie Woman: The Odyssey of Indenture* (Chicago: University of Chicago Press, 2014), 127.

5. Madhavi Kale, *Fragments of Empire: Capital, Slavery, and Indian Indentured Labor in the British Caribbean* (Philadelphia: University of Pennsylvania Press, 1998), 172.

6. Stuart Hall, with Bill Schwarz, *Familiar Stranger: A Life between Two Islands* (Durham, NC: Duke University Press, 2017), 69.

7. David Vincent Trotman, *Crime in Trinidad: Conflict and Control in a Plantation Society 1838–1900* (Baltimore: Johns Hopkins University Press, 1986); Jan Breman, *Imperial Monkey Business: Racial Supremacy in Social Darwinist Theory and Colonial Practice*, CASA Monographs 4 (Amsterdam: VU University Press, 1990); John Kelly, *A Politics of Virtue: Hinduism, Sexuality, and Countercolonial Discourse in Fiji* (Chicago: University of Chicago Press, 1991); Walton Look Lai, *Indentured Labor, Caribbean Sugar: Chinese and Indian Migrants to the British West Indies, 1838–1918* (Baltimore: Johns Hopkins University Press, 1993).

8. Trotman, *Crime in Trinidad*, 195.

9. Edgar L. Erickson, "The Introduction of East Indian Coolies into the British West Indies," *Journal of Modern History* 6, no. 2 (1934): 131.

10. Denise Helly, ed., *The Cuba Commission Report: A Hidden History of the Chinese in Cuba* (Baltimore: Johns Hopkins University Press, 1993); Lisa Yun, *The Coolie Speaks: Chinese Indentured Laborers and African Slaves in Cuba* (Philadelphia: Temple University Press, 2008).

11. Erickson, "Introduction of East Indian Coolies," 131.

12. Rex Nettleford, *Mirror Mirror: Identity, Race, and Protest in Jamaica* (1970; repr., Kingston: LMH Publishing, 1998), 183–184.

13. Erickson, "Introduction of East Indian Coolies," 145.

14. D. W. Comins, *Notes on Emigration from India to Trinidad* (Bengal Secretariat Press, 1893), 4.

15. Breman, *Imperial Monkey Business*.

16. Simone Browne, *Dark Matters: On the Surveillance of Blackness* (Durham, NC: Duke University Press, 2015), 16.

17. Browne, 17.

18. Kelly, *Politics of Virtue*, 69–70.

19. Hugh Tinker, *A New System of Slavery: The Export of Indian Labour Overseas, 1830–1920* (London: Oxford University Press, 1974).

20. Hall, *Familiar Stranger*, 17.

21. Ashutosh Kumar, *Coolies of the Empire: Indentured Indians in the Sugar Colonies, 1830–1920* (Cambridge: Cambridge University Press, 2017), 8.

22. C.O.111/373, Government House, British Guiana, correspondence between Sir John Scott and Earl Granville, November 8, 1869.
23. C.O. 295/445, *Memorandum on East Indian Immigration to the West Indies, West Indian No. 152* (London: Colonial Office, 1906), 5.
24. *Report of the Committee: Emigraton from India to the Crown Colonies and Protectorates, Part III* (London: His Majesty's Stationary Office, 1910), 136.
25. "The Campaign against State-Aided Immigration, Petition to the Secretary of State," *Daily Chronicle*, May 21, 1903.
26. C.O. 295/445, "*Memorandum*," 1906, pp. 5–6.
27. C.O. 111/269, Letter to W. B. Wolseley from C.A. Goodman, September 27, 1849.
28. C.O. 111/269, Letter to Wolseley from Goodman, September 27, 1849.
29. William Grant Sewell, *The Ordeal of Free Labor in the British West Indies* (New York: Harper & Brothers, 1861), 121, 128.
30. Sewell, *Ordeal of Free Labour*, 123–124.
31. Sewell, 134.
32. Verene Shepherd, *Maharani's Misery: Narratives of a Passage from India to the Caribbean* (Barbados: University of the West Indies Press. 2002), 5.
33. Look Lai, *Indentured Labor, Caribbean Sugar*, 118–119.
34. C.O. 295/447, Letter to the Under-Secretary of State for the Colonies, June 24, 1908.
35. C.O. 295/447, Letter to the Under-Secretary, June 24, 1908.
36. C.O. 295/447, Letter to the Under-Secretary of State, July 6, 1908.
37. Daniel Hart, *Trinidad and the Other West India Islands and Colonies*, second edition (Trinidad: The Chronicle Publishing Office, 1866), 84.
38. C.O. 111/269, Letter from Henry Barkly to Earl Grey, October 30, 1849.
39. C.O. 111/269, Barkly to Earl Grey, December 10, 1849.
40. Emigrants' Information Office, *The West Indies: General Information for Intending Settlers* (London: Hismjatesty's Stationary Office, 1904), p. 17.
41. *Port of Spain Gazette*, September 13, 1884, quoted in Bridget Brereton, *Race Relations in Colonial Trinidad 1870–1900* (Cambridge: Cambridge University Press, 1979), 187.
42. Mandy Banton, *Administering the Empire, 1801–1968: A Guide to the Records of the Colonial Office in the National Archives of the UK* (London: University of London School of Advanced Study, Institute of Historical Research, 2008), 21.
43. Brereton, *Race Relations in Colonial Trinidad*, 184.
44. Alan Richardson, "Romantic Voodoo: Obeah and British Culture, 1797–1807," in *Sacred Possessions: Vodou, Santeria, Obeah, and the Caribbean*, ed. Margarite Fernandez Olmos and Lizabeth Paravisini-Gebert (New Brunswick, NJ: Rutgers University Press, 1997), 171–194; Diana Paton, "Witchcraft, Poison, Law, and Atlantic Slavery," *William and Mary Quarterly* 69, no. 2 (2012):

235–264; Jerome Handler and Kenneth Bilby, *Enacting Power: The Criminalization of Obeah in the Anglophone Caribbean, 1760–2011* (Kingston, Jamaica: University of the West Indies Press, 2011).

45. C.O. 372/10, *Notes on the West Indian Riots 1881–1903*, 1905, 1.
46. C.O. 372/10, *West Indian Riots* 1905, 1.
47. Donald Wood, *Trinidad in Transition: The Years after Slavery* (Oxford: Oxford University Press, 1968), 152; Carlton Robert Ottley, *A Historical Account of the Trinidad and Tobago Police Force from the Earliest Times* (Port of Spain: published by the author, "Compiled on a special assignment from the Government of Trinidad and Tobago"), 1964.
48. C.O. 111/393, Letter to I. M. Grant, Government Secretary, from St. J. Loughran, November 30, 1872.
49. C.O. 111/393, Letter to Grant from Loughran, November 30, 1872.
50. Bridget Brereton, *Race Relations in Colonial Trinidad 1870–1900* (London: Cambridge University Press, 1979), 187.
51. Brereton, *Race Relations in Colonial Trinidad*, 187.
52. "Proclamation, by the Queen in Council, to the Princes, Chiefs, and People of India" (Allahabad: Governor-General), November 1, 1858. House of Commons Parliamentary Papers Online, 2005.
53. "Proclamation," House of Commons Parliamentary Papers Online 2005, 1–2.
54. "Proclamation," House of Commons Parliamentary Papers Online 2005, 2.
55. Brinsley Samaroo, "The Caribbean Consequences of the 1857 Revolt," in *Indian Diaspora in the Caribbean*, ed. Ratan Lal Hangloo (Delhi: Primus, 2012), 90.
56. Samaroo, "Caribbean Consequences," 87.
57. C.O. 111/393, "The Coolie Riots in Essequebo: A Report of the Proceedings and Evidence at the Inquest on the Bodies of Five Rioters, Killed by the Fire of the Police" (Georgetown: *The Colonist* Office, 1872), pp. 19, 23.
58. Reverend Kenneth Grant, *My Missionary Memories* (Halifax, Nova Scotia: Imperial Publishing Co., Limited, 1923), 93–94. Grant arrived in Trinidad in 1870; he stated that the "riot" occurred as he "approached the middle of our second decade in mission work," which dates this event to approximately 1884—the year of the infamous "Hosay Riot," or massacre. But given the amount of plantation unrest that characterized the sugar colonies in the West Indies, Grant could have been referring to another such incident.
59. Wood, *Trinidad in Transition*, 154–155.
60. Biswamoy Pati, "Introduction: The Nature of 1857," in *The 1857 Rebellion*, ed. Biswamoy Pati (New Delhi: Oxford University Press, 2007): xiii–xiv, xx.
61. Thomas R. Metcalf, *The New Cambridge History of India, III.4, Ideologies of the Raj* (Berkeley: University of California Press, 1995), 45.
62. C. S. Adcock, *The Limits of Tolerance: Indian Secularism and the Politics of Religious Freedom* (New York: Oxford University Press, 2014), 33; Ilyse R.

Morgenstein Fuerst, *Indian Muslim Minorities and the 1857 Rebellion: Religion, Rebels, and Jihad* (London: I. B. Tauris, 2017), 113.

63. *Report of the Committee: Emigration from India to the Crown Colonies and Protectorates, Part 3* (London: His Majesty's Stationary Office, 1910), 127.

64. Gisli Palsson, *The Man Who Stole Himself: The Slave Odyssey of Hans Jonathan* (Chicago: University of Chicago Press, 2016), 18.

65. Robert Dirks, *Black Saturnalia: Conflict and Its Ritual Expression on British West Indian Slave Plantations* (Gainesville: University Press of Florida, 1987), ix.

66. Jim Masselos, "Change and Custom in the Format of the Bombay Mohurrum during the Nineteenth and Twentieth Centuries," *South Asia: Journal of South Asian Studies* (Nedlands, Australia) 5, no. 2 (1982), 54n.

67. Ottley, *Historical Account of the Trinidad and Tobago Police Force*, 31.

68. *The Creole*, April 19, 1867, part 1.

69. C.O. 113/5, No. 16, British Guiana, Court of Policy, "An Ordinance to Provide for the Due Regulation of the Festivals and Processions of East Indian Immigrants in this Colony," 1869, p. 1.

70. *Report of the Committee*, p. 127.

71. John Cowley, *Carnival, Canboulay, and Calypso: Traditions in the Making* (Cambridge: Cambridge University Press, 1996), 84.

72. C.O. 295/301, Trinidad Despatch No. 5279, Letter from Governor Freeling to the Earl of Derby, March 8, 1884.

73. C.O. 295/301, Letter from Freeling to Derby, March 8, 1884.

74. Nicholas Dirks, "The Policing of Tradition: Colonialism and Anthropology in Southern India," *Comparative Studies in Society and History* 39, no. 1 (1997): 184.

75. Bridget Brereton, *Race Relations in Colonial Trinidad 1870–1900* (Cambridge: Cambridge University Press, 1979), 184.

76. Trotman, *Crime in Trinidad*, 101.

77. Trotman, 270.

78. C.O. 295/306: 227.

79. C.O. 295/306, "Report," Lionel M. Fraser, Inspector of Prisons, April 15, 1885.

80. Kelvin Singh, *Bloodstained Tombs: The Muharram Massacre 1884* (London: Macmillan, 1988).

81. "The Hosein Calamity," *Port of Spain Gazette*, November 8, 1884, 4.

82. C.O. 298/38, Trinidad Minutes of Executive Council 1880–1891, "Hosea Festival," July 10, 1884.

83. "The Coolie Immigrants," *Port of Spain Gazette*, October 18, 1884.

84. "Coolie Insubordinations, Especially in Reference to Their Manifestation at the Moharrum," *Port of Spain Gazette*, November 8, 1884.

85. "Coolie Insubordinations."

86. C.O. 295/303, "The Mayor of San Fernando to the Administrator," December 17, 1884, pp. 667–669.

87. C.O. 295/303, "Proposed Volunteer Corps at San Fernando," December 17, 1884, p. 664.
88. C.O. 295/301, dispatch no. 6135, "Police Force. Reports on Necessity for increase of and drill in use of firearms," March 25, 1884.
89. *Port of Spain Gazette*, March 1, 1884.
90. "The Tadjah riot in Trinidad," *The Argosy*, February 28, 1885.
91. Sir H. W. Norman, *Report on the Coolie Disturbances in Trinidad*. Council Paper, January 13, 1885, p. 3.
92. James McNeill and Chimman Lal, *Indian Immigration: Report to the Government of India on the Condition of Indian Immigrants in West Indian Colonies* (Port of Spain, Trinidad: Government Printing Office, 1915), 23.
93. McNeill and Lal, *Indian Immigration*, 22.
94. McNeill and Lal, 18.
95. Basdeo Mangru, *Benevolent Neutrality: Indian Government Policy and Labour Migration in British Guiana 1854–1884* (London: Hansib, 1987), 170.
96. Mangru, *Benevolent Neutrality*, 170.
97. Richard Robert Madden, *A Twelve Months' Residence in the West Indies during the Transition from Slavery to Apprenticeship* (New York: Negro Universities Press, 1835), 108; Bryan Edwards, *The History, Civil and Commercial, of the British West Indies*, vol. 2, book 4 (London, 1819), 108–109.
98. Greg Grandin, *The Empire of Necessity: Slavery, Freedom, and Deception in the New World* (New York: Metropolitan Books, 2014), 191.
99. Madden, *A Twelve Months' Residence*, 108.
100. Also see, for example, Aisha Khan, "Realizing a Muslim Atlantic," *Maydan*, July 16, 2020 (https://themaydan.com/2020/07/realising-a-muslim-atlantic/).

### 3. The Performance of Shadows

1. Stuart Hall, with Bill Schwartz, *Familiar Stranger: A Life between Two Islands* (Durham, NC: Duke University Press 2017), 104.
2. Donald Wood, *Trinidad in Transition: The Years after Slavery* (Oxford: Oxford University Press, 1968), 150.
3. Diana Paton, "The Racist History of Jamaica's Obeah Acts," *The Gleaner*, October 8, 2019, http://jamaica-gleaner.com/article/news/20190616/diana-paton-racist-history-jamaicas-obeah-act
4. Paton, "Racist History."
5. Reverend H. V. P. Bronkhurst, *The Colony of British Guiana and Its Labouring Population* (London: T. Woolmer, 1883), 356.
6. Basdeo Mangru, *Benevolent Neutrality: Indian Government Policy and Labour Migration in British Guiana 1854–1884* (London: Hansib, 1987), 171.

7. Jose Muñoz, "Ephemera as Evidence: Introductory Notes to Queer Acts," *Women and Performance: A Journal of Feminist Theory* 8, no. 2 (1996): 10–11.

8. Nicholas Dirks, "The Policing of Tradition: Colonialism and Anthropology in Southern India," *Comparative Studies in Society and History* 39, no. 1 (1997): 185.

9. C.O. 111/373, Letter from E.J. Williams to Governor Barkly, Georgetown, March 1, 1853.

10. C.O. 111/373, Williams to Barkly, March 1, 1853.

11. C.O. 111/373, Government Notice, March 24, 1853, S. Gardiner Austin, Immigration Agent General.

12. C.O. 111/294, Government House, April 14, 1853, Barkly to Newcastle.

13. C.O. 260/81, 111/294, Government House, April 14, 1853, Barkly to Newcastle.

14. Bryan Edwards, *The History, Civil and Commercial, of the British West Indies*, vol. II, chapter 3 (1801; repr., London, 1819), 111–112.

15. Jerome Handler and Kenneth Bilby, *Enacting Power: The Criminalization of Obeah in the Anglophone Caribbean, 1760–2011* (Kingston, Jamaica: University of the West Indies Press, 2012), 46.

16. Bronkhurst, *The Colony of British Guiana and Its Labouring Population*, 382.

17. Ittai Weinryb, introduction to *Agents of Faith: Votive Objects in Time and Place*, ed. Ittai Weinryb (New York: Bard Graduate Center Gallery, 2018), ix, xi.

18. Edwards, *History, Civil and Commercial*, vol. I, appendix, 538.

19. Fraud had long been marked in European thought as a serious breach of moral imperatives. In Dante Alighieri's *The Divine Comedy* (1320), for example, Dante divides the afterlife into Hell, Purgatory, and Paradise. Hell, or *Malebolge*, has ten (descending) ditches or trenches, each of which contains a different kind of fraudulence and its own form of punishment. The fourth ditch—below panderers and seducers (first ditch), flatterers (second ditch), and "simony," or crimes against the Church (third ditch)—is reserved for astrologers, seers, and sorcerers. Their eternal punishment for presuming to see into the future is to walk backward because their heads are twisted around to face that direction.

20. Edwards, *History, Civil and Commercial*, vol. II, book IV, 114–117, italics original.

21. Diana Paton, *The Cultural Politics of Obeah: Religion, Colonialism, and Modernity in the Caribbean World* (Cambridge: Cambridge University Press, 2015).

22. Hall, *Familiar Stranger*, 104.

23. The reverse was also possible. In his analysis of forms of speech in West Indian slave societies, Miles Ogburn writes that the "use by obeah men and women in Barbados and Jamaica of everyday, if liminal, materials—feathers, bones, bottles, eggshells, grave dirt, beads—to manage the power of the spirits suggests the transformation of these objects into something more than material through the performance of ritualized forms of speech and action." Miles Ogburn, *The*

*Freedom of Speech: Talk and Slavery in the Anglo-Caribbean World* (Chicago: University of Chicago Press, 2019), 156.

24. C.O. 297/8, *An Ordinance*, No. 6, Governor Arthur Gordon, Trinidad, 1868, p. 6.
25. Kelly Wisecup and Toni Wall Jaudon, "On Knowing and Not Knowing about Obeah," *Atlantic Studies* 12, no. 2 (2015): 137.
26. Wisecup and Jaudon, "On Knowing and Not Knowing," 130.
27. Richard Robert Madden, *A Twelve Months' Residence in the West Indies during the Transition from Slavery to Apprenticeship* (New York: Negro Universities Press, 1835), 76.
28. Madden, *Twelve Months' Residence*, 76.
29. Madden, 76.
30. C.O. 139/108, *Jamaica—Law 5 of 1898*, "The Obeah Law."
31. David Trotman, *Crime in Trinidad: Conflict and Control in a Plantation Society 1838–1900* (Baltimore: Johns Hopkins University Press, 1986), 225.
32. Stephen Greenblatt, *The Swerve: How the World Became Modern* (New York: W. W. Norton, 2011).
33. C.O. 260/81, January 9, 1854, Letter to Col. Colbrooke from Lt. Gov. Richard Donnell. (Donnell is also identified as MacDonnell [for example, in the *Dictionary of Canadian Biography*, http://www.biographi.ca/en/bio /macdonnell_richard_graves_11E.html].)
34. Ludwig Wittgenstein, *Philosophical Investigations*, ed. G. E. M. Anscombe and R. Rhees, trans. G. E. M. Anscombe (1953; repr., Englewood Cliffs, NJ: Prentice Hall, 1958).
35. Mary Douglas, *Purity and Danger: An Analysis of the Concepts of Pollution and Taboo* (London: Routledge and Kegan Paul, 1966), 53.
36. Douglas, *Purity and Danger*, 53–54.
37. Dirks, "Policing of Tradition," 192.
38. Stanley Tambiah, *Magic, Science, Religion, and the Scope of Rationality* (New York: Cambridge University Press, 1990).
39. John Savage, "'Black Magic' and White Terror: Slave Poisoning and Colonial Society in Early 19th Century Martinique," *Journal of Social History* 40, no. 3 (2007): 653.
40. C.O. 260/81, January 9, 1854, Letter to Col. Colbrooke from Lt. Gov. Richard Donnell.
41. James McNeill and Chimman Lal, *Indian Immigration: Report to the Government of India on the Condition of Indian Immigrants in West Indian Colonies* (Port of Spain, Trinidad: Government Printing Office, 1915), 18.
42. McNeill and Lal, *Indian Immigration*, 27.
43. Margarite Fernandez-Olmos and Lizabeth Paravisini Gebert, *Creole Religions of the Caribbean: An Introduction from Vodou and Santeria to Obeah and Espiritismo* (New York: New York University Press, 2011), 133.

44. Emile Durkheim, *Elementary Forms of Religious Life*, ed. Mark Cladis, trans. Carol Cosman (New York: Oxford University Press, 2001), xiv, xxii.

45. W. S. F. Pickering, *Durkheim's Sociology of Religion: Themes and Theories* (London: Routledge and Kegan Paul, 1984), 195.

46. Emile Durkheim, "Individual and Collective Representations," in *Sociology and Philosophy*, by Emile Durkheim (Glencoe, IL: Free Press, 1953), 25.

47. Durkheim, *Elementary Forms of Religious Life*, xxii.

48. Ann Warfield Rawls, *Epistemology and Practice: Durkheim's "The Elementary Forms of Religious Life"* (Cambridge: Cambridge University Press, 2004), 216.

49. Tambiah, *Magic, Science, Religion*, 31.

50. Emile Durkheim, *The Elementary Forms of Religious Life*, ed. Karen E. Fields (New York: Free Press, 1995), 41.

51. Durkheim, *Elementary Forms* (1995), 40.

52. Durkheim, 42.

53. Dirks, "Policing of Tradition," 211.

54. Anne Laura Stoler, *Along the Archival Grain: Epistemic Anxieties and Colonial Common Sense* (Princeton, NJ: Princeton University Press, 2009), 39.

55. Bryan Edwards, *An Historical Survey of the French Colony in the Island of St. Domingo* (London: John Stockdale, 1797), 63.

56. Daniel Hart, *Trinidad and the Other West India Islands and Colonies*, 2nd ed. (Trinidad: Chronicle Publishing Office, 1866), 83.

57. Hart, *Trinidad and Other West India Islands*, 101.

58. Goolam Vahed, "Muharram in Diasporic Setting [*sic*] in the Twenty-first Century," in *Indentured Muslims in the Diaspora: Identity and Belonging of Minority Groups in Plural Societies*, ed. Maurits S. Hassankhan, Goolam Vahed, and Lomarsh Roopnarine (New Delhi: Manohar, 2016), 305, 306.

59. Hall, *Familiar Stranger*, 39.

60. Hall, 51, 57.

61. Hall, 37.

62. Christine Barrow, "Anthropology, the Family, and Women in the Caribbean," in *Gender in Caribbean Development*, ed. Patricia Mohammed and Catherine Shepherd (Barbados: University of the West Indies Press, 1988), 157; Thomas Simey, *Welfare & Planning in the West Indies* (Oxford: Clarendon, 1946); Walter Guinness, Lord Moyne, *West India Royal Commission Report* (London: H.M.S.O., 1945).

63. Richard Price, "Studies of Caribbean Family Organization: Problems and Prospects," *Daedalo* 7, no. 14 (1971), 27.

64. Christine Barrow, *Family in the Caribbean: Themes and Perspectives* (Kingston, Jamaica: Ian Randle, 1996), 459.

65. C.O. 950/98, "West India Royal Commission, Seventh Session Held in Jamaica," November 10, 1938.

66. C.O. 950/98, West India Royal Commission," p. 1. I could not determine from the document why "Mr. Lewis" was selected as an expert.
67. Myalism is an Afro-Atlantic religious tradition concerned with the power of ancestors that generally involves drumming, dancing, spirit possession, and use of herbs. Pocomania also is concerned with ancestor veneration and spirit possession, and it involves elements of Christian revivalism.
68. C.O. 950/98, "West India Royal Commisson," p. 10.
69. C.O. 950/98, "West India Royal Commission," p. 9.
70. Hall, Familiar Stranger, 109.
71. C.O. 950/98, "West India Royal Commission," p. 11.
72. C.O. 950/98, "West India Royal Commission," pp. 11–12.
73. C.O. 950/98, "West India Royal Commission," p. 12.
74. C.O. 950/98, "West India Royal Commission," p. 13.
75. C.O. 950/98, "West India Royal Commission," p. 26.
76. C.O. 950/98, "West India Royal Commission," p. 27.
77. C.O. 950/98, "West India Royal Commission," p. 27.
78. C.O. 950/98, "West India Royal Commission," p. 41.
79. C.O. 950/98, "West India Royal Commission," p. 41.
80. C.O. 950/98, "West India Royal Commission," p. 41.
81. C.O. 950/98, "West India Royal Commission," p. 44.
82. C.O. 950/98, "West India Royal Commission," pp. 42–44.
83. C.O. 950/98, "West India Royal Commission," pp. 61–63.
84. C.O. 950/98, "A Memorandum Presented by the Leaders of Certain Christian Bodies in Jamaica to the Chairman and Members of the West Indian [sic] Royal Commission," 1938, p. 19.
85. C.O. 950/98, "A Memorandum," p. 20.
86. C.O. 950/98, "A Memorandum," p. 23.
87. Michel-Rolph Trouillot, "North Atlantic Universals: Analytical Fictions, 1492–1945," *South Atlantic Quarterly* 101, no. 4 (2002): 849.
88. Hall, *Familiar Stranger*, 48.
89. Hall, *Familiar Stranger*, 48.
90. Hall, *Familiar Stranger*, 109.
91. Hall, *Familiar Stranger*, 117.

## 4. The Trials of Obeah Today

1. Among the most notable proponents of this point of view is Stuart Hall. See, for example, "Cultural Identity and Diaspora," in *Colonial Discourse and Postcolonial Theory: A Reader*, ed. Patrick Williams and Laura Chrisman (London: Harvester Wheatsheaf, 1990), 222–237.

2. "Trinidad and Tobago" indicates the Republic; "Trinidad" indicates either the Republic or that island alone; usage will be clear according to context.

3. *Daily Express*," PM: T&T a Mecca for Shouter Baptists," March 30, 2015, 9.

4. *Daily Express*, "Ahmed, Rowley Extend Greetings to Baptists," March 30, 2015, 8.

5. *Daily Express*, March 30, 2015, 8.

6. *Daily Express*, March 30, 2015, 31.

7. "Obeah Threats for Cops," Gyasi Gonzales, *Saturday Express*, April 7, 2018, 8.

8. Ria Taitt, "Rowley Hits Out at 'Obeah' Ad . . . Blames Contractor," *Daily Express*, September 3, 2015, 9.

9. Diana Paton, *The Cultural Politics of Obeah: Religion, Colonialism, and Modernity in the Caribbean World* (Cambridge: Cambridge University Press, 2015), 283.

10. Paton, *Cultural Politics of Obeah*, 283.

11. Paton, 284.

12. Musab Younis, "Against Independence," review of *Freedom Time: Negritude, Decolonisation and the Future of the World*, by Gary Wilder, *London Review of Books* 39, no. 13 (2017): 27.

13. Rex Nettleford, *Mirror Mirror: Identity, Race, and Protest in Jamaica* (1970; repr., Kingston, Jamaica: LMH Publishing, 1998), 173.

14. Nettleford, *Mirror Mirror*, 176–177.

15. Nettleford, *Mirror, Mirror*, 174.

16. Nettleford, 177.

17. Nettleford, 176.

18. Nettleford, 178.

19. Nettleford, 175.

20. Nettleford, 177.

21. Nettleford, 175.

22. Nettleford, 210–211.

23. Kei Miller, "The Banning of the Drums; or 'How to Be a Good Nigger in Jamaica,'" *Under the Saltire Flag* (blog), July 13, 2014, https://underthesaltireflag.com/2014/07/13/the-banning-of-the-drums.

24. Stuart Hall, with Bill Schwartz, *Familiar Stranger: A Life between Two Islands* (Durham, NC: Duke University Press 2017).

25. Yvonne Brewster, introduction to *For the Reckord: A Collection of Three Plays by Barry Reckord*, ed. Yvonne Brewster (London: Oberon Books, 2010), 11.

26. Brewster, introduction to *For the Reckord*, 11, 13.

27. Amanda Bidnall, *The West Indian Generation: Remaking British Culture in London 1945–1065* (Liverpool: Liverpool University Press, 2017), 204.

28. Brewster, introduction to *For the Reckord*, 15.

29. Bidnall, *West Indian Generation*, 208.

30. Brewster, introduction to *For the Reckord*, 15.

31. Bidnall, *West Indian Generation*, 214.

32. Richardson would go on to become one of Britain's leading theater and film directors in the 1960s.

33. Bidnall, *West Indian Generation*, 205.

34. Bidnall, 207.

35. *Hampshire Telegraph Post*, May 9, 1958, quoted in Bidnall, 216.

36. Barry Reckord, *Flesh to a Tiger*, in *For the Reckord: A Collection of Three Plays by Barry Reckord*, ed. Yvonne Brewster (London: Oberon Books, 2010), 33.

37. Reckord, *Flesh to a Tiger*, 21.

38. Reckord, 22.

39. Reckord, 24–25.

40. Reckord, *Flesh to a Tiger*, 28–29. A balm yard is the location in a neighborhood where obeah healing rituals are practiced. Zora Neale Hurston's explanation of balm yards is instructive: "[They] are deep in the lives of the Jamaican peasants. A Balm Yard is a place where they give baths, and the people who operate these yards are to their followers both doctor and priest. Sometimes he or she diagnoses a case as a natural ailment, and a bath or series of baths in infusions of secret plants is prescribed. More often the diagnosis is that the patient has been 'hurt' by a duppy, and the bath is given to drive the spirit off." Zora Neale Hurston, *Tell My Horse: Voodoo and Life in Haiti and Jamaica* (1938; repr., New York: Harper and Row, 1990), 5.

41. Reckord, *Flesh to a Tiger*, 31.

42. Reckord, 31.

43. Reckord, 32.

44. Reckord, 33.

45. Reckord, 33–34.

46. Reckord, 44.

47. Reckord, 67.

48. Reckord, 47.

49. Reckord, 47.

50. Paton, *Cultural Politics of Obeah*, 208–240.

51. Ludwig Wittgenstein, *Philosophical Investigations*, trans. G. E. M. Anscombe, ed. G. E. M. Anscombe and R. Rhees (1953; repr., Englewood Cliffs, NJ: Prentice Hall, 1958).

52. Brewster, introduction to *For the Reckord*, 15.

53. Candace Ward, *Crossing the Line: Early Creole Novels and Anglophone Caribbean Culture in the Age of Emancipation* (Charlottesville, VA: University of Virginia Press, 2017), 57.

54. Janelle Rodriques, "Obeah(man) as Trickster in Cynric Williams's *Hamel, the Obeah Man*," *Atlantic Studies* 12, no. 2 (2015): 219.

55. Ward, *Crossing the Line*, 57.

56. Ben Child, "A Bulletproof Black Man: Luke Cage Is the Superhero America Needs Now," *The Guardian*, September 30, 2016, https://www.theguardian.com /tv-and-radio/2016/sep/30/luke-cage-netflix-marvel-a-bulletproof-black-man-the -superhero-america-needs-now.

57. *Luke Cage*, season 2, episode 2, "Straighten It Out," directed by Steph Green, written by Akela Cooper, released June 22, 2018, on Netflix.

58. *Luke Cage*, season 2, episode 7, "On and On," directed by Rashaad Ernesto Green, written by Nicole Mirante-Matthews, released June 22, 2018, on Netflix.

59. *Luke Cage*, season 2, episode 9, "For Pete's Sake," directed by Clark Johnson, written by Matt Owens and Ian Stokes, released June 22, 2018, on Netflix.

60. Aisha Harris, "'Luke Cage' Season 2: A New Villain and Respectability Politics," *New York Times*, June 21, 2018, https://www.nytimes.com/2018/06/21 /arts/television/luke-cage-season-2-netflix.html.

61. *Luke Cage*, season 2, episode 3, "Wig Out," directed by Marc Jobst, written by Matt Owens, released June 22, 2018, on Netflix.

62. Max Romeo and the Upsetters, "I Chase the Devil" (composed by Max Romeo and Lee Perry).

63. Capoeria is an Afro-Brazilian martial art that involves graceful and acrobatic dance movements.

64. The association between Jamaica and botanicals has a long history, doubtless one that goes back to the slavery era. A century after emancipation, Zora Neale Hurston opened her monograph *Tell My Horse* with this message: "Jamaica, British West Indies, has something else besides its mountains of majesty and its quick, green valleys. . . . Jamaica has its 'bush.' That is, the island has more usable plants for medicinal and edible purposes than any other spot on earth." Hurston, *Tell My Horse*, 3.

65. *Luke Cage*, season 2, episode 4, "I Get Physical," directed by Salli Richardson-Whitfield, written by Matthew Lopes.

66. *Luke Cage*, season 2, episode 19, "The Basement," directed by Millicent Shelton, written by Aïda Mashaka Croal.

67. *Luke Cage*, season 2, episode 12, "Can't Front on Me," directed by Everardo Gout, written by Aïda Mashaka Croal.

68. *Luke Cage*, "Can't Front on Me."

69. *Luke Cage*, season 2, episode 8, "If It Ain't Rough, It Ain't Right," directed by Neema Barnette, written by Nathan Louis Jackson.

70. *Luke Cage*, season 2, episode 11, "The Creator," directed by Stephen Surjik, written by Nicole Mirante-Matthews and Matthew Lopes.

71. *Luke Cage*, season 2, episode 10, "The Main Ingredient," directed by Andy Goddard, written by Akela Cooper.

72. *Luke Cage*, "For Pete's Sake"; *Luke Cage*, "If It Ain't Rough, It Ain't Right."

73. *Luke Cage*, "For Pete's Sake."

74. *Luke Cage*, season 2, episode 26, "They Reminisce over You," directed by Alex Garcia Lopez, written by Cheo Hodari Coker.

75. Andray Domise and Sharine Taylor, "To the Producers of Marvel's Luke Cage: Enough with the Ja'Faikans," *Vice*, June 27, 2018, https://www.vice.com/en_ca /article/8xep35/to-the-producers-of-marvels-luke-cage-enough-with-the-jafaikans.

76. Domise and Taylor, "To the Producers of Marvel's *Luke Cage*."

77. "Review: 'Luke Cage' Season 2 Claims the Throne," *Black Nerd Problems*, http://blacknerdproblems.com/luke-cage-season-2-review/.

78. Jerome Handler and Kenneth Bilby, *Enacting Power: The Criminalization of Obeah in the Anglophone Caribbean, 1760–2011* (Kingston, Jamaica: University of the West Indies Press, 2012), 106.

79. *Luke Cage*, "The Creator."

80. A "reading" is a spiritual consultation done during a specified time in a person's life.

81. *Luke Cage*, "I Get Physical."

82. For example, Psalms 118:22–23.

83. Katherine Gerbner, "'They Call Me Obea': German Moravian Missionaries and Afro-Caribbean Religion in Jamaica, 1754–1760," *Atlantic Studies* 12, no. 2 (2015): 174.

84. Jane Beck, "The Implied Obeah Man," *Western Folklore* 35, no. 1 (1976): 23.

85. Beck, "Implied Obeah Man," 24.

86. Beck, 25, 32.

87. Jerome Handler and Kenneth Bilby, *Enacting Power*, 107.

88. *Her Majesty the Queen v. Marlon Rowe*, Docket: C36577, Court of Appeal for Ontario.

89. *Her Majesty the Queen v. Evol Robinson, Jahmar Welsh, and Ruben Pinnock*, Dockets C49453, C49268, C49887, Court of Appeal for Ontario.

90. "5 Top Birthplaces of Immigrants Living in Brampton: Over Half of Population Canadian Immigrants," *Brampton Guardian*, October 26, 2017, https://www.bramptonguardian.com/news-story/7684236-5-top-birthplaces-of -immigrants-living-in-brampton/.

91. Noreen Ahmed-Ullah, "How Brampton, a Town in Suburban Ontario, Was Dubbed a Ghetto," *Globe and Mail*, June 3, 2016, https://www .theglobeandmail.com/news/toronto/brampton-a-story-of-political-importance -power-and-ethnic-enclaves/article30273820/.

92. *Her Majesty the Queen v. Marlon Rowe*, Docket C36577, Court of Appeal for Ontario, p. 3.

93. *Marlon Rowe*, Applicant's Memorandum of Argument, Court of Appeal for Ontario, part 1, paragraph 8; *Marlon Rowe*, Docket C36577.

94. *Marlon Rowe*, Docket C36577, pp. 3–4.

95. *Marlon Rowe*, Applicant's Memorandum of Argument, part 1, paragraph 8.

96. *Marlon Rowe*, Docket C36577, p. 13.

97. *Marlon Rowe*, Docket C36577, p. 5.

98. *Marlon Rowe*, Applicant's Memorandum of Argument, part 1, paragraph 12.

99. *Marlon Rowe*, Docket C36577, pp. 5–6.

100. *Marlon Rowe*, Applicant's Memorandum of Argument, part 1, paragraph 15.

101. *Marlon Rowe*, Applicant's Memorandum of Argument, part 1, paragraph 12.

102. *Marlon Rowe*, Applicant's Memorandum of Argument, part 1, paragraphs 13, 16.

103. *Marlon Rowe*, Docket C36577, p. 6.

104. *Marlon Rowe*, Applicant's Memorandum of Argument, part 1, paragraph 18.

105. *Marlon Rowe*, Docket C36577, pp. 6–7.

106. *Marlon Rowe*, Applicant's Memorandum of Argument, part 1, paragraph 18.

107. *Marlon Rowe*, Docket C36577, p. 7.

108. *Marlon Rowe*, Applicant's Memorandum of Argument, part I, paragraph 18.

109. *Marlon Rowe*, Applicant's Memorandum of Argument, part I, paragraph 19.

110. *Marlon Rowe*, Docket C36577, pp. 8–9.

111. *Marlon Rowe*, Docket C36577, p. 9.

112. *Marlon Rowe*, Applicant's Memorandum of Argument, part 1, paragraph 19.

113. *Marlon Rowe*, Docket C36577, pp. 9-10.

114. *Marlon Rowe*, Docket C36577, pp. 9–10.

115. *Marlon Rowe*, Docket C36577, p. 9.

116. *Marlon Rowe*, Applicant's Memorandum of Argument, part 3, Brief of Argument, paragraph 27.

117. *Marlon Rowe*, Applicant's Memorandum of Argument, part 3, Brief of Argument, paragraph 28.

118. *Marlon Rowe*, Applicant's Memorandum of Argument, part 1, paragraph 19.

119. *Marlon Rowe*, Docket C36577, p. 10.

120. *Marlon Rowe*, Docket C36577, p. 15.

121. *Marlon Rowe*, Applicant's Memorandum of Argument, part 3, paragraph 26.

122. *Marlon Rowe*, Docket C36577, p. 11.

123. *Marlon Rowe*, Applicant's Memorandum of Argument, part 3, paragraph 23.

124. *Marlon Rowe*, Applicant's Memorandum of Argument, part 3, Brief of Argument, paragraph 23.

125. *Marlon Rowe*, Docket C36577, p. 19.

126. See, for example, Court of Appeal for Ontario, Her Majesty the Queen and Jahmar Welsh, Appellant's Factum, C49268, pp. 20–23.

127. Some of this discussion is drawn from Aisha Khan, "Dark Arts and Diaspora," *Diaspora* 17, no. 1 (2012): 40–63.

128. "Witch Ruse Breached Rights, Court Told," Toronto Star, December 18, 2012, GT1, GT2, https://www.thestar.com/news/crime/2012/12/17/police_officer _breached_religious_rights_by_posing_as_obeah_man_court_hears.html.
129. *Marlon Rowe*, Applicant's Memorandum of Argument, part 3.
130. "Witch Ruse Breached Rights," GT1, GT2.
131. Court of Appeal for Ontario, Her Majesty the Queen and Evol Robinson, C49453, Part I, Statement of the Case, p. 6.
132. Court of Appeal for Ontario, Her Majesty the Queen and Evol Robinson, part 2, Summary of the Facts, p. 53.
133. Court of Appeal for Ontario, Her Majesty the Queen and Evol Robinson, part 2, p. 52.
134. African Canadian Legal Clinic, Statement of the Case, October 31, 2012, p. 12.
135. Court of Appeal for Ontario, Her Majesty the Queen and Evol Robinson, part 2, p. 52.
136. Court of Appeal for Ontario, Her Majesty the Queen and Jahmar Welsh, Appellant's Factum, C49268, p. 3.
137. Court of Appeal for Ontario, Her Majesty the Queen and Evol Robinson, part 3, p. 78–79.
138. Court of Appeal for Ontario, Her Majesty the Queen and Jahmar Welsh, Appellant's Factum, C49268, p. 3.
139. African Canadian Legal Clinic, Statement of the Case, October 31, 2012, pp. 13, 11.
140. African Canadian Legal Clinic, Statement of the Case, October 31, 2012, p. 1.
141. African Canadian Legal Clinic, Statement of the Case, October 31, 2012, pp. 13, 5, 4, 13.
142. Court of Appeal for Ontario, Her Majesty the Queen and Evol Robinson, part 2, p. 53.
143. "Witch Ruse Breached Rights," GT2.
144. "Witch Ruse Breached Rights," GT2.
145. Kamari Clarke, "How Police Use Religion to Deceive Suspects," *Huffington Post*, March 21, 2013, https://www.huffingtonpost.ca/kamari-clarke/police -religion-_b_2917615.html.
146. Stephan Palmié, "Which Centre, Whose Margin? Notes toward an Archae-ology of US Supreme Court Case 91-948, 1993 (*Church of the Lukumí, vs. City of Hialeah, South Florida*)," in *Inside and Outside the Law: Anthropological Studies of Authority and Ambiguity*, ed. Olivia Harris (London: Routledge, 1996), 156.
147. Field notes, December 19, 2012, Ontario Court of Appeal.
148. Field notes, December 20, 2012, Ontario Court of Appeal.
149. "Witch Ruse Breached Rights," 1.

150. Field notes, December 18, 2012, Ontario, Canada Court of Appeals, Toronto.
151. Jane Beck, "The Implied Obeah Man," *Western Folklore* 35, no. 1 (1976): 23–33.
152. Field notes, December 18, 2012, Ontario Court of Appeals.
153. *Syndicat Northcrest v. Anselem* (2004) 2 S.C.R. 551, para. 1, in Canadian Civil Liberties Association, Argument, part 2, p. 12, October 31, 2012.
154. Kamari Clarke, "Beyond Genealogies: Expertise and Religious Knowledge in Legal Cases Involving African Diasporic Publics," *Transforming Anthropology* 25, no. 2 (2017): 135.

## 5. The Spirit of Hosay Today

1. All names in this chapter are pseudonyms except those of public figures.
2. Satnarine Balkaransingh, *The Shaping of a Culture: Rituals and Festivals in Trinidad Compared with Selected Counterparts in India, 1900–2014* (Hertford-shire, UK: Hansib Publications, 2016), 254.
3. *Port of Spain Gazette*, September 10 and 24, 1897; quoted in Balkaransingh, *Shaping of a Culture*, 255.
4. Desiree Seebaran, "Getting to the Heart of Hosay," *Trinidad Guardian*, May 9, 2013, B2.
5. Terry Joseph, "Religions Unite for Hosay," *Trinidad Guardian*, June 17, 1994, 7.
6. Clarendon Parish was still keeping "Hosay culture alive" in 2019. "Leroy Jagasar Keeps the Hosay Culture Alive in Clarendon," *Jamaica Gleaner*, October 26, 2019, http://jamaica-gleaner.com/article/news/20191026/leroy-jagasar.
7. Robert Lalah, "A Grand Old Time for Clarendonians at Hussay Festival," *Weekly Gleaner*, September 7–13, 2006, 12.
8. Guha Shankar, "Imagining India(ns): Cultural Performances and Diaspora Politics in Jamaica," PhD diss., Department of Anthropology, University of Texas, Austin, 2003, 97.
9. "March to Mark Jahaji Massacre," *Trinidad and Tobago Newsday*, October 23, 2009, section B, p. 9.
10. Noor Kumar Mahabir, "The Bloodiest Massacre in Colonial TT," *Trinidad and Tobago Newsday*, October 29, 2009, p. 10.
11. Eintou Springer, "Re-enact Hosay Riots," *Newsday*, March 3, 2010, section A, p. 12.
12. "Quo vadis, Hosay?," *Trinidad Guardian*, July 19, 1991, p. 8.
13. Louis B. Homer, "Bloody End to 1884 Hosay March," *Daily Express*, November 7, 2011, 9.
14. Louis B. Homer, "Bloody End," 9.
15. Robert Dirks, *Black Saturnalia: Conflict and its Ritual Expression on British West Indian Slave Plantations* (Gainesville: University Press of Florida, 1987).

16. Desiree Seebaran, "Getting to the Heart of Hosay," *Trinidad Guardian*, May 9, 2013, B2.

17. Wayne Bowman, "Hosay Begins Tomorrow," *Daily Express*, October 21, 2015, section 2, p. 10.

18. Colin Clarke and Gillian Clarke, *Post-Colonial Trinidad: An Ethnographic Journal* (New York: Palgrave Macmillan, 2010), 121.

19. Clarke and Clarke, *Post-Colonial Trinidad*, 122.

20. See, for example, Aisha Khan, *Callaloo Nation* (Durham, NC: Duke University Press, 2004).

21. For example, Khan, *Callaloo Nation*.

22. Seebaran, "Getting to the Heart of Hosay," B2.

23. Kim Johnson, "Live from St. James Hosay: Under the Crescent Moon," *Trinidad Express*, July 4, 1993, 4.

24. "Wining" is a party dance move that involves gyrating the hips—hence its description as "win[d]ing," as with a watch or clock.

25. Prayers blessing food intended for distribution among family, neighbors, and friends.

26. The imambara is an enclosed space where some Hosay rituals are performed and tadjahs built.

27. Khan, *Callaloo Nation*.

28. Michel-Rolph Trouillot, "Anthropology and the Savage Slot: The Poetics and Politics of Otherness," in *Recapturing Anthropology*, ed. Richard G. Fox (Santa Fe, NM: School of American Research, 1991), 17–44.

29. See, for example, Aisha Khan, "Aftermath: Life and Post-Life in Atlantic Religions," in *Passages and Afterworlds: Anthropological Perspectives on Death and Mortuary Rituals in the Caribbean*, ed. Maarit Forde and Yanique Hume (Durham, NC: Duke University Press, 2018), 243–260.

30. The *chowk* is a consecrated platform or otherwise demarcated space where the tadjah is placed when it is taken out of the area where it is being built and where drumming, prayer, and the distribution of melida (sweets) to those who have gathered there takes place.

31. In reference to the imam praying over her, she also used the word *jharray*, reciting holy scripture from the Quran (or Hindu sacred texts), and blowing or sweeping away the malady using a peacock feather or a few broom straws, or with a few breaths.

## 6. Identifications

1. Ta-Nehisi Coates, *Between the World and Me* (New York: Spiegel and Grau, 2015), 7.

2. Matthew Restall, *When Montezuma Met Cortés: The True Story of the Meeting That Changed History* (New York: HarperCollins, 2018), 62–63.

3. Also see Rogers Brubaker and Frederick Cooper, "Beyond 'Identity,'" *Theory and Society* 29, no. 1 (2000): 1–47, for a thoughtful discussion of the challenges posed by the concept of identity.

4. Michel Foucault, *Michel Foucault: Beyond Structuralism and Hermeneutics*, ed. Hubert L. Dreyfus and Paul Rabinow (Chicago: University of Chicago Press, 1982), 213.

5. Foucault, *Beyond Structuralism*, 214.

6. Judith Butler, *The Psychic Life of Power: Theories in Subjection* (Palo Alto, CA: Stanford University Press, 1997), 100.

7. Butler, *Psychic Life of Power*, 104.

8. Butler, 105.

9. Foucault, *Beyond Structuralism*, 216.

10. Asad Haider, *Mistaken Identity: Race and Class in the Age of Trump* (London: Verso, 2018), 10–11.

11. Haider, *Mistaken Identity*, 11.

12. Haider, 11.

13. Kwame Anthony Appiah, *The Lies That Bind: Rethinking Identity, Creed, Country, Color, Class, Culture* (New York: Liveright, 2018), xvi.

14. Appiah, *Lies That Bind*, 218.

15. Appiah, 218.

16. I borrow the notion of "intimate" global histories from Lisa Lowe, *The Intimacies of Four Continents* (Durham, NC: Duke University Press, 2015).

17. Stephan Palmié, "Which Centre, Whose Margin? Notes toward an Archaeology of US Supreme Court Case 91–948, 1993 (Church of the Lukumí vs. City of Hialeah, South Florida), in *Inside and Outside the Law: Anthropological Studies of Authority and Ambiguity*, ed. Olivia Harris (London: Routledge, 2012), 15.

18. Stuart Hall, "The West and the Rest: Discourse and Power," in *Essential Essays*, eds. Stuart Hall and David Morley (Durham, NC: Duke University Press, 2019), 144.

19. C. L. R. James, *The Black Jacobins: Toussaint L'Ouverture and the San Domingo Revolution* (1963; repr., New York: Vintage Books, 1989); Sidney Mintz, "Enduring Substances, Trying Theories: The Caribbean Region as Oikumene," *Journal of the Royal Anthropological Institute* 2, no. (1996): 289–311; Trouillot, *Silencing the Past*.

20. Michel Foucault, *The Archaeology of Knowledge* (New York: Pantheon 1972), 144.

21. Brackette Williams, *Stains on My Name, War in My Veins: Guyana and the Politics of Cultural Struggle* (Durham, NC: Duke University Press, 1991).

22. Jerome S. Handler and Kenneth M. Bilby, *Enacting Power: The Criminalization of Obeah in the Anglophone Caribbean 1760–2011* (Mona, Jamaica: University of the West Indies Press, 2012), 106.

23. Ludwig Wittgenstein, *Philosophical Investigations*, eds. G. E. M. Anscombe and R. Rhees, trans. G. E. M. Anscombe (Englewood Cliffs, NJ: Prentice Hall, 1958).

24. Foucault, *Foucault Reader*, 32–50.

25. Michel-Rolph Trouillot, "Culture on the Edges: Creolization in the Plantation Context," in *The African Diaspora and Creolization*, ed. Karl Eric Boucicaut (Broward County, FL: A.C.T.I.O.N. Foundation, 2006). .

26. Or, sometimes, it is more of a compromise: socially constructing the biogenetic material deeply recessed within us.

27. John Kirkpatrick, "Trials of Identity in America," *Cultural Anthropology* 4, no. 3 (1989): 304.

28. Michel-Rolph Trouillot, "North Atlantic Universals: Analytical Fictions, 1492–1945," *South Atlantic Quarterly* 101, no. 4 (2002): 850.

29. Quoted in Sylvia Hui, "Nobel Prize-Winning Author V. S. Naipaul Dies at 85," https://www.seattletimes.com/nation-world/family-nobel-prize-winning-author -v-s-naipaul-dies-at-85/.

30. Denise Helly, introduction to *The Cuba Commission Report: A Hidden History of the Chinese in Cuba* (Baltimore: Johns Hopkins University Press, 1993).

31. Edward Jenkins, *Lutchmee and Dilloo: A Study in West Indian Life* (1877; repr., London: Macmillan, 2003); Harriet Beecher Stowe, *Uncle Tom's Cabin, or Life among the Lowly* (1852; repr., Edinburgh: Black and White Publishing, 2015).

# ACKNOWLEDGMENTS

The idea for this book emerged from my long-standing curiosity about the contradictions that are generated by the concept of identity when it is simultaneously a foundation for equality and an instrument through which power hierarchies are reinforced. Many societies in the Americas place great philosophical value on heterogeneity (the culturally, linguistically, racially, and ethnically diverse populations that together comprise these societies' national identities) and at the same time have political cultures that reflect ideological investments in creating and maintaining racial, ethnic, and religious boundaries that represent groups and communities as homogeneous—separate and distinct. I wanted to explore these issues by looking at the ways race as an aspect of identity and religion as an aspect of identity are mutually defining and mutually dependent in terms of their meaning and their power. The next step was to find illustrative cases; as an anthropologist I am interested in quotidian, local, on-the-ground experience, in the present and historically. I considered two examples that I thought had rich possibilities, obeah and Hosay, which are good illustrations of heterogeneity-homogeneity tensions. Both are commonly understood to have culturally and racially diverse constituencies, yet both are commonly identified as, respectively, "African" and "Indian." I soon realized that rather than isolate one and focus on it alone, positioning them in terms of what I call a parallax view could better reveal the limitations as well as potentials of identity, one of Western epistemology's most cherished concepts.

In his book *Killers of the Flower Moon*, David Grann writes that in Osage tradition, clans included members known as the Travelers in the Mist. They were responsible for guiding the clan through "sudden changes or venturing into unfamiliar realms." I want to borrow this Osage concept, as throughout this project I have felt like a "traveler in the mist." This has been so not in terms of leadership—quite the contrary—but rather in terms of an anthropologist venturing into what were for me unfamiliar realms: historiography, a regional bird's-eye view rather than one trained on a single site, and different ways to think about identity categories and their intersections. From the moment I began to think in concrete terms about what a book of this kind might entail, to working out key arguments and details, to wrapping up its final lines, I have at times found this travel exhilarating. At many other times it has felt daunting, the "mist" thick and overwhelming. Yet the journey launched, I pushed on, and it came to fruition.

I incurred a lot of debt along the way. My appreciation, as deep as it is, can never express completely the extent of my gratitude and awe at the generosity and support I have been shown. I begin with indebtedness that started accumulating long ago: to friends in the Caribbean, particularly in Trinidad, who in some cases think of me "like a family," for over three decades of answering my questions, listening to my speculations, tolerating my bewilderments, and celebrating my epiphanies. For all of this and more, I thank you, now and always.

A residential fellowship at Harvard University's Radcliffe Institute for Advanced Study, a National Endowment for the Humanities Summer Stipend award, and a fellowship from New York University's Center for the Humanities helped me get this book underway. A National Endowment for the Humanities Faculty Award and an NYU Center for the Humanities grant allowed me to finish it. I sincerely thank my department chair at the time, Susan Antón, for the leave to make the most of these fellowships; to say that they were crucial to this enterprise would be putting it mildly.

At the Radcliffe Institute I was in excellent company among colleagues who inspired and buoyed me. I especially would like to thank Jon Stewart, Bob Orsi, Rebecca Carter, Tomiko Brown Nagin, Anthony Tan, Steve Epstein, Jennifer Hughes, Hala Zriqat, and Nancy Cott for our extended conversations about some of the ideas I was grappling with, which helped me to turn tentative hunches into more robust arguments. While in Cambridge I had the pleasure of meeting historian Vince Brown. Our conversations were among the most encouraging, generous, and stimulating of my fellowship stay. I also had the good fortune of working with three sharp and conscientious Harvard University student research assistants: Diana Gerberich, Marty Berman, and Kayla Hollingsworth. Their excitement about my project and their dedicated searches for, and through, various archive collections served the development of this book very well.

The librarians at Trinidad's National Archives and at the University of the West Indies, St. Augustine, Alma Jordan Library, West Indiana and Special Collections Division, were once again indispensable in helping me to locate relevant archival data. Along with the librarians at the National Archives at Kew, London, and the British Library, they were gracious guides as I worked on coming up with uncommon or unexpected materials as well as collecting the staple sources of nineteenth- and twentieth-century West Indian historiography.

The following people went far above and beyond ordinary collegial support in reading all or parts of the manuscript. I will never forget that Bruce Grant, Kate Crehan, Barbara Weinstein, and Maarit Forde trained their expertise and attention on my work even with their own hands full, simply to help me produce a better book. Their constructive critiques permeate each chapter. These kinds of unmitigated generosity are not always the case in academia, and I seem to have the extraordinary luck of finding myself among ex-

### Acknowledgments

traordinary people. Among the latter also are Kamari Clarke, who invited me to join her on a visit to Toronto to meet the defense attorneys and attend the court session of one of the obeah appeals cases I write about in this book; and Laurie Lambert, who brought Netflix's *Luke Cage* to my attention and read that section of the manuscript. I also want to express my gratitude to colleagues who responded with alacrity when I asked them questions about topics in their special areas of expertise: Joseline Santos, Sebastián Calderon Bentin, Brinsley Samaroo, Terry Harrison, Elayne Oliphant, David Ludden, Michael Gilsenan, Tom Beidelman, Tejaswini Ganti, Carl Ernst, Allyson Purpura, Scott Williams, Andrew Sartori, Diana Paton, Jane Anderson, Wayne Modest, and Steve Stuempfle. Sarah Goode has my sincere thanks for her notations on fraud in Dante's *Divine Comedy*. My editors at Harvard University Press, Heather Hughes and Sharmila Sen, have been with me through this project from the beginning. The copyediting by Don Burgard and Tammy Parker Song was crucial, as was Alexander Trotter's indexing work at the end. My sincere thanks also go to my anonymous reviewers, who gave me invaluable constructive critique to help me better express the story that I wanted this book to tell.

Finally, this book is for my mother. Her steadfast, sage counsel throughout my life—"Don't let the bastards get you down" and "This too shall pass"—has gotten me through all kinds of mists.

# INDEX

Abel, Peter, 44–45

Africans: African Americans, 117; African culture seen as atavistic, 92; enslavement of, 3; formerly enslaved, 1; Hosay and African Muslims, 163; occult practices associated with, 10; as potential collaborators with Indians, 23

Afro-Caribbean peoples, 57, 58, 59

agency, 28, 40, 82, 172; alternative forms of, 4; binary interpretation of, 180; confrontation as manifestation of, 181; nonconformist kinds of, 138; obeah devotees allegedly robbed of, 91; religion and, 139; rogue individual and, 19

Ahmed, Reziah, 101

Amazon rainforest ("the bush"), 68, 94

Amin, Imam, 152, 159, 163–165

Anguilla, 5

animism, African, 61

Anna Regina plantation (British Guiana), 44

anthropology, 26, 27

Appiah, Kwame Anthony, 178–179

Austin, S. Gardner, 69

Austin-Broos, Diane, 17

Bahadur, Gaiutra, 31

Barbados, 5, 77, 80, 89, 199n23

Barkly, Henry, 41, 67, 70–71

Barrow, Christine, 90

Beck, Jane, 121–122

Bell, Hesketh, 20

Bequia, 121

*Between the World and Me* (Coates), 170

Bidnall, Amanda, 107

Bilby, Kenneth, 182

Bisnath, Jameel, 148

blackness, 17, 81, 105; African Muslims and, 61; Africanness and, 111; blurred racial boundaries and, 59; heritability and, 91, 106; in *Luke Cage* series, 114–115, 117; of obeah, 128, 173; Orientalism and, 118; in postwar Britain (UK), 106; racial surveillance of, 34; rogue individual and, 21; shared between coolies and former slaves, 33

Black Power movements, 149

Blavatsky, Madame, 24

Borofsky, Robert, 16

Brazil, 43, 118

Brereton, Bridget, 46

Brewster, Yvonne, 111

British Greater Caribbean, 30

British Guiana, 11, 52; "coolies" from India sent to, 3; Gladstone Experiment in, 32–33; hookswinging ritual in, 64–65, 67–68; Hosay in, 6; Ordinance No. 16 (1869), 35, 52; Ordinance No. 25 (1891), 36; "riots" in, 44. *See also* Guyana

Bronkhurst, Reverend H.V.P., 3, 11, 12, 20, 64–65

Brown, Vincent, 31

Browne, Simone, 33–34

Buckridee, 23–24

Burnham, Forbes, 103

Bushe, John Scott, 57

Butler, Judith, 177, 179

Canboulay, 53, 78; Riot (Trinidad, 1881), 44, 52

Campbell, John, 23, 24

Canada, court cases in, 99, 120–139

Candomblé, 118

capitalism, 23, 30, 34–35, 96

capoeira, 115, 205n63